PARTNERSHIP OR CONFRONTATION?

Poor Lands and Rich

PARTNERSHIP
OR
CONFRONTATION?

Poor Lands and Rich

Paul Alpert

The Free Press   *New York*
Collier–Macmillan Limited   *London*

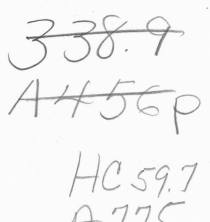

To my daughter,
Sylvie Alpert Bryant,
whose assistance in editing this
book has been invaluable

TABLE OF CONTENTS

INTRODUCTION

THE CONFLICT of ideologies between East and West, capitalism versus collectivism, has been the main political problem of our century. But the intensity of this conflict, particularly as it relates to the socialist countries of Europe, is diminishing gradually. A conflict of far greater scope is emerging as the major threat to peace, continued progress, and the very survival of our civilization. This is the conflict between the North and the South, between the rich minority, which includes socialist USSR and Eastern Europe, and the vast, rapidly growing majority of the underdeveloped poor in Asia, Africa, and Latin America, the proletariat of humanity.

This conflict is of recent origin. It started once the scientific and industrial revolution opened the way to economic progress in the West. It became acute only when political emancipation and the transmittal of information through mass media aroused a passionate yearning in the underdeveloped countries for the fruits of development in power and wealth.

The potential danger of this confrontation seems more imminent when one considers that the poor nations are also "under-civilized" in the values of our modern world. Yet to some extent they still are dependent both politically and economically on the rich countries. The great majority of them are colored, while with the exception of Japan, all the rich countries are white. Thus the opposition between rich and poor is further complicated by its racial overtones.

The problem facing the poor nations is not purely an economic one. While economic growth is an essential part of development, decisive changes in all other fields, in values and attitudes of life and work, in political and social institutions are also necessary. The whole fabric of civilization in the developing countries needs to be transformed and modernized.

The experience of the last 50 years has proven the existence of various political alternatives for achieving economic development. The decision to adopt a socialist or a capitalist approach to development, or an intermediary method, depends more on a country's political orientation than on the state of the economy.

Each country must also determine the degree to which it wants to rely on help from the outside. Economic development can be achieved by a "go it alone" policy, as in the Soviet Union and even more in China, in isolation from, and actual opposition to, the rich countries. The other option is to co-operate with the rest of the world, to invite assistance.

While such a decision must be made by the poor countries, of necessity it must be influenced by the attitude of the wealthy ones, and their willingness to provide co-operation and assistance.

It is in the interest of the world community, both the "have" and the "have not" nations, that the process of development be achieved in a climate of co-operation rather than hostile confrontation. If peace can be maintained only through an equilibrium between East and West, then only the "peace making" affirmation of solidarity between the North and the South, the rich and the poor, can promote true development and ensure the future: a world in which to live in, as well as a world worth living in.

Definitions: *GOALS AND POLICIES OF ECONOMIC DEVELOPMENT*

Economic development has been steadily gaining in momentum since the end of World War II. Affecting as it does more than two thirds of the world's population, economic development will probably be the most important factor of change for the rest of our century and longer.

In this book we would like to analyze the different political and economic aspects of the development process. It is not our purpose, however, to judge the moral value of economic development, which intends basically to achieve freedom from want. Should the Third World—that is, the developing countries—follow in the footsteps of the wealthy developed countries and allow their efforts to be guided only by material criteria and incentives? Should they, by the same token, make short shrift of the non-material values in their traditional society, those which had brought neither prosperity nor progress in the past, but had ensured a certain degree of stability and security? The growing discontent with the values and achievements of the "affluent" society in the West indicates that material progress alone does not guarantee happiness, nor even contentment.

In solving gradually the problems of poverty and destitution, material progress inevitably creates new ones. But at the stage where developing countries find themselves today, improvement in economic conditions is an absolute necessity. Without it progress in other fields may be extremely difficult. In a speech to the Royal Economic Society, J. M. Keynes once said that although economic prosperity should not be considered equivalent to civilization, it did create a basis for civilization. In his discussion of the ethics of development Denis Goulet expresses the same idea somewhat more concisely: "Man must have enough in order to be more."[1]

The basic purpose of economic development is easy to define. It is simply to modernize the developing countries and to raise them to the level of the advanced industrialized nations. Under this general heading, however, there can be great differences with emphasis placed on one or another of the myriad aspects of the overall process of

1. Denis L. Goulet, *The Cruel Choice*, Atheneum, New York, 1971, p. 28.

growth and change. This diversity is reflected in the great variety of policies which can be pursued.

The traditional goal of economic development has been to improve the standard of living. Usually this suggests increased private consumption and a higher quality of consumer goods. Economic development also implies higher standards of collective consumption, with improved public services in education, health, welfare, and utilities. In the world of today—although other goals may be given higher priority in some cases—these are still vital objectives and are sought in various ways. A developing country can choose to emphasize the importance of increasing private income and wealth and may select a policy which seeks the maximum expansion of production. Alternatively, the decision may be to stress a more equal distribution of private income. This will occur when a government redistributes income and/or when maximum efforts are made to increase employment. One should note here that greater employment will not necessarily result in the highest possible rate of increase in production, or in the growth of income.

Another major aim of development is to extend national power. Developing countries suffer from a humiliating inferiority in economic and military power. Their need for power will even take precedence over their yearning to improve conditions of life, when they feel that their national independence is being threatened by this inferiority. Eventually, of course, the two objectives can become complementary, rather than contradictory. The establishment of a modern and productive economy will create a base for both increased wealth and increased power.

Social revolution is also a basic goal of development in a number of countries. It may reflect the philosophical orientation of the government and the ruling party, which considers it more important than improved material standards, and therefore gives it higher priority. But irrespective of the ideological commitment, social revolution may be considered essential in putting into effect the political and social changes without which development could not succeed. In many cases both arguments coincide.

All human and material resources must be fully mobilized in order to achieve any of the goals of economic development. The productive effort must be intensified and made more efficient. Consumption must be reduced in relative, if not in absolute, terms to free maximum savings for investment. These efforts and sacrifices can be made voluntarily or imposed by coercion.

When the main thrust of the development process is toward greater personal income and wealth, the ingenuity of private entrepreneurs is mainly responsible for this increase in productivity. Private consumption is governed by the laws of the market, the law of supply and demand. Therefore, the burden of restricted consumption is borne by those who have the weakest bargaining power in the economy, usually domestice wage earners and/or overseas suppliers. The savings are derived mainly from entrepreneurial profits and are reinvested in order to generate further profits.

When countries aspire to increase their national power, their economic policies comply with this goal. Industries which are essential to defense are expanded at the expense of those which could produce consumer goods. The ensuing sacrifices are accepted by different classes of the population, more or less on a voluntary basis. Savings amassed by private entrepreneurs or derived from taxes are invested in accordance with government directives.

In countries whose objective is socialization, the government both directs and operates all economic activities. Drastic sacrifices in consumption are exacted of the population as a whole. While such sacrifices may be made voluntarily by those who share the government's ideological persuasion, usually the most severe ones are imposed on those classes which are least in favor of government policies. In a socialist economy all savings are collected and reinvested by the government.

Before we delve into the problems that developing countries face today, we need to examine briefly as background:

(1) the period which preceded the start of development, when progress was impossible in the confines of a static and stagnant civilization;

(2) chief examples of the various forms of development which have proved successful—the spontaneous evolution of Western capitalism; the nationalistic flowering of Japan; the growth of a socialist economy in the Soviet Union;

(3) the initial stages of development in the countries of the Third World, which were launched and conducted by Western powers to further their own interest.

Part One

Background

Chapter 1. *THE PREDEVELOPMENT SOCIETY*

THE CONCEPT of economic development presumes the existence of a flexible society which will accept and facilitate change, technical and economic innovation. This prerequisite is taken so much for granted in the twentieth century that its absence appears absurd and difficult to imagine. But throughout most of history it has not been found anywhere in the world. Only in the relatively short span of the last two centuries has it been present even in the most advanced countries. In the developing countries of Asia, Africa, to a lesser extent in Latin America, only a few decades ago, the whole structure of society was based on tradition, tradition usually sanctified by religion and therefore immutable. Any proposal for altering traditional views was considered heretical and as such punishable. In Western Europe, as late as the middle of the seventeenth century, Galileo was tried and forced to renounce his theory that the earth rotated around the sun. The prevailing conviction that methods of production already in existence are best and therefore to be strictly followed—as was the case with the guilds of the Middle Ages—obviously was a powerful impediment to any change or improvement.

Another obstacle was the dominant role that non-economic values played in this predevelopment civilization. Basic economic activities, especially agriculture, had to be performed in order to satisfy material needs. Because of the scant yield of the work, these basic activities occupied the great majority of people full-time. But material values, the desire for material success, played a relatively small part in the life and aspirations of the people. To be sure, individual enrichment seems unlikely, if one remembers the context of stagnant production techniques and the small scale of the market place. International trade was only a minor exception to this general rule and involved only luxury items.

Society was dominated by the upper classes; their material wants were indulged by the masses to the highest extent possible within the confines of existing technology. But the services which this élite performed were considered of a higher order and more important than material things. Most frequently these functions were religious. To serve as an intermediary between mankind and the Deity, to ensure mankind's protection, to provide thus the assurance of eternal life, were the main responsibilities of the clergy. A particularly striking example was the hereditary caste of Brahmans in India. Protection from outside aggression and the maintenance of a modicum of order were offered by military or civilian élite groups, feudal, tribal, or governmental, as was the case of ancient Egypt, Persia, and China, in particular where the Mandarin class could rule on the basis of their mastery of traditional knowledge and wisdom.

As long as such civilizations existed, this hierarchy of values and functions was generally accepted as a natural, God-given state of affairs, even by those at the lowest rung of the ladder. The masses permitted their menial toil to provide the resources for the luxurious consumption of the upper classes and for all investments which were made in these societies. With only the minor exception of dams and irrigation canals in a few river basins, all investments were made in accordance with prevailing values—in temples, fortresses, castles, etc.

There was considerable diversity in the organization of economy in predevelopment societies. They included such extremes as feudal land ownership and craft guilds during the Middle Ages in Western Europe, and the state socialism of pre-Columbian Peru, where all land belonged to the Inca who determined the remuneration of every group. Whatever the particular institution of each of these societies, the general objective was to establish through fixed rules a stable framework for production and distribution of goods and services. And one must admit that on the whole they were successful, especially since excessive population growth was restrained by famine, epidemics, and war. This stability was shaken from time to time by catastrophies, frequently the result of climatic conditions, such as droughts, and these natural events occasionally precipitated man-made disasters. The droughts which occurred in the plains of Central Asia in the fourth century forced their nomadic inhabitants to look westward for better pastures and led them to invade Europe, the cause ultimately of the downfall of the Roman Empire.

These societies did thus more or less attain their goal of stability, but there was no concern with economic progress: therefore, it could not and did not materialize.

Chapter 2. *PRECEDENTS FOR ECONOMIC DEVELOPMENT*

WHICH TYPES of economic development have evolved in the past? To what extent do they relate to the problems now facing developing countries? Can previous policies and methods be imitated in today's world?

In the development of Western Europe, we see the first example of the modernization of an entire society and its economy. It was a spontaneous and slow process which only gradually gained momentum, and it was accompanied by a parallel change in cultural values and institutions.

The starting point for this development is found in the early sixteenth century, when important changes occurred in several directions to cause the disintegration of the closed, static, and rigid society of the Middle Ages. Thus the revival of rational thought in the Renaissance opened the way to scientific investigation, and as a consequence, to technical innovation. The Reformation tore down many of the barriers which religious authorities heretofore had placed in the path of economic development, such as the prohibition of interest-bearing loans. Simultaneously the discoveries of new lands opened up new vistas and invalidated the old concepts of a narrow restricted world, so that further change and progress could now be envisioned. Opportunities multiplied for economic expansion and enrichment through international trade. With more possibility for improving material conditions, material values grew in importance and motivated increasingly the behavior of individuals and the policies of their governments. In the countries of northern Europe, which became the pioneers of the new capitalist economy, the Protestant ethic sanctified material success. Success was now considered a proof of righteousness and a manifestation of Divine Blessing. This was in sharp contrast to the previous exaltation of monastic poverty which had discouraged the drive for material success, the motor of progress in an economy of private enterprise. Now this new conciliation of religious and material motives added a powerful incentive to economic development.

The necessary conditions for the Industrial Revolution, which then led to the establishment of the modern capitalist economy, evolved slowly and gradually. The creation of strong centralized national states fostered the growth of large-scale industries, to meet both the needs of national defense and of the royal courts. Improvement in security conditions and in means of transportation, at first by water and later by land, as well as the disappearance of tolls and other obstacles to domestic trade, expanded markets for agricultural and industrial products.

Finally, the development of overseas trade, through the discovery of new markets for European goods and new sources of supply for exotic products and precious metals, brought to the fore a new class of capitalist entrepreneurs who evolved new business techniques and accumulated vast capital resources. When the right moment had come, these entrepreneurs were prepared to meet the demand for new products, and the growing need for products previously imported, such as Indian cotton goods. In their new manufacturing ventures they introduced technological innovations and thus started the Industrial Revolution.

Three important factors contributed to the tremendous industrial expansion which took place in Western Europe and the United States in the nineteenth century. First, all legal and institutional obstacles to free enterprise, which had been introduced previously to ensure social stability or to protect labor (e.g., guilds, minimum wage laws, etc.) now disappeared. Then the revolution in navigation through the invention of steamships, and the widespread adoption of free trade policies created a world market economy. The free movement of goods, capital, and persons brought about international specialization of labor. Goods and services were exchanged on a world scale determined by the comparative advantage of each region. This world trade involved mainly an exchange of manufactured goods from the industrialized countries—primarily at first Great Britain, where the Industrial Revolution started—for the primary products of other nations. Naturally this trade was particularly profitable for the West which had organized it to further its own interests. A general climate of monetary stability, ensured throughout most of the period by the operation of the universal gold standard, also encouraged industrial expansion.

During this whole period the growth of population had not created a problem for economic development. Population had increased very rapidly, compared to the rate of growth experienced in the periods both before and after the Industrial Revolution. But only rarely had its increase exceeded an annual rate of 15 per thousand. Moreover, the decline in the death rate, due to better living conditions and improved hygiene, had been very gradual. It accelerated only when the economy was already developing at a rapid pace and thus able to absorb a large labor force and to benefit from a greater number of consumers. Under such conditions a rapid increase in population could be on the whole a positive factor to stimulate development, not an impediment.

In addition, migration to the nearly empty spaces of the Americas and Australia provided a major outlet during that period for the excess population of Western Europe. In these new countries population growth was even more a prerequisite for development. By expanding the overseas markets and the sources of supply available to the older industrial countries of Western Europe, the increase in population of the New World stimulated international trade and the progress of the world economy.

One should note here that the development of the West was achieved essentially by private enterprise, through the initiative and the resources of private entrepreneurs. Governments to be sure played an important role in providing the institutional framework, in particular security, legal protection, administrative services, a monetary basis, and frequently, tariff protection. In some important areas, in the construction of railroads, for example, direct or at least indirect government subsidies were available. Still, on the whole, governments took second place to private enterprise.

The financing of this economic development is an important point. What resources provided the funds for the investments which this development required?

During the period preceding the Industrial Revolution, the capital of entrepreneurs, which was later used to establish their manufacturing enterprises, came largely from profits accumulated through overseas trade with the underdeveloped countries. This trade was conducted under conditions of outright colonial domination, or at the very least of complete monopoly of the markets of the underdeveloped countries, both for the purchase of primary products and for the sale of manufactured goods. The slave trade was a most profitable activity from the seventeenth to the early nineteenth century. But even apart from the slave trade this overseas trade involved a gross exploitation of the underdeveloped trading partners of the West.

After the start of industrialization, exploitation of the populations of overseas countries gradually ceased to be the main source of profits, and consequently of investment capital. Still the inequality in the trading relationships persisted, though it became less scandalous. To a great extent this inequality has continued up to the present and is reflected in the generally unfavorable terms of trade for primary exports from developing countries.

With the start of industrialization a more important source of funds for development investments was found by exploiting the domestic labor force of the new industries. This became apparent as soon as centralized factories, using power-driven machinery, began to replace the workshops of the craftsmen who had formerly worked on their own or for entrepreneurs under the old "putting out" system. In these new factories productivity was immediately and substantially increased. Yet the bargaining power of the workers who were employed in these factories, and were deprived of all legal protection, was extremely weak. Thousands of farm workers had fled to the cities after having been driven off the land in England by the enclosure laws. The level of wages, determined by the law of supply and demand, was very low—at, and often below, the subsistence level. Working conditions for women and children, as well as for grown men, were appalling. The time lag between the considerable increase in productivity, which occurred at the start of industrialization, and the beginning of fairer employment practices, extended for over half a century. This excess of entrepreneurial profits provided vast and growing resources which could be used, and were indeed used—in a society which still attached considerable importance to the Calvinist virtues of hard work and thrift—for productive investment. To a large extent these profits provided the financial base for an extremely rapid rate of development and industrialization.

Only gradually did the exploitation of labor diminish, in part as a result of more humane laws, but largely because of the growing power of organized labor. Then, too, employers realized that wages could be an important source of consumer income and that the products of the industries could be marketed to their own workers. This became a significant argument in opposing the heretofore excessively low wages. In today's consumer society, wage exploitation has survived, if at all, only as a marginal phenomenon. The financial resources which pay the cost of further economic development are principally drawn from the savings of business enterprises or of the general public.

In conclusion, one can say that this first example of successful economic development can offer some limited guidelines to the developing countries of today. It reveals the importance of various prerequisites for development: the existence of a functioning institutional framework, the accumulation of savings to the point where they can be utilized for productive investment, the initiation of innovating entrepreneurs. Conditions in the developing countries, however, are very different today from what prevailed in the West at the start of its development. Their needs are also far more pressing. They will not be satisfied with a slow gradual rate of development. Their governments can no longer play a marginal role in directing and organizing their economy. It is not possible, as it was in the past, to rely on the exploitation of foreign labor for necessary financial resources. They are also unwilling to impose the heavy burden of such exploitation on their own people without their explicit approval or at least without their tacit acceptance.

The development of Japan was the result of a deliberate effort, undertaken by the government, supported by the dominating élite and willingly accepted by the mass of the population.

Its main purpose was political rather than economic: the increasing encroachments of the West, since the forced opening of Japan to Western trade by Commodore Perry in 1854, had deeply humiliated an intensely nationalistic nation. Japan had been proud of having remained isolated for two centuries from the barbarians overseas. In the second half of the nineteenth century the specter of foreign colonization or at least of losing their complete independence suddenly loomed large. The examples of other Asiatic countries were well understood by the leaders of Japan. India's ancient and advanced culture had not prevented her from becoming an outright colony. Even nearer home, China had had to consent to restrictions on her right of sovereignty and to a loss of territory. There was a mortal danger that by remaining faithful to traditional forms of life and civilization Japan would become unable to withstand the pressures of the West with its modern technology and its new institutional structures. Already Japan had been forced to accept unequal treaties which gave extraterritorial rights to foreigners and restricted its right to impose custom duties.

In order to safeguard her independence, Japan decided on a total transformation of her institutions in all major areas, political and economic, as well as military. The object was to imitate the West wherever appropriate, in order to reduce the imbalance of power. Under somewhat similar circumstances other countries have also attempted to transform their entire institutional structure. The most obvious examples of revolutions initiated from above are those of Russia under Peter the Great and Turkey under Kemal Ataturk. But Japan's modernization was by far the most successful.

A major reason for her success was that this project of revolutionary transformation received the nearly unanimous support of all classes of Japanese society. Even those who stood to lose their dominant position and their *raison d'être*, the "Daymios," the feudal princes of Japan, and the "Samurai," did not oppose it. One of the first and most important measures taken was the abolition of the feudal system. The Daymios surrendered both their private armies and their power of taxation. The Samurai, a hereditary class of warriors who received a government stipend for their services, were now replaced by a modern standing army. They gave up their functions, privileges, and status, as well as their livelihood, when the loss of their regular stipend was compensated only by the payment of a relatively modest lump sum.

Another important feature in this program was the introduction of the basic framework of a capitalist society. The new order permitted freedom of occupation, and allowed an open market to set the level of prices and wages. Modern legal, administrative, and financial institutions came into being and included the creation of a central banking system and a stable currency.

The theory of copying Western institutions in order to catch up with the West went as far as an attempt to establish a pseudo-constitutional form of government with an elected legislature. But this last innovation proved contrary to the spirit of Japanese nationalism which venerated the divine origin of the Emperor in whose name and on whose order the modernization had begun. Moreover, it became obvious that the parliamentary system would not strengthen the nation. It was more likely, on the contrary, to increase the difficulty of maintaining a strong and stable government, which was essential to the consolidation and the growth of power of the country. Although a parliament was in fact established, it remained of little importance until the total breakdown of traditional nationalism after the defeat of World War II.

As far as economic policies were concerned, the free enterprise system which had produced such outstanding results in the West also became the basis of Japan's modern economy. But Japanese policies were extremely pragmatic and were governed by expediency rather than absolute adherence to principle. In the absence of an established class of private entrepreneurs with capital and experience in modern industry, the government did not hesitate to take the initiative in industrial development. It invested heavily not only in the creation of modern means of transport, such as railroads and shipping lines, but also in mines, iron and steel manufactures, and shipyards—areas which would be important to national defense. It created banks to finance agriculture, industry, and foreign trade. Thus the government paved the way for further investments by private capital in these and other related activities.

The economic development of Japan was achieved without the aid of private foreign investment. Direct foreign investments in particular were considered dangerous to national economic independence and were therefore discouraged, an attitude which has not been totally abandoned even today. Only a relatively small amount of capital was raised in foreign markets, mainly by government loans.

Foreign exchange, however, was needed to pay for imports, particularly of capital goods, and it was obtained from the proceeds of exports, which grew at a very rapid rate. The main export items were at first labor-intensive agricultural products. In the absence of synthetic fabrics, there was a vast demand for silk in Western Europe and even more in the United States. Later Japan started increasingly to export labor-intensive industrial products: textiles, cheap chinaware, etc. The availability of cheap labor gave Japan an obvious advantage over her more advanced trading partners. But her success in the international marketplace was due even more to the organization of her manufactures. Many of them were initially cottage industries, located in the countryside and employing on a full-time or part-time basis members of peasant families who needed some extra income, however small it might be. These cottage industries required little capital or overhead facilities, such as transport and housing. The workers lived at home or, as was the case with larger plants and in particular with female workers, in dormitories owned and operated by the factories. There was a close co-ordination between the cottage industries and large-scale plants in the same fields. The former often acted as subcontractors, supplying factories with individual parts. The cost of production could thus be kept low and this made Japan's exports particularly competitive in foreign markets. In addition, Japanese industry was practically the first to create special export corporations with government sponsorship and assistance. This made it easier for small producers to gain access to foreign markets.

Particularly important in the development of Japan was the effort made to introduce a comprehensive and well integrated system of education. In a relatively short time this produced universal literacy and insured an adequate supply of well trained technical and managerial personnel for Japan's economy.

The real cost of Japan's development, especially in its early stages, was borne mainly by the rural population. At that time it represented the great majority of the people. The feudal dues which had been paid in kind were replaced by a fixed land tax payable in money, increasing

the effective fiscal burden on the peasants. It is true that this tax, since
it was assessed on an acreage basis, provided an incentive for more
intensive production, and consequently for more income. But in actual
fact all the increase in income was syphoned off for tax payments; at
one time the land tax amounted to 80 per cent of total government
revenue. The greater agricultural production provided the extra food
needed to feed the growing urban population. Migration to the cities
of surplus farm workers provided the cheap labor required by the
new urban industries.

But on the whole the success of Japan's industrial development
was not due to the dumping of cheap goods on foreign markets or to
the exploitation of cheap labor. That was the explanation which was
put forward by the older industrial countries of the West that were
suffering from the successful competition of Japanese products, both
on the international scene and within their own boundaries. The standard of living for the mass of the Japanese people, especially for the
urban and rural working classes, did not deteriorate during this period
of development. But neither did it change significantly. The level and
the habits of private consumption remained stable, and it was this
maintenance of the status quo, while productivity was increasing
rapidly because of modernization, which provided for a long time vast
surpluses available for investment. The high rate of investment over
a long period of time was a major factor in Japan's success.

As we pointed out earlier, the task of transforming and modernizing Japanese society and the economy was generally embraced by
the people as a whole. No one doubted that it was indispensable, to the
nation's survival and glory. Furthermore the basic system of values—
an intense quasi-religious nationalism, with the Emperor embodying
the divine character of the nation—had remained unchanged, this in
spite of technological and economic innovations. Thus all considered
it their patriotic duty to participate in the modernization effort, and
they accepted any sacrifices which this might involve.

This sense of duty was particularly felt by the Samurais who,
with the loss of their privileged status, transferred their energies to
their new careers as business managers. Their success in this field,
and the knowledge that their contribution was adding to the greatness
of the nation, gave them a deep satisfaction. Yet in spite of the new
wealth which their business careers brought them, they maintained for
quite a long time their traditionally rather modest standards and
habits of life.

Patriotic and religious feelings also motivated the working classes,
who accepted obediently the fact that in this changing economy their

material resources were not increasing in relation to the productivity of their labor. But the survival of a paternalistic tradition in the new industrial framework was the determining factor. In accordance with this semi-feudal tradition, the employers were actually responsible for their workers, and this gave them a considerable degree of security. This paternalistic tradition exists even today to a great extent and it is probably still an important element in the tremendous industrial expansion of Japan.

Even if one sets aside Japan's extraordinary performance in the period right after World War II, her economic development has been outstandingly successful. In a relatively short span of 50 to 60 years she was able to reach the level of the most highly industrialized countries of the West. Such achievement seems particularly striking when one remembers that mere economic growth was not her only or even most important goal. A major portion of Japan's total investments was spent on expanding the armed forces and on developing a colonial empire. Later events were to prove the futility of those efforts. However, the very fact that Japan was able to challenge—and at first with some success—the world's greatest power, is an indication of the economic and military power that she acquired in the process of development.

Japan offers an example which many of the developing countries today might like to imitate. They share the same aspirations. The desire to achieve or to consolidate their national independence is common to all of them, even if the developing countries attribute much more importance to improving rapidly the standard of living than did Japan a hundred years ago. But only a few, so far, have been able to impose this discipline of hard work and limited consumption on their people as a national duty in order to free savings for the purpose of development. Quite the contrary. Now the revolution of "rising expectations" creates an irresistable urge to greater consumption, which will not wait until an expanded economy can afford it. Just as important, and as difficult to reproduce totally, would be Japan's happy transformation of her outmoded élite into a class of modern, efficient entrepreneurs and managers. Still the pragmatic character of her development, her emphasis on education, her decisions not to concentrate on replacing imports but instead to pay for them by generating exports which would be competitive on the world market, are all aspects which developing countries could study with profit.

The October Revolution of 1917 which established the Soviet government had one main objective, the creation of a communist society. This goal obviously included public ownership of all means of production and the abolition of a capitalist system under which the Russian economy during the preceding decades had made considerable headway. While still underdeveloped, especially as regards its peasant agriculture, Russia in 1917 was well beyond the "take-off" point of self-generating economic development.

The introduction of communism had far deeper implications, however. What was involved was the substitution of collective solidarity for individualistic egoism, the abandonment of material incentives and the attempt to establish an equalitarian society. It was assumed that improvements in the standard of living for the working masses would be reached as a matter of course, when the new collectivist economy had gone into operation.

During the first phase of Soviet rule, the period of "war communism," political motives and objectives dominated government policies. All industrial plants were nationalized and estates were divided up among the peasants without thought to the probable effect on industrial and agricultural production. It is true, however, that these measures only legalized a spontaneous and rather chaotic takeover of factories and land, which had already occurred and which could not have been prevented.

This course was reversed drastically only in 1921 when a protracted civil war, the confiscation of food from the peasants by the government, and mismanagement in the factories operated by workers' committees brought the country to the verge of total economic collapse and to a disastrous famine. Economic recovery became the sole consideration for the survival of Soviet power. Lenin introduced, therefore, the New Economic Policy (NEP), which involved a partial return to the system of private enterprise. Peasants were authorized to sell their food surpluses on the open market; small industrial and commercial enterprises were returned to private management. But as Lenin pointed out to colleagues who feared a complete return to capitalism, this policy was intended only as a breathing spell until the economy recovered sufficiently to permit the launching of a new socialization effort. Lenin's objective was achieved. Under the NEP the Russian economy recovered rapidly, and by 1926 it had reached its highest prewar level. Still one notes that the revival of agricultural production was due mainly to the "kulaks," a new class of efficient peasants whose increasing wealth and power presented a serious danger to the Soviet government.

The first Five-Year Plan was started in 1927–1928 and saw the beginning of massive industrialization. Three main considerations motivated Stalin, who had initiated it.

First and foremost was national power. When her hopes of world revolution, which in the early post World War I period had seemed near fulfillment, faded away, Soviet Russia found herself to be a socialist island surrounded by hostile capitalist states. She therefore thought it essential to strengthen her military capability. To this end a massive effort was made to build up heavy industry, in order to ensure the production of capital goods in time of peace, and an adequate supply of armament in case of war. For that reason the development of new industrial centers in the Urals and in Siberia was given a high priority; both regions would be safer in an invasion than the already industrialized areas of European Russia.

Stalin's first Five-Year Plan was also concerned with the elimination of the private sector that had been revived during the NEP. To establish a fully collectivistic economy, the government would take over all small industrial and commercial enterprises. It counted on improving the rate of productivity on the farms by consolidating small farms into large collective units. The mechanization of agriculture would create a surplus of workers who could migrate to the cities and provide the labor needed by the rapidly developing industries. The proportion of industrial workers would increase in ratio to peasants. This was judged essential by the government who feared peasants and looked upon them as the class most bound by tradition and hostile to the collectivist spirit.

A definitely low priority was given to all major items of private consumption. This included even food, which had to be strictly rationed. The manufacture of industrial consumer goods increased at a far slower rate than did capital goods. Little investment was made in housing during the early period. But there was a strong emphasis on expanding public services such as education—which was justifiably considered of particular importance, not only to improve the cultural level of the country but primarily to increase productivity—health, and social security.

In its attempt to develop heavy industry on a large scale, the Soviet Union reaped an unqualified success. It became in only 30-odd years the world's second largest industrial power, not only in the production of basic industrial materials such as steel and coal, but also in some highly sophisticated fields, usually those related to defense, such as atomic energy and the exploration of outer space.[1]

1. In other fields they seem to fall behind, as in the science of computers.

It is interesting to note that under Stalin especially, Soviet policy abandoned in part its equalitarian principles in order to attain maximum production. Extremely high premiums were granted to workers who exceeded their individual quotas, and to managers who succeeded in "overfulfilling" the production plans for their factories.

Production of light consumer goods developed much more slowly and did not approach consumer demand, either in quantity or even more in quality. Although this is gradually improving the Soviet Union is still far from attaining the affluence of the consumer society that exists in the United States, in Western Europe, and lately even in Japan.

The collectivization of agriculture encountered at first a stubborn resistance on the part of most peasants and particularly the wealthy kulaks, who were its principal victims. It was finally imposed, but the government's triumph resembled more a military victory than a land reform leading to greater production. The back of the opposition was broken by mass deportation to forced labor camps. The results were severely reduced harvests and the mass slaughter of livestock. In the early 1930's the total breakdown of food production gave rise to a famine in the richest grain producing areas of southern Russia. Subsequently government policy was somewhat modified, and farmers were allowed to retain small individual plots which they could cultivate for their own account. But in spite of further technical improvements and additional concessions to farmers, such as minimum wages and pensions, agriculture remains today the most laggard sector of the Soviet economy. The area under cultivation is enormous, but the needs of the population are barely met; there is only a relatively small surplus left over for export, this in a country that before the revolution had been one of the world's major food exporters. In contrast to the United States and to Western Europe, agriculture in the Soviet Union is still a labor-intensive proposition and productivity on the farms remains low.

The cost of development in the Soviet Union was financed largely through a drastic reduction in private consumption. In the early stages of their industrialization a feeling of dedication and enthusiasm amidst the communist youth, the "komsomol," made this to some extent possible. But principally it was imposed on the people through coercion, strict rationing backed by terror. The magnitude of the sacrifices enforced on Soviet consumers can be seen in the size of the "turnover" tax on all consumer items including food. At its maximum in 1935 it represented 64 per cent of the sales price.

Naturally the heaviest sacrifices were exacted from the "class enemies," mainly the peasants who had resisted collectivization, who formed the majority of inmates in the slave labor camps, and who furnished labor for public works such as canals.

Of the three main goals of Soviet development—namely, national power, a socialist transformation of society, and improvement in the welfare of the people—the last, not surprisingly, was the least stressed. It is therefore only natural that results in this area have proved the least satisfactory. But such a conclusion must be somewhat qualified. Goods required for private consumption were available only at a very minimal level. But as soon as it became at all feasible, public collective services were started in a lavish, almost luxurious style. The object was to substitute for individual satisfaction of the kind derived from private ownership of a car for instance, or landscaping of the family plot, as in American suburbs, the sense of a collective pride in elaborately decorated subways and in beautifully landscaped streets with fountains and playgrounds. This was done in the newly built sections of cities in the Soviet Union.

There has been considerable change during the last two decades, and especially since Stalin's death in 1953. Some contradictory trends have become apparent in the goals of Soviet development. National power remains still of paramount importance, as witnessed in the high priority of heavy industry and fields related to defense. But after more than a generation of continued hardships and austerity, there is a strong and ultimately irresistible yearning for higher standards of consumption. This general feeling is shared by the two upper layers of the technocracy and bureaucracy which are gradually becoming the most influential sectors of the Soviet Union. Soviet consumers, who are now well informed about progress in the West, cannot accept that 50 years after the victory of socialism their country, which has achieved such outstanding triumphs in space, is still unable to provide a varied diet, good quality clothing, durable consumer goods, decent housing, and a car for each family—i.e., the standard of living which even workers in capitalist countries either already enjoy or are rapidly attaining.

Under this pressure a higher priority is being gradually given to the needs of the consumer. Considerable efforts, as yet not completely successful, have been made to increase agricultural production. Substantial quantities of special foodstuffs and consumer goods are being imported, from other socialist countries, from developing countries and even from the West, including butter from Denmark and poultry from France. Large-scale investments have been allocated to promote an expanded manufacture of consumer goods and to accelerate the construction of housing. To stimulate efforts in the field, privately financed and owned apartments have been authorized.

Such attempts to meet the demands of individual consumers, started under Khrushchev, have continued and even grown under his successors. A significant step in this direction was the decision to build —with technical assistance of a major capitalist manufacturer, Fiat of Italy—a factory for the mass production of family-size passenger automobiles. It represents a deliberate choice to adopt the consumer-oriented approach of the capitalist countries in the field of motorization which to some extent at least is the symbol of the twentieth century. From the point of view of orthodox communists, this is indeed a revisionist heresy and a betrayal of the socialist ideal. This is of course the argument put forth by China.

The increasing importance of consumer goods, which must suit the tastes of the public, has called for far greater sophistication in the Soviet economy; this creates considerable difficulties in maintaining a centralized system of planning for industrial production. Earlier, when the public willingly bought up any consumer goods it could find regardless of quality, and when the main objective was still to increase as rapidly as possible the output of basic industrial products, there was no problem. The new challenge, not only of producing but above all of having to sell consumer goods, necessitates a greater reliance on the market. To this end a scheme of granting greater autonomy to individual plants has been introduced. Material incentives for managers and workers have been offered in a great number of factories.

This more flexible system of planning has had apparent success, both in the Soviet Union and in other socialist countries, in Hungary in particular. But it has encountered considerable ideological opposition because of its appeal to material incentives. There is also the fear that more liberal economic policies may lead to demands for a similar political liberalization. Therefore increasing attention has been paid to emphasizing the socialist reasons for achieving the goal of an improved standard of life, an objective which is still considered valid.

The pattern of development in the Soviet Union is quite attractive to the developing countries. Obviously the cost in human suffering and hardship has been high. Individual rights have been denied—rights which, to be sure, few if any in the developing countries are enjoying in any event, with the possible exception of the ruling élite. On the other hand, the Soviet Union has taken gigantic strides in education, medical care, social security, and has established a basic equality for everyone which enhances the self-respect of the people. In becoming one of the world's greatest industrial powers it has at least formed a basis for future improvement in lagging standards of living.

The Soviet Union's appeal is particularly strong for those countries whose governments or youthful élites accept the ideological goals of a socialist revolution. The Soviet example is also of great interest, however, for those who do not necessarily share the socialist ideal, but simply despair of achieving both economic and social development by more humane methods. In the face of powerful obstacles such as the egoistic opposition of the upper classes, the Soviet approach seems to them a very viable solution.

Chapter 3. *THE START OF DEVELOPMENT OF THE THIRD WORLD*

THE DEVELOPMENT, or the modernization, of countries in Asia, Africa, and Latin America first began through contact with Western countries. From the start, as early as the sixteenth century, these contacts—with very few exceptions, notably Japan—were made on an unequal basis. The underdeveloped countries lost in the process. This unequal relationship was not always due to an inferior civilization, or even, to some extent, to inferior technology. Initially, for instance, India's textiles and China's paper and pottery were far superior to what the West could produce. The decisive factor was the question of armaments, and principally of fire arms.

These contacts were invariably sought by the Western countries. In some instances they went as far as to force the underdeveloped countries to open their ports to Western traders. This was the case with China and Japan as late as the middle of the nineteenth century. Out of such encounters the West was able to obtain at most advantageous terms the products of the underdeveloped countries, and in the final analysis to exploit natural and human resources.

The circumstances governing these trading relationships varied widely. In some cases, as in Mexico and Peru, outright conquest completely destroyed existing institutions, and was followed by actual plunder of the gold and silver treasures of the Aztecs and Incas. In most other countries the first contacts were through trade, which led gradually to greater economic and political influence, then to partial or even complete domination, as happened in India and Indonesia. But even when these relationships involved legitimate trade, the West set up a system of monopoly which they jealously protected to safeguard for themselves both the purchase of exotic goods and the sale of their own products. This monopoly was imposed by force. The Portuguese and the Dutch wiped out the Arab traders who previously had controlled the Indian Ocean. Each Western country excluded from its sphere of influence traders from competing nations, and a number of wars were fought for these reasons from the sixteenth to the eighteenth century.

Force was also applied in making indigenous producers obey the policies which the monopolies dictated. Thus the Dutch destroyed spice plantations at Amboina, in Indonesia, in order to reduce the supply and maintain high prices on the world market.

The most logical method—in that day's inhuman view of foreign trade—was to take advantage of the availability in some overseas areas of cheap labor and in others of virgin land for growing tropical crops such as sugar, coffee, or cotton for the world market— i. e., for Western industries or consumers. Thus Negro slaves were imported from Africa and brought to the fertile lands in the southern part of the United States, the islands of the Caribbean, and Brazil. Later a somewhat less barbaric combination of labor and natural resources evolved. Indentured Indian or Chinese coolies were re- cruited to cultivate the rubber plantations of Malaya and Indonesia. Rural Africans from South and Central Africa worked for a pittance in the gold and diamond mines of the Transvaal.

Another approach was to compel the local population to grow export products for the world market, at the risk sometimes of severely reducing essential food crops. The Dutch enforced the mandatory delivery of export products until the latter part of the nineteenth century. Under this scheme only coffee, sugar, and spices could fill the tax requirements. A similar method of imposing the cultivation of coffee and cotton was applied in the Portuguese colonies of Africa and was only officially abolished in 1954.

The most brutal aspects of this exploitation of natural and human resources had nearly all disappeared by the end of World War II. But the imbalance in trade relations between the developed industrial powers of the West and the developing countries remained.

This was a natural consequence of the former's political and economic domination. The Western countries encouraged the under- developed nations to produce and export primary agricultural and mineral products, foodstuffs, and raw materials in order to obtain cheap sources of supply to meet their own needs. To this end they supplied investment capital, usually from private sources, but some- times from government funds, as in the case of several oil companies, in particular the Anglo—Persian Oil Company. These investments directly financed the operations of mines and plantations, or were used to develop essential ancillary facilities, such as harbors, railroads, power plants, and telecommunications.

Foreign-owned enterprises were frequently also foreign-operated; the owners provided their own managers in order to ensure efficiency of operation. They formed a powerful enclave within the indigenous economy and had little if any connection with its other sectors. A substantial part of the profits naturally was transferred abroad, to pay interest and dividends on the initial investment. Thus, as originally intended, most of the benefits that could be derived from the establishment of these new endeavors were reaped by the countries of the investors and the initiators, and not by the developing countries where they were located.

By the end of World War II, which marked also the end of the period during which their development was directed by Western industrial countries, the underdeveloped nations found themselves in a peculiar position. They had become completely export-oriented. The production of primary products designed for export was the strongest sector in their economy and the only one able to compete on the world market. But it was dominated by foreign interests, and its profits did not stay in the country.

Moreover, they were now totally dependent on the world market. Any fluctuation in the industrial activity or in the purchasing power of the developed countries was immediately reflected in the volume and prices of their exports. Their whole economy was affected. Yet the greater part of their economy was still concentrated on meeting their domestic needs, and it remained underdeveloped, even prim- itive, as in the case of their largely subsistence agriculture. There was thus a total imbalance in their economy. Later on, however, usually after they had achieved independence, this modern and effi- cient export sector would enable them to earn the foreign exchange required to finance a more balanced development of their economy.

As a consequence of their domination by the West they had acquired an economic infrastructure. Although it was insufficient and concentrated mainly in transport and power, it would prove most useful in their further development. The underdeveloped countries which had been administered before their independence by dem- ocratic countries, such as Britain and France and, in the case of the Philippines, by the United States, had also inherited from their masters a competent public administration, an essential prerequisite of de- velopment. A system of public education had been established. Though it was limited in scope, it still made available to these countries the necessary minimum of trained personnel at the time of their in- dependence.

Another positive aspect of their relations with the West should be mentioned here. Whatever the cost in terms of economic exploita- tion and political domination might have been, the West did provide a short cut to the assimilation of our modern scientific civilization. This proved crucial for the further development of those countries which had previously been particularly backward. The benefits that they derived could be compared to those reaped by the Celtic and Germanic tribes of Western Europe when they were conquered by the Romans. One reaches the same conclusion when one examines the position of underdeveloped countries which had no contact at all with the West, such as Nepal or Yemen.

On the other hand, the Western powers were most reluctant to encourage changes in traditional cultural patterns which later proved to be an impediment to development; they did little to modify religious taboos or the caste system in India, tribal organization, or the institutions of land tenure. Initially the West was interested solely in the maintenance and the development of trade. Later, and particularly in countries which the Western powers administered directly, they became concerned also with law and order. However, as long as traditional institutions, archaic and absurd though they might be by Western standards, did not conflict with these goals, the principle of Western policy was not to interfere. A minimum of interference would encounter only a minimum of resistance and thus facilitate administration. The major task of removing these obstacles in the indigenous societies was therefore barely started during the period of Western domination. It remained one of the major problems for countries of the Third World when they became independent.

The most important political legacy at the end of Western domination was a widespread feeling of resentment and suspicion toward private Western capital; to a lesser degree it extended to all foreign economic interests.

There was, to be sure, great respect and frequently even admiration—especially among the western-education élites—for the cultures of their former colonial masters, a culture which they in great part had themselves adopted. There was also some recognition of the efforts which had been made by Western governments in the last stages of colonization. But these countries were essentially far more conscious of the economic exploitation which they had had to endure during this period. One must remember that this experience was their first exposure to large-scale capitalist enterprise, as their own domestic concerns were either small or non-existent. It is not surprising, therefore, that most of the newly independent countries viewed all large-scale capitalism with suspicion, if not outright hostility. They aspired to become free from domination by foreign capital by nationalizing or at least limiting foreign investments already in existence and by prohibiting or strictly regulating new investments. They wanted their own governments to take on the major responsibility of owning and running large-scale enterprises. In the field of international trade, they sought the same independence from the world market by concentrating their efforts on diversification and industrialization.

Part Two

The Domestic Problems of Development

Economic development in broad terms is an international phenomenon. But if an underdeveloped country intends to preserve its independence, the nature of its own development is essentially a domestic problem. The direction of its development policies must be determined in the context of its own needs and objectives, and not by a foreign government, however well intentioned, nor even by an international organization.

Only if development is basically a national undertaking can it enjoy the active support of the people which it requires in order to succeed. Obviously economic development policies must be pursued in the framework of the world economy, and not in a vacuum. They must therefore take into consideration relations with other countries, in fields such as trade, aid, or foreign investments. Even though external contributions to development may be substantial, however, the domestic character of development still remains foremost.

As stated earlier, there are considerable differences among the various underdeveloped countries, both in the goals of their development and in the policies they pursue. But there is a great similarity in the major problems which they must face and solve. These can be analyzed, therefore, without reference to specific countries. In this part we will also examine problems which are of special relevance to particular regions.

Chapter 4.   *HUMAN PROBLEMS*

a.   Changes in values

THE MOST IMPORTANT ASPECTS of development relate to human values, and to the attitudes and capabilities of the population. The crucial factor in the transition from a static predevelopment state to a phase of development was a change in the system of values, which put greater emphasis on material factors, and the acceptance of a new concept of progress. The prospect of change and improvement in economic and social conditions was a powerful incentive for increased effort. Entrepreneurs were thus stimulated to take risks and to innovate; farmers felt encouraged to intensify the cultivation of their land. The possibility of greater income became a reason to eschew immediate consumption in order to invest the money saved and build for the future.

Needless to say, the attraction of such material incentives was strongest in countries with an economy of free enterprise. There the entrepreneurs, the dynamic movers of progress, were bound to reap immediate benefits from this change.

In countries with what David Apter called a "mobilization type of society" the goals of development were collective in nature rather than individualistic.[1] Improvement in the standard of living would come of itself to individuals once these goals were attained. The prospect of change and progress in these countries had its main impact in giving their governments a justification for urging the people on to greater efforts, either by persuasion or by coercion.

b.   Utilization of human resources

Another essential element of development is the maximum utilization of human resources. Population, mainly in the form of unskilled manpower, is the major resource of underdeveloped countries; usually it is their only wealth and often it far surpasses their requirements. Whatever the structure of their economy may be, therefore, it becomes absolutely necessary for all underdeveloped countries to make maximum use of all available manpower in their plan of economic development.

The object is to take advantage of the overabundance in manpower to create additional capital, the one factor of production most lacking in underdeveloped countries. But in order to obtain this result labor cannot be granted normal wages. It must be supplied free of charge or at least remunerated at the mininum subsistence level.

In the past the contribution of labor to the growth of capital investment was supplied through forced labor, mainly of slaves. Forced labor was used extensively, especially in the construction of religious buildings—most important then in the context of the pre-

1. David E. Apter, *Some Conceptual Approaches to the Study of Modernization*, Prentice-Hall, Englewood Cliffs, N.J.: 1968, p. 357.

vailing value system—and in building economically productive projects, such as dams and roads. In some cases, however, this labor was furnished voluntarily. Thus for centuries every pilgrim who visited the abbey of Mont St. Michel in Brittany donated several days of his time to work on the construction of the sanctuary. More recently, a milder version of forced labor was imposed in lieu of a tax. Peasants in France before the revolution of 1789 had to work a few days a year on building the highways in their respective provinces. Through the use of this *"corvée du roi,"* for which a cash payment could be substituted, France was able to establish a system of roads that in the eighteenth century was the finest in continental Europe.

There was no special provision for the mobilization of labor during the Industrial Revolution. But the extremely low wages of that time can be considered as a forced contribution of labor to savings and investment. Similarly the retention of a modest level of consumption in Japan during its period of industrialization can be interpreted as a contribution to saving and investment.

In the Soviet Union, on the contrary, mobilization of the labor force, both voluntary and forced, was quite extensive. Great efforts were made in the early stages to persuade workers and partisans of the communist youth movement to make a voluntary sacrifice by working on holidays. To be sure, the contribution of forced labor was more important. According to the findings of the International Labour Office, at its peak in the 1930's the inmates of forced labor camps numbered in the millions. Political and economic reasons prompted this massive use of forced labor. It enabled the Soviet government to neutralize the potential danger of the kulaks and other hostile elements who formed the vast majority of the forced laborers. They were used in large-scale labor-intensive projects, such as building canals and lumbering in the cold northern forests. It was a most economical method of production at a time when capital was scarce and unskilled labor plentiful. The large-scale use of forced labor camps was finally abandoned by Khrushchev when the danger of active political opposition to the government had largely disappeared. In addition, the use of forced labor had become inefficient and wasteful in the new Soviet economy, which had a relative abundance of capital goods but suffered from a shortage of labor.

The unemployed or the underemployed in developing countries must be used to make an important contribution to their development. In nearly all of them there is a surplus of agricultural workers estimated at 30 per cent, even up to 50 per cent in some of them, of the labor force, who are supported by the framework of the traditional family social security system. In addition to these disguised unemployed, most farmers are idle during part of the year when no agricultural work can usefully be performed.

René Dumont, one of the world's foremost specialists in agricultural development, estimated from pilot surveys made that peasants in tropical Africa are only engaged in agricultural work during 100 to 150 days of the year. This represents a maximum of 1,000 man hours.[2] He feels that it should be possible to require all African adults, in addition to their normal work in the fields, to contribute 50 to 60 days per year for productive "human investment" projects. This would bring tropical Africa rapidly to the "take off" stage. Up to now, however, no African country has succeeded even in approaching this level of human investment.

The mobilization on a voluntary basis of this surplus labor force is derived from a tradition of solidarity within the local community which exists in most pre-industrial societies. With its help community development projects can be set up. Such projects are organized by local initiative, through the efforts of the people themselves, and need only the technical organizational, and financial assistance that government can provide. The emphasis in such projects is on self-reliance and the maximum active participation of the local population. Thus the most successful projects of this kind are usually limited in scale, those which are of direct use to the people, such as the construction of feeder roads to connect previously isolated villages with markets, of small dams, the digging of wells, irrigation ditches, and fish ponds. Competent, and above all dedicated, government officials are absolutely essential to provide guidance for village community development workers. India, for instance, failed in her attempt to organize community development work on a national basis. Although she established a large bureaucratic superstructure, the lack of dedication on the part of too many officials doomed any program to stimulate active local participation.

Large-scale projects, such as the building of dams for hydroelectric power stations through labor-intensive methods, must obviously be organized by the government itself. This was done successfully both in India and in China. Wages must of course be paid on such projects, but part of the workers' remuneration can be given in the form of food. Here foreign assistance to provide the extra food which may be in short supply in the particular country is most useful. The United States does this in its Food for Peace Program, for example,

2. René Dumont, *L'Afrique Noire est mal partie,* Editions du Seuil, Paris, 1966, pp. 195–96.

and the United Nations has its World Food Programme. The amount actually paid out in cash may not exceed the cost of relief payments which the workers would anyway receive if they remained unemployed.

The custom of putting draftees to work on public projects during, or in lieu of, their military service is another, somewhat less voluntary, form of using surplus labor for investment. It has a long tradition. Some of the roads built by the Roman legions are still being used throughout Western Europe. The use of draftees for productive civilian service is spreading and in Africa it is particularly evident in Tunisia, the Ivory Coast, and Guinea. In Iran draftees with a minimum of high school education are also being used successfully as primary teachers in the drive for literacy. Where the use of forced labor is unacceptable, utilization of draftees for mandatory work on development projects may be a productive and convenient method of mobilizing labor.

c. *The paramount importance of education*

Education is the natural method of transmitting knowledge and understanding. The lack of a comprehensive educational system, equipped to offer each person the kind of education most suited to his needs and capabilities, is the major cause for the cultural lag of the underdeveloped countries. In order to create an intellectual basis for the modernization of the society and the economy, such an educational system must be established.

General literacy, the first result of a universal elementary education, is of tremendous cultural and political importance. It is the basic tool with which the people can grasp the aims and methods of change and progress. It permits the dissemination of the government's views and of those held by groups representing different shades of public opinion. Although the written word has lost its monopoly of the sources of information and indoctrination with the advent of mass media communication, it is still very important. Naturally its effect depends on the level of literacy within the population.

The impact of education on the economy is even more visible. Competent personnel must be trained at all levels to man administrative and technical posts, both in government and in the private economy. A literate working force must be educated to understand and to apply instructions in an efficient modern industrial economy.

A close correlation can always be seen between the establishment and the expansion of educational services and rapid economic development, with Japan and the Soviet Union as outstanding examples.

A study was made to compare the productivity of educational expenditure with that of investment in physical plant and equipment in the United States.[3] The results demonstrated that the measurable yield of investment in education was at least on a par with other forms of investment. Moreover, this took into account only the direct increase in personal income resulting from education, not its effect on the economy as a whole. Yet the latter can be even more important in developing countries where new industries owe their start to the presence of a few or even a single key person.

The governments of developing countries are under strong pressure from their own people to emphasize education, irrespective of these economic reasons. Throughout the Third World there is an irresistible urge for education. Even illiterate peasants in the most rural backward areas demand education for their children, as an entree into the modern world and a means of assuring social advancement.

But the experience of many developing countries during the last two decades has shown that great care must be taken to plan educational development and to co-ordinate it with the needs of the economy and its capacity to absorb trained personnel. Otherwise very serious economic, social, and political problems may arise.

The traditional expectations which the start of development rendered obsolete have been the cause of some of these difficulties. In the still recent, and remembered, past, when illiteracy was the general rule, graduation even from primary school guaranteed advancement to the ranks of the privileged. The post of clerk in the colonial administration offered an income and status infinitely superior to that of most subsistence farmers. But as soon as primary education expands—even before it becomes universal—such social promotion is no longer assured. As primary school graduates refuse to stay in traditional agriculture and flock into the cities, they can find jobs only if the urban economy has grown sufficiently to provide suitable openings. Even when available, the jobs open to them come with far less privileges and glamour than in the past.

The resulting phenomenon of growing unemployment among young graduates of primary schools has already become quite serious in the big cities of many developing countries. This obviously represents a waste of the resources spent on their education. Their discontent and resentment create a serious threat to the stability of the country and impede its further development.

3. Gary S. Becker, "Underinvestment in College Education," *American Economic Review*, March 1960, pp. 346–54.

The rapidly growing number of high school, and in particular university, graduates, who have studied abroad and in the newly established national institutes, pose an even greater problem. In too many cases their qualifications are not in line with the requirements of the economy. There is an excessive concentration in the liberal arts and a relative scarcity of engineers and especially agronomists. This reflects traditional prejudices and habits of thought in the predevelopment society. The disregard for practical considerations results in the unemployment of highly trained individuals and the loss of any return on the large sums paid out for their education. It causes the brain drain, the emigration of graduates to developed countries, where there are more opportunities. The brain drain and the unemployment of graduates reflect the misuse of the limited resources which the developing countries have for the higher education of their people. Curiously it is the richer developed countries who profit. In many cases, furthermore, the benefits are not inconsiderable. Thus in medicine a large proportion of the interns in hospitals, both in the United States and Great Britain, are former students from the developing countries.

There is considerable disenchantment in several African countries with the results from the massive campaign to carry out the decisions of the Conference of African Ministers of Education, held in 1961, in Addis Ababa. A great effort was made to increase rapidly the enrollment of students in primary education, before a sufficient number of teachers could be trained. Thus they graduated masses of semi-illiterates. Yet in spite of their poor schooling, these youths considered that the jobs which their parents held in traditional agriculture were beneath them. They were not sufficiently qualified, however, to meet the standards of jobs in the modern sector, even if such jobs had been available. On the other hand, the high cost of the initial investment and the recurrent expenditure which this low quality education still entailed placed a heavy burden on the economy; it swallowed a disproportionate share of the budget for economic development. This slowed down the expansion of the modern sector of the economy and reduced its ability to utilize profitably new graduates of the educational system.

It seems essential, therefore, for developing countries to plan the development of their education system so that the maximum rate of growth can be attained, while still taking into account the needs and the absorptive capacity of the economy. For this purpose surveys which anticipate long-term requirements of trained manpower seem most appropriate and should be incorporated within the overall plan of economic development as was done in Nigeria. In the case of Nigeria not all of the predictions materialized, and not all of the measures which the survey recommended were adopted. Still, such comprehensive surveys provide a necessary framework and avoid gross miscalculations. A general plan of education development for all developing countries during the decade of the '70's has been prepared by UNESCO.

Arthur Lewis (in a "Letter to the Editor," in *The Economist*, January 18, 1959, p. 118) points out the need, borne out by experience, of proceeding with a balanced expansion of education at all levels. Both the base and the summit of the educational pyramid must be enlarged together. The alternative method of concentrating first on primary education before undertaking the establishment of secondary schools, and subsequently, universities, was tried in the Congo by the Belgian colonial administration. It proved to be a costly political and economic mistake. When the Congo won its independence, the country found itself bereft of adequately trained nationals to work in the government and direct the economy.

Special attention must also be paid to fill the most serious gaps in educational development. These are to be found at present in the training of teachers and in technical and secondary education. These are recognized as serious impediments to economic development, and the International Bank, for one, is supplying aid in this field with low-interest loans.

It is necessary to determine at the outset the extent to which higher education should be provided by the establishment and expansion of national or regional institutions, and the relative importance of overseas fellowships. The maximum use of local institutions is desirable, but only when they are set up to meet real needs. Sometimes the existence of a national university is considered a status symbol, and they are founded for reasons of prestige. They must offer high quality education at a reasonable cost, but because of their limited enrollment, the cost per student may initially be higher than in institutions overseas. For this reason the creation of regional institutions by neighboring countries seems most logical. This approach was followed by the former territories of French Equatorial Africa at the time of their independence, when they established a common university, with each faculty in a different country.

In the rural areas, primary education must be organized in such a way as to encourage graduates to remain in their villages, and at the same time equip them with the necessary knowledge to improve and modernize methods of cultivation. FAO and UNESCO, the agencies of the United Nations which specialize respectively in agriculture and education, are providing the developing countries with guidelines for this purpose.

The establishment and expansion of what may be called a conventional system of education, as outlined above, can only proceed at a relatively slow pace, if only for financial reasons. It will not answer the tremendous clamor for literacy which is spreading throughout the Third World. To meet this demand new and unorthodox methods, which involve little financial responsibility for the economy, must be devised.

Such methods are directed primarily at adult education, and use secondary, often even primary school graduates, to teach evening classes. In some cases one finds children instructing their parents. This approach has been tried successfully in the Soviet Union in particular to eradicate illiteracy. It has also been used in some developing countries such as Indonesia.

d. *Population and family planning*

The high and increasing rate of population growth is a major obstacle to economic development in most developing countries. In many of them, most notably in India and Pakistan, the present density of population may already be considered excessive in relation to the existing level of technology and the present structure of their economy.

Previously, in the predevelopment period, very high birth rates were matched by correspondingly high death rates, the result of poor food and primitive hygiene. Famines due to the failure of crops, mass epidemics—such as the Black Death which reduced Europe's population by one fourth in the fourteenth century—and protracted wars such as the Hundred Years War in France and the Thirty Years War in Germany, were additional curbs on population growth. On the whole population remained stable or increased at a very slow rate, more or less in step with the equally slow progress of the economy. There was thus a balance between the size of the population and the resources of the economy.

This equilibrium disappeared rapidly after World War II, principally because of the dramatic reduction in the death rate due to the effective use of DDT to wipe out malaria and the introduction of antibiotics. In only three decades the average death rate dropped from 25 to 30 per thousand to less than 10 per thousand. The birth rate, however, remained at its previous high level, or at best declined slowly.

The position in which the Third World found itself after the end of World War II is somewhat similar to that envisioned by Malthus at the end of the eighteenth century. Writing at the start of the Industrial Revolution, Malthus drew a gloomy picture of a population which was multiplying at a geometrical rate of progression and was growing beyond its ability to support itself. His predictions did not materialize in the West because of a combination of favorable factors. The most important of these was the progress in industrial and agricultural technology which led to an enormous expansion of production. This increased the resources to sustain a growing population and created an even greater demand for additional labor with the advantage of a large domestic market. A rapidly burgeoning population thus became an asset, stimulating rather than impeding development. The countries of Western Europe with a high rate of population growth, such as Britain and Germany, expanded their economies more rapidly than did France, whose population remained stable.

Emigration overseas, in particular to the United States, reduced the impact of population growth and provided an important safety valve. It was especially valuable to countries with a stagnant economy, such as Ireland during the potato famine of the 1850's, where a situation similar to the one described by Malthus already existed.

Finally, although improvements in hygiene and living conditions brought about a gradual decline in the death rate before the birth rate itself started to slow down, the death rate still remained high. It took Western Europe and North America more than a century to reduce it from 20 per thousand to 10 per thousand or slightly below. Thus the actual increase in population rarely exceeded 15 per thousand and was slower than that of developing countries today.

The decline in the birth rate in the West occurred only after economic development had engendered substantial changes in living conditions and above all in popular attitudes. Attitudes are usually slower to alter than material conditions, and it may take the life span of a whole generation for people to adjust.

But in the West people came to realize that the advantages of a large family, which had existed in a more primitive civilization, had by now largely disappeared. The prohibition of child labor and compulsory education meant that a large number of children in one household, far from being an asset, imposed a heavy burden. Each additional child reduced the family's per capita income, and as consumer goods became available to the masses, limited as well the per capita consumption. Even the natural desire of parents to secure better opportunities for their offspring could be more easily satisfied in a smaller family. The traditional religious view, that nature should determine the size of the family, gradually lost its hold. It had only been valid as long as the mortality was so high that a maximum birth rate was essential simply to maintain the level of the population. Now a more rational attitude prevailed, and by the early part of the twentieth century family planning was being practiced in most Western countries, if not openly acknowledged.

Since then the level of birth rate has varied in accordance with popular temper. Thus during the depression of the 1930's it declined in several countries to a level below the death rate. In the post World War II period it rose substantially and started to decline again significantly in the second half of the 1960's. Since the Industrial Revolution it has not exceeded the death rate to the extent that it might create a serious population problem, and it is not likely to do so in the near future.

The transition from a very high birth rate in the predevelopment period to one governed by rational motives was a relatively painless evolutionary process in the West. It occurred without assistance or direction on the part of public authorities.

This is not the case with the countries of the Third World, where the problem of population is far more serious than it ever was in the West. They are faced with an unprecedented explosion of population. The average rate of population growth for all developing countries reached 20 per thousand in the 1950's, jumped to 25 per thousand in the first half of the next decade, and at the writing of this book is now 26 per thousand.[4]

To complicate matters further, most of the major developing countries with large populations have also a density of population which is as high or higher than that of developed countries after a century of economic development. Thus in 1968 the number of inhabitants per square kilometer was 160 in India and 125 in Pakistan, compared with 227 in Great Britain, 175 in Italy, and only 91 in France. The situation in a number of smaller developing countries, with population densities such as 374 in Taiwan, 306 in Puerto Rico, and 396 in Mauritius, is even more serious. Furthermore, unlike Western Europe, developing countries cannot hope to alleviate the pressures of excess population through large-scale emigration.

The result is that the growing need for more food and basic necessities, just to maintain existing standards of consumption, actually holds back any real improvement in living conditions of the people.

4. Organization for Economic Co-operation and Development (OECD) 1970 Review of Development Assistance, Paris, 1970, p. 13.

Production is indeed growing but the increase is absorbed by the extra mouths added each year. The developing countries, like Alice in Wonderland, must work harder and harder just to preserve the status quo.

Family planning is the obvious solution, but it is a far more difficult task for them than it was in the West. The developing countries cannot afford a gradual evolution in popular thinking. Time is running out for them and economic development must go hand in hand with a change in attitude which would permit family planning. It must be an act of faith, for it must take place before any improvements in the standards of living can occur.

The adoption of a policy to restrict the birth rate thus becomes an essential part of economic and social development, and no longer a result. Such a policy must include a massive effort of persuasion and education, and the means of supplying the necessary tools. There has been considerable opposition in the past in many developing countries to family planning. In part this opposition was based on religious grounds. It is still the official position of the Catholic church. Moreover, leaders in some developing countries thought that the strength of sheer numbers might compensate to some extent for technical and military inferiority. It is now widely accepted, however, that excessive population growth has a negative rather than a positive impact on a country's economy and that it weakens a country both militarily and politically. Consequently, in many areas this resistance to family planning has subsided. It has now become possible to offer large-scale aid in family planning to developing countries. The international agencies of the United Nations family have been active in this field. The Scandinavian countries—pioneers in this area—and the United States, among others, have set up major bilateral aid programs.

But in this field, as in others, it is the domestic policies of developing countries which carry the most weight. Only in Algeria in Africa, in Mexico, and in some other countries of Latin America with record rates of population growth is this problem not given high priority. There are programs for educating both sexes in birth control and for the distribution of contraceptives. In addition, techniques such as paying bonuses for voluntary sterilization have been introduced in several countries, including India.

Up to now, however, the impact of family planning on population growth has been very limited, at least for the major developing countries with the most serious problems. As can be seen from Table I on page 35, it was most successful in urban centers such as Hong Kong and Singapore, between 1950 and 1969, and in some small countries where industrial development brought about noticeable improvements in living conditions. The most impressive example of family planning is Japan's declining birth rate, which occurred under similar circumstances.

Fortunately for developing countries, extraordinary progress has been made recently in the yield of major cereals, the "Green Revolution," which will be discussed in a later chapter. This has allowed the Third World a breathing spell. It has postponed the realization of the Malthusian threat of a famine due to an increase in population exceeding the expansion of food production. One can only hope that the developing countries will use the time thus gained to good advantage for strengthening their programs of family planning.

It is interesting to note that in spite of the opposition of the social-

Table I

BIRTH RATES, DEATH RATES, GROWTH AND DENSITY OF POPULATION

	Birth Rate (per thousand)		Death Rates (per thousand)		Growth of Population (per thousand)		Density of Population (inhabit. per square klm)
	1950	1969	1950	1969	1950	1969	1968
AFRICA							
Algeria	39.5	40.9*	14.7	10.4*	24.8	30.5*	
Mauritius	49.7	27.2	13.9	8.0	35.8	19.2	396
UAR	44.4	36.8	19.1	14.4	25.3	22.4	32
LATIN AMERICA							
El Salvador	48.5	41.9	14.7	9.9	33.8	32.0	153
Guatemala	50.9	42.5*	21.8	13.3*	29.1	29.2*	45
Jamaica	33.1	34.3*	11.9	7.7*	21.2	26.6*	175
Mexico	45.5	42.2	16.2	9.1	29.3	33.1	24
Puerto Rico	39.0	24.5	9.9	5.6	29.1	18.9	306
ASIA							
Ceylon	39.7	31.8*	12.4	7.9*	27.3	23.9*	182
China (Taiwan)	43.3	25.6	11.5	5.3	31.8	20.3	374
Hong Kong	26.8	20.7	8.2	4.8	18.6	15.9	
Japan	28.2	18.3	10.9	6.7	17.3	11.6	273
Singapore	45.4	22.2	12.0	5.1	33.4	17.1	

* 1968

Source: United Nations Demographic Yearbooks, 1960 and 1969.

ist countries to family planning—the Marxist doctrine does not recognize the danger of overpopulation—the impact of industrialization and urbanization has effected a reduction in the birth rate of the Soviet Union similar to that of the West at the same stage of development. From 1963 to 1968 one can observe a considerable difference between the annual growth of 0.9 per thousand in the European part of the Soviet Union and the 17 per thousand in the Asian part—which includes mainly the developing regions of the USSR. In the Ukraine, the most industrialized of the republics of the USSR, the birth rate in 1968 was 14.9 per thousand, equivalent to the lowest ever recorded in Western Europe.[5] .

Without publicizing its views on family planning, Communist China has apparently succeeded in substantially reducing the birth rate, both in the urban and the rural areas. This result seems to have been achieved by postponing marriages (the recommended age for men is 28, and for women 26), by making available free contraceptives, and by promoting sterilizations.[6] The disappearance of traditional ways of life and customs, the fact that communal nurseries take care of small children and that women as well as men now work outside the home, the assurance that the elderly will be supported out of public funds and no longer must rely on their children, have destroyed the incentive for large families.

e. Employment and unemployment

One of the most serious effects of sudden overpopulation in developing countries is the sharp increase in unemployment. This includes both the registered unemployed in cities and the even greater number of disguised unemployed or under-employed still on the farms. As can be seen in Table II, the rate of growth of the labor force is far higher in developing than in developed countries. Accordingly, a study published in 1970 by the OECD emphasized the fact that the question of employment is the most urgent of those which the Third World will have to face in the next two decades.[7]

As we mentioned before, this rising rate of unemployment is particularly serious because it affects mainly the youth, the new graduates of the expanded educational system. Their growing number greatly exceeds the opportunities that are open to them in the modern

5. *United Nations Statistical Yearbook, 1969*, United Nations, New York, 1970.
6. *The New York Times*, 21 April 1971; *The New Republic*, 1 May 1971.
7. *The OECD Observer*, December 1970, Paris.

Table II

ESTIMATES OF GROWTH OF THE LABOR FORCE
IN LESS DEVELOPED COUNTRIES: 1950–1980

	Annual Percentage Rates of Growth	
	1950–1965	1970–1980
Developed countries	1.1	1.0
Less developed countries	1.7	2.3
REGIONS		
Middle South Asia[a]	1.4	2.0
South East Asia[b]	1.9	2.5
Other East Asia	1.8	3.1
South West Asia[c]	1.9	2.8
West Africa	2.2	2.3
East Africa	1.3	1.8
Central Africa	1.0	1.2
North Africa	1.1	2.6
Tropical South America	2.7	3.0
Central America	2.8	3.4
Temperate South America	1.5	1.5
Caribbean	1.8	2.3

Source: Derived from data shown in J. N. Ypsilantis, "World and Regional Estimates and Projections of Labour Force," ISLEP document 1966. Reproduced in *The OECD Observer,* December 1970.

Note: Excludes Sino-Soviet countries.

[a] Includes Ceylon, India, Iran, and Pakistan.
[b] Includes Burma, Cambodia, Indonesia, Malaysia, the Philippines, and Thailand.
[c] Middle East countries.

sector, mainly industry and public services. If one assumes a rate of growth of 2 per cent of the labor force—which is rather moderate in light of the estimates in Table II—and the modern sector to account for 20 per cent of total employment—which will not likely be surpassed at the beginning of development—employment in the modern sector would have to grow at a rate of 10 per cent per annum to absorb all the new job applicants. Such a rate of increase has occurred only in quite exceptional cases up to now, and will probably not be duplicated in the near future.

The rise in registered unemployment has been most serious in Asian countries (see Table II), where the density of population and its growth in absolute figures has also been highest. But this phenomenon is felt increasingly in other areas as well, especially in Latin

America, and even in Africa where it is of more recent origin.[8] Thus
it has been reported that out of 160,000 students graduating each year
in Kenya after seven years in primary school, only 60,000 will find
employment outside of traditional agriculture, or be able to continue
their education.[9] Moreover, by 1980 the number of school "leavers"
is expected to reach 300,000.

There is no easy formula to prevent the majority of these youths
from drifting into the cities. They are attracted there by the prospects
of a modern and more exciting life, in contrast to the dreary traditional
routine of their ancestral villages. But most of them, who manage at
best to obtain casual employment, find themselves uprooted and
alienated, condemned to a life of misery and semi-starvation in shanty-
towns surrounding the modern cities, where luxury housing is spreading. They must inevitably form a socially unstable, dangerous, frequently criminal element, with deep resentment and hostility toward
a society which appears to have rejected them. Thus any attempt to
overturn this society will find in them a receptive audience and a
ready tool.

Various approaches are being tried to alleviate this situation. For
the most part, however, because of the shortage of financial resources,
they are on too small a scale to make a decisive impact.

Table III

UNEMPLOYMENT
(number of registered applicants for work or registered unemployed)
(in thousands)

	1953	1961	1968
Burma	3.6	5.8	70.1
Ceylon	52.6	151.2	265.6
Ghana	6.1	14.7	17.6
India	477.6	1,753.9	2,902.8
Korea (South)	—	226.0	496.0
Malaysia (West)	—	37.9	127.6
Mauritius	1.2	2.2	9.1
Philippines	—	750.0	1,051.0
Singapore	—	53.4	65.4
U.A.R.	—	211.4	268.0
Zambia	—	3.4	12.9

Source: *United Nations Statistical Yearbook*, 1969, United Nations, New York,
1970, table 22.

8. Official statistical data for Latin America are not available.
9. *The New York Times*, 11 February 1971.

The most desirable goal would be to create maximum employment in the rural areas with a level of productivity and income that would be superior to that of traditional agriculture. This would avoid the danger inherent in uprooting the young; by slowing down urbanization this would reduce obligatory expenditure for urban housing and public services, such as transportation, sanitation, schools, and hospitals.

The method used in Kenya is to take advantage of the technical assistance provided by the International Labour Organisation to encourage the development of local craftsmen who could use modern yet inexpensive tools; this would provide the basic consumer goods (furniture, clothing, etc.) for which markets already exist in the village communities. Similar attempts on a larger scale have been made in a number of developing countries, particularly in Indonesia, by establishing cottage industries or by modernizing traditional ones to help them compete in cost and quality with more mechanized industries. Cottage industries of this kind are being frequently organized into co-operatives. It is in their interest to co-operate and co-ordinate their production with larger urban enterprises, for which they can profitably serve as subcontractors and supply parts. This method, as we stated previously, was used with great success in Japan, and is still quite common in the watch industry in Switzerland. It has the additional advantage of providing part-time employment to under-employed farmers during the slack season.

Major efforts must also be made to provide productive employment for the urban unemployed. There have been attempts to develop labor-intensive industries (which will be discussed in a later chapter), and to utilize unemployed workers for large-scale labor-intensive public works, such as the construction of roads and dams.

These projects and others along the same line, such as the construction of low-cost housing and the eradication of slums by the workers who live in them, must be undertaken on a much larger scale than before to make a significant dent in the problem of mass unemployment.

Chapter 5. *POLICY PROBLEMS*

a. Development by Government and/or private enterprise

Confronting the developing countries in their selection of appropriate development strategies is the problem of determining the respective functions of government and private enterprise. Is development to rely on the initiative of private individuals seeking to maximize their profits? Or should it be conducted under the direction and control of government, with the object of strengthening the military and economic power of the state, or effecting revolutionary changes in the structure of the economy?

The choice in this field is usually determined by the prevailing ideology, by the goals of the particular development program, and by the availability of both human and material resources in the private sector.

The active participation of private enterprise in development implies the existence of an economy which is not purely collectivistic in character, and which therefore will allow the presence of a private sector. There are some exceptions to this but they remain limited and temporary. The most important of these exceptions is the existence of a private sector in the agriculture of all socialist countries—ranging from the cultivation of small family plots in the Soviet Union to private ownership of most farmland in Poland. Another encroachment of private enterprise in the socialist economies in recent years has been the assistance provided under contract by foreign corporations to establish large manufactures; the French Renault Company has recently committed itself to assisting with the construction of a large truck factory in the Soviet Union.

Private enterprise can be expected to initiate development only in areas and for projects where profits are sufficiently certain and attractive. This is not the case with transport, or many other fields where development is particularly necessary. Thus in most countries of the West, railroads were started by private companies only with the guarantee that special privileges and facilities would be granted by the governments. In the United States, railroads were awarded extensive and highly profitable land grants. Even the establishment of new industries catering to the domestic market will attract private enterprise only if the government provides tariff protection to ensure profitability. Similarly, in a number of developing countries such as Puerto Rico, Jamaica, and other former British territories, special tax exemptions had to be introduced in order to lure private enterprise into particularly important fields such as export industries.

Economic development by private enterprise implies the existence of a class of dynamic entrepreneurs who are willing to engage in new ventures, when these offer attractive profit prospects and when they can mobilize the necessary financial resources. As we stated earlier, these prerequisites were generally found in the West; in Japan the government had to lead the way into industrial development before private enterprise could follow suit.

Since World War II, the entrepreneurial role of government has considerably expanded in the West's economic system of private enterprise. In both Great Britain and France important activities such as coal mining, railroads, and electric power have now been taken over by the government. The reasons for this nationalization are political to a great extent. Under the constitution of the Fourth Republic in France, all economic activities which became private monopolies had to revert to the nation. In some cases, however, the main objective was economic. National ownership of coal mining in Great Britain permitted its rationalization, which was not feasible as long as coal mining was controlled by a multitude of private companies.

Government, moreover, has had to assume the risk-taking function of the entrepreneur for projects of national importance which private enterprise is unwilling or unable to handle. This will occur when the size of the venture would tax the resources of even the largest private corporations or when profit expectations are inadequate. Thus during World War II the United States government had to finance out of public funds the expansion and construction of aircraft and aluminum plants; they were operated, however, by the major private firms which were active in these fields, and were eventually sold to them. Similarly governments are underwriting the cost of projects undertaken in the national interest, such as the stillborn SST in the United States and its competitor the "Concorde" financed jointly by the French and British governments. The actual work of development and construction is being done by the private corporations, which will also reap the eventual profits.

In the event of failure, on the other hand, it is increasingly up to the government to assume the cost of bailing out large private corporations. These rescue operations were frequent during the depression of the 1930's in Western Europe, and we have seen some striking examples recently, the Rolls Royce Company in Great Britain and the Penn Central Railroad in the United States, to name only two. It may be quite proper for a government concerned with the public welfare to offer assistance in such cases. Essential services must be maintained, and the government must avoid the massive lay-offs which would occur with the disappearance of an important industry. But it has been pointed out that such operations do amount to a rather unilateral socialization of the losses incurred by private enterprise.

In the developing countries the entrepreneurial functions of government are bound to be more prominent. The domestic private sector has neither the ability nor the necessary resources to assume the responsibility of handling the formidable task of economic development at the desired speed. Entrepreneurial talent and acquisitive astuteness can certainly be found, especially among the traders and money lenders in Asia and Africa and the latifundia (large estates) owners of Latin America. But the money-making activity of these groups has usually made only a marginal contribution to their country's economic development. It seems unlikely that they would take the initiative in areas where heavy investment is needed and where profits are lower and less certain than what they have been accustomed to.

Many developing countries have decided, moreover, as a matter of basic policy, to have public ownership of fundamental economic activities. This would permit them to direct their economic programs themselves and attain their objectives, free from the influence of private interests, domestic or foreign. In addition to railroad transportation and electric power these basic activities frequently included such heavy industries as steel and machinery.

In view of the scale of the operation and the limited domestic market (India and Brazil are the major exceptions), public ownership makes good sense. There is room only for a small number of plants, in many cases for one only, to meet fully the demand. Thus there is no possibility of competition and it is in the interest of economic development not to maximize profits through high prices or rates. Services and products should be available at the lowest price possible to further the development of the other sectors. Because of its greater resources and powers, the government furthermore is in a better position than domestic private enterprise to obtain outside technical and financial assistance—including loans from institutions such as the World Bank. It can even co-operate in large ventures with foreign capital, as was the case with mining in particular, e.g., in several African countries.

Conventional government institutions, which apply normal ad-

ministrative rules and procedures, are not geared to undertake entrepreneurial responsibilities. Special institutions such as "Development
Corporations" have been established in a number of developing countries in order to promote development of the economy as a whole, or of
a particular sector, usually the industrial sector. These corporations
are autonomous bodies, free from administrative regulations, with
great flexibility in making decisions and in applying normal business
methods. They can be fully government-owned or established in association with either foreign or domestic private interests. Some of the
most successful institutions, such as the Nacional Financiera in Mexico
use their capital as a revolving fund. When one of their enterprises has
become self-supporting, they sell it to domestic investors in order to
use the proceeds for new ventures.

Private enterprise has an important role to play in areas where
large-scale operation would be neither feasible nor desirable and
when, therefore, private monopolies are not likely to evolve. Agriculture, for instance, remains under private ownership and operation
in all countries where the economy is not fully socialized. But the
system of land tenure and the methods of cultivation must be modernized.

Manufacturing is another field where private enterprise may have
some advantage over the government. As entrepreneurs, private industrialists must take risks, and this can be a positive factor. The private
entrepreneur has direct responsibility for the success of his enterprise,
in his personal capacity as owner, or professionally as a corporate
representative. This responsibility leads him to examine carefully
the potentials of the venture and to apply himself in order to ensure
maximum efficiency of operation.

The public official in charge of launching a new enterprise probably has the same education and degree of technical competence as
his private counterpart. But he has no personal interest or responsibility
for the project. He will not suffer if it fails or benefit directly from its
success. No matter how conscientious he may be, his involvement is
likely to be less personal. Moreover, decisions affecting government-
owned enterprises are frequently based on other than purely economic
grounds. In large part, they may be political reasons. National prestige
is an important consideration. The creation of their own airlines by
so many small developing countries can be explained only by their
desire to have such a status symbol. Even when these ventures are
proven failures and become a drain on the public treasury, impeding
rather than promoting development, they are not discontinued; the
recognition of failure would suggest a loss of face for the government.

The examples of Ghana and Indonesia would indicate that revolution sometimes has to occur before a project of this kind can be scrapped.

There is room both for public and for private enterprise in the developing countries which permit a private sector. When both concentrate their activities in areas for which they are best equipped, they are most likely to produce the happiest results for economic development.

b.   Laissez-faire, or planning?

The decision to formulate specific plans for economic development reflects the concern of the great majority of developing countries to make effective use of their limited resources, and in particular of their capital, for them the scarcest of all commodities.

In the West economic development came in response to the price mechanism of the market. Government policies on tariffs, subsidies, and taxes influenced its course. But even when these measures were intended to guide development in a particular direction the notion of co-ordinating the development for the whole economy was never envisaged. In Japan too, while government directives stimulated progress in the most important sectors of the country, there was no overall plan. The rest of the economy was left to cope with the dictates of the market.

It is generally recognized, however, that in developing countries the law of the market place does not operate properly. Because of the existence of bottlenecks, the stimulant of higher prices does not create an increase in production which would be sufficient to establish an equilibrium between supply and demand. Moreover, there is little reason to believe that the allocation of resources, as dictated by the market, would favor activities essential for economic development rather than luxury housing, for instance, which would be a wasteful use of capital. Most important, reliance on the market cannot achieve the maximum mobilization of resources which is necessary to produce the rapid rate of development that the people of the developing countries are demanding. This is the rationale behind the development plans of nearly all the developing countries. Even the oil-producing countries, who are not short of capital, have adopted it.

Development plans are borne out of the joint effort of policy makers, who determine the goals of development, and planners, who map out the details on the basis of the goals that have been picked and the policies they imply.

Generally, as we indicated at the outset, the most important objective of a development plan is to achieve a high rate of economic growth, reflected in the growth of per capita income. Other major goals are maximum increase in employment, industrialization, possibly including specific production targets for key industries, and improvement in the balance of payments by replacing imports or developing exports. These objectives may not always be consistent with one another. For example, a maximum increase in employment by using labor-intensive methods can result in a smaller increase in production than would otherwise be the case if more advanced and expensive equipment were used. It is up to the policy makers to set the priorities.

Planners estimate the extent to which investment, foreign exchange, and skilled manpower will be needed to implement the plan. But the selection of the particular measures to make these resources available is a political decision. Should the investment capital be found in private savings and, thus, should there be incentives to encourage the accumulation of private capital? Should there be direct restriction on consumption through rationing? Another possibility would be to levy taxes, but on income or on consumption? Foreign exchange could be derived from foreign aid, private investments, or trade. If it is to be through trade, should the emphasis be placed on creating new industries, on restricting imports, or on developing exports? The latter might well be at the expense of the starving domestic consumer. Should the labor force be lured into specific fields (e.g., electronics) and areas (regions with a difficult climate) with wage differentials? An alternative would be to impose mandatory assignments and conscription. These are only some of the choices which are available to policy makers in determining development plans.

Ultimately it is the responsibility of planners to make the necessary adjustments so that a proper balance can be established between requirements and the available resources. They are the ones who select the specific projects which have the best chance of achieving the desired goals.

In establishing a system of classification of the numerous development plans in both developing and developed countries, there are two important criteria. On the one hand there is the degree of comprehensiveness and complexity of the plan, and on the other the imperative nature of its provisions.

As we pointed out earlier, development planning is an approach which seems appropriate to the problem of limited resources in developing countries. But there is not the same justification for the common practice of even the smallest and most backward of these countries to demand the preparation—usually by international experts recruited for this purpose—of elaborate plans based on complex econometric models. Indeed such plans may be premature and out of line with the real needs and potential of the countries involved.

These complicated plans require complete sets of accurate and detailed statistical data on all sectors of the economy. This data does not exist at the start of development, when statistical services are usually at an embryonic stage. Thus there is no adequate basis for a complex plan of development, and at this point attention should be given rather to improve statistical services. It should also be remembered that subsistence agriculture is the most important activity at this stage of development and does not lend itself to systematic planning.

At the outset, then, developing countries can formulate plans only for utilizing resources which are available for public investment. The first realistic development plans therefore are usually public investment programs. In many cases the policies which dictate these investments are fairly easy to determine and do not require complex calculations. Thus a small landlocked African country, where the lack of roads hampers the exportation of products, has no choice but to put the primary emphasis on creating transportation. Econometric calculations are useful there, however, to ascertain the kind of transportation which should be developed.

As the country develops and its economy becomes more complex, as more complete and accurate statistical data are made available, the need for more sophisticated planning increases. At the same time, the possibility of carrying out such plans becomes more real. Obviously in the larger and more advanced developing nations—India, Pakistan, and most of the countries of Latin America—this stage was reached a long time ago.

In countries where most economic activities are privately owned and operated, it is not usually mandatory for the private sector to follow the development plan. The plans are indicative rather than imperative. They indicate the direction which should be followed, and the objectives which are both feasible and desirable. The plan serves as a comprehensive market survey for the private sector and provides guidelines for its expansion. Usually the government provides various incentives such as cheap credit and tax rebates to encourage the private sector to move in accordance with the plan. France, for example, is offering considerable rebates to industries which go along with its plan of decentralization. The government, on the other hand, may discourage private business decisions which are contrary to the policies laid down in its plan. Again, in the case of France, an additional tax is imposed on new industries which settle in the overcrowded region of Paris.

For the public sector, on the contrary, development plans are usually mandatory. The government is committed to carry out its own plan of action, particularly if it has been approved by the legislature. But the financial implications of the plan must be worked out in its program of public investment, and the actual decision is made yearly in allocating specific sums in the annual budget. These sums may vary according to the government's financial position, or for other reasons, and they may not necessarily carry out the provisions of the plan.

In countries where the economy is entirely controlled by the government all enterprises must adhere to the development plan. The plan enacted into law is binding on all public institutions and enterprises. In these "centrally planned economies" (thus identified in the system of classification devised by the United Nations), the plan determines and spells out in considerable detail the policies and targets to be reached by the individual enterprises. Any major discrepancy between the anticipated objectives and the results represents an important failure under these conditions.

This type of plan has been instrumental in guiding the industrial development of the Soviet Union. It was successful as long as its principal objective remained a rapid increase in the output of heavy industry. But, as we stated earlier, it encountered serious difficulties when the production of consumer goods grew in importance. Attempts to decentralize planning in Russia have been made with the intent to consider more the wishes of consumers.

c. *Priorities for development—agriculture and/or industry?*

The question of priorities is a major policy decision which determines the direction that economic development will take. The relative importance of the main sectors of the economy must be weighed and the distinction made, in particular, between industry and agriculture. There is a great divergence of views on this matter, both for political and economic reasons. Each alternative has its drawbacks and the choice can only be made on the basis of the objectives which have been set and the various economic and political factors involved.

It is generally recognized that early emphasis on industrial development, in particular on heavy capital goods industry, produces

a high rate of economic growth. These industries are capital intensive
and operate at a high level of technology, characteristics which ensure
a correspondingly high level of productivity. Employing relatively few
workers, their labor costs are usually low in proportion to their overall expenditure; thus they offer the opportunity of large savings available for reinvestment and they facilitate an accelerated rate of development. Equally important is the fact that these industries introduce into
the economy a nucleus of high level technology which subsequently
makes possible further progress in other sectors. Viewed from a
different angle these industries represent considerable economic power
and in their ability to manufacture armanents they have the potential
for military power. One must bear in mind also the more spectacular
aspects of industrialization, those that serve to dramatize the results
of development, such as the establishment of large modern plants.
They arouse the enthusiasm and fan the pride of the people, ensure
their continuing support and acceptance of the sacrifices which as
consumers they must make for the cause of development.

On the other hand, the establishment of heavy industries is
extremely expensive for a developing country. It requires heavy
financing, and more important, takes out of the economy a great
deal of scarce capital in proportion to the value of additional output
thus obtained. With only rare exceptions, such as contributions of
foreign aid, this places a very heavy burden on the rest of the
economy.[1] Restrictions may have to be imposed on the consumption
of even essential products, so that these can be exported to pay for
the import of equipment. This was done in the Soviet Union when it
first started to industrialize. Other sectors of the economy and, in
particular, agriculture, may be neglected. In the case of agriculture,
it may not only have to forego investment funds for further development, but may even be deprived of the minimum resources required
to maintain its output. Exclusive concentration on heavy industry at
the expense of agriculture tends to lead to a drastic decline in farm
production. This happened in the Soviet Union and caused the severe
famine of the early 1930's. A similar downgrading of agriculture in the
Argentine in the late 1940's and early '50's led to the decline for a long
time of the country's main export activities: livestock breeding and
grain production. Finally heavy industry, by employing relatively few
workers, makes only a minor contribution to solving the paramount
problem of unemployment. One must conclude thus that heavy industry offers only limited advantages to the masses in the developing

1. The Soviet Union has financed the construction of iron and steel factories
in India with long-term and low-interest credit.

countries on a short-term basis, although the rapid growth of the economy which it fosters will be beneficial to the nation in the long run.

Emphasis on agriculture, on increasing agricultural production, inevitably augments the income of the major part of the population employed on the farms. But the problem arises of mobilizing this additional income for investment. Usually the extra food which is produced is seized by the peasants to supplement their own diet, especially when they have had to survive in the past on a marginal level of subsistence. Only with considerable difficulties, by designing taxes to provide incentives for increased output and encouraging private savings, can governments manage to preserve for investment a sizable portion of the farmers' additional income.

Agriculture on the other hand, does not require much capital, with the exception of monies needed for irrigation, in proportion to the value of the additional output obtained. A limited amount spent on seeds, fertilizer, and agricultural machinery, together with inexpensive technical assistance, can considerably increase the volume of the crop. It is therefore very economical usually to focus on development efforts for agriculture.

To a great extent the effect that this modernization and increase of agricultural production will have on employment depends on the particular system of land tenure. When most of the land is concentrated in large farm holdings, technological progress can lead to the displacement of workers by machines, and to an accelerated flight from the land into the city slums. Land reform, on the other hand, can increase the demand for farm labor.

In the face of these conflicting arguments, governments often base their decision on political reasons. The socialist countries give absolute priority to heavy industry, in order to accelerate growth, to gain economic and military power, and to expand the industrial proletariat. Generally the governments whose aim it is to strengthen their national independence share the same bias. When they have to pay greater heed to the needs and wishes of the present generation of voters, then more attention is given to progress in agriculture. Even for them, however, the appeal of industrialization is irresistible.

On the whole the preference for industrial development seems well justified. Industrialization is the key to a modern economy. But great care must be taken to ensure a parallel development of agriculture. There must be adequate food supplies for the growing population; a decline in export crops, which are the main source of essential foreign exchange, cannot be tolerated.

d.   Problems of agricultural development

It is evident that non-agricultural activities are bound to progress
at a more rapid pace than agriculture, the traditional occupation of
the predevelopment society. Still, as can be seen from Table IV, agriculture will remain the predominant sector of the Third World as a
whole.

Table IV

AGRICULTURAL AND NON-AGRICULTURAL POPULATION

	Agricultural				Non-agricultural	
	1962	1985	1962	1985	1962	1985
	Million		Per cent		Million	
Asia and Far East	583	880	70	60	250	591
Latin America	99	144	44	33	127	289
Africa south of Sahara	163	250	82	70	36	107
Near East and northwest Africa	88	114	65	45	47	140
Total for developing countries (excluding Mainland China)	985	1,388	67	55	460	1,127

*Source: A Strategy for Plenty: The Indicative World Plan for Agricultural
Development, Food and Agriculture Organization* (FAO), Rome, 1970, p. 32.

The major objective of agricultural development will be therefore
to produce enough food and raw materials for industry to meet the
demand of the whole population, which will increase by over 70
per cent by 1985. A large proportion of agricultural production is still
coming from subsistence agriculture, especially in Africa south of the
Sahara, and in India. The increase in production for the market,
therefore, will have to be even more substantial. Just as important, and
probably more difficult to resolve, is the problem of providing employment to an agricultural population growing by 40 per cent—that is,
for around 400 million people during that same period.

The high yield cereals which have been developed recently in
pilot stations, for wheat in Mexico and rice in the Philippines, have
somewhat alleviated the Malthusian fear. These new varieties not only
produce higher yields, but mature more rapidly, so that two harvests
can be reaped in a year when the water supply is adequate. FAO has
estimated that from a purely technical point of view enough of these
cereals, which provide the basic calories in the developing countries,

could be obtained if by 1985 the new strands were planted in one third of the area now devoted to cereals. This is in contrast to the 5 per cent of 1968.[2] Once this was achieved, further efforts could be made to improve the diet by emphasizing the production of protein rich foods such as milk products and meat.

But mere technical feasibility does not guarantee that the necessary increase in agricultural production will occur. According to FAO it should proceed at an annual rate of 3.7 per cent, compared with 2.7 per cent in the preceding decade (1955/57 to 1965/67). There are other complex economic, social, political, and institutional requirements. Max Millikan points out that "Agriculture is a systems problem; it will perform effectively only if a whole range of interacting conditions is satisfied."[3] Farm machinery, seeds, and fertilizers must be made available, as well as technical assistance. Farmers must be able to get credit at reasonable terms and need the incentive of remunerative prices and an equitable system of land tenure which will guarantee fair compensation for their labor.

What is required essentially to meet these conditions are financial resources. While this necessarily involves greater expenditure, still, according to the FAO estimates, it represents only an annual investment of about $4 per person in agriculture during the period of 1962 to 1985. The provision of credit and above all the establishment of a satisfactory system of land tenure which will be both just and economically efficient would imply major institutional changes of great political importance.

For an adequate system of agricultural credit, to provide short-term loans for the purchase of seeds and fertilizers, longer ones to cover the cost of irrigation and equipment, it is necessary to purge a country of usurious money-lenders. India offers a striking example of the crushing burden which such usury imposes on peasants and tenant farmers in both Southern Asia and Latin America. Even in the mid-1950's in India, after a rather comprehensive land reform had been carried out, 70 per cent of all argricultural credit was still coming from money-lenders at monthly rates of 2 to 5 per cent.[4] But it is obviously not enough just to eliminate such practices. There must be something else to take their place. The services which they

2. *A Strategy for Plenty: The Indicative World Plan for Agricultural Development*, Food and Agriculture Organization, Rome, 1970, p. 12.

3. Max F. Millikan and David Hapgood, *No Easy Harvest*, Boston, Little, Brown and Co., 1967, p. vii.

4. Paul Alpert, *Economic Development: Objectives and Methods*, Free Press, New York, 1963, p. 162.

rendered to the farmers at exorbitant prices must be provided on more reasonable terms; this can be done through co-operatives or government banks. The eviction of money-lenders can spell disaster for agricultural production if no other system has been set up.

There is a close connection between agricultural credit and the marketing of crops, and these new credit institutions should therefore actually undertake to purchase the produce which they have financed, and supply the farmers with the necessary seeds, fertilizers, and herbicides. Thus more than just large financial resources are needed to replace the money-lenders. The ability to administer and organize is crucial, but it cannot be taken for granted in many developing countries. Obviously it also presents a major political problem.

Land reform is even more difficult from the economic and particularly the political standpoints. It is intended to increase the efficiency of cultivation, and this is certainly the case where the system of traditional land tenure has been ownership of land by practicing "shifting cultivation." It is still prevalent in some regions of Africa south of the Sahara and represents an extremely wasteful use of land resources. Marked improvements can also be confidently expected when reform is aimed at large Latifundia estates with largely absentee landlords who devote little attention to the efficiency of the cultivation, and invest little to improve the productivity of their land. Their tenants or farm laborers, who are practically serfs, have neither the resources to invest in improving their land nor the incentive to do so. All benefits thereof would be reaped by their landlords. The reversion of the land to the "tillers" will stimulate the farmers to exert greater effort when it becomes their advantage to obtain maximum output. Large estates can be carved up into small family-size farms or preserved as large-scale units, organized into collective or co-operative farms. Production will be maintained and in the long run probably increased if the necessary ancillary facilities mentioned above, such as cheap credit, marketing facilities, as well as technical advice and guidance, are available.

But today the rural population is determined to break up the large estates even when the system operates efficiently, and when increased productivity cannot reasonably be expected from this change. Their demand expresses the craving of peasants in all countries and in all times for land of their own. It reflects their persistent resentment and hatred of the large landowners—even if these no longer dominate or oppress—and their rage to destroy the landed estates.

Governments of developing countries can withstand such demands only at their peril. When the tide of popular feeling runs high, it would even be dangerous for the preservation of law and order and peaceful development to postpone satisfying such demands. One might recall in this connection that in October 1917 Russia's first democratic government collapsed in large part because of Alexander Kerensky's decision to postpone land reform until a Constituent Assembly could vote on the matter.[5] A similar development occurred recently in Chile, where discontent with the slow progress of land reform was certainly an important factor in the defeat of President Frei and his party in the 1970 elections, and in the victory of the leftist candidate.

The choice of subdividing expropriated estates or operating them as single units is made generally more for political than for economic reasons. In countries where there is a deep attachment to individual ownership of land, the trend is usually toward subdivision. This was the general pattern of the initial stage of land reform in Eastern Europe, where collectivization was strenuously resisted. In some socialist countries, in particular Poland, private ownership of farms was even restored when the pressure for collectivization subsided after Stalin's death. In addition, the results from collective farming in even the most highly developed socialist countries of East Germany and Czechoslovakia are far from satisfactory. Production is far below the level attained in the privately owned farms of Western Europe, a discrepancy which did not exist before World War II.

But the optimum size of farms is rapidly growing as farm equipment becomes more sophisticated and expensive and economies of scale assume a larger role in agriculture. In the United States this is leading to the decline of the family farm and to the establishment of very large farm units, owned sometimes by corporations. In some countries of Western Europe, for example France and West Germany, it has fostered the creation of group farms where farmers pool their land and equipment and act as a single unit. The consolidation of small farms into larger units has begun voluntarily in Asia, especially in Taiwan and Thailand.

It is true that the problem of economies of scale generally has not yet occurred in the peasant agriculture of most developing countries. But in certain instances, as in the case of plantations, the land which has become available through expropriation must not be divided if efficiency is to be maintained. A government-appointed manager is put in charge of the whole operation—if there is a short-

5. Paul Alpert, *Twentieth Century Economic History of Europe*, Schuman, New York, 1951, p. 38.

age of competent managers, the previous manager may remain temporarily. The manager must account to the government—in state farms where farm workers receive a wage—or to all the members in collective farms. In the latter instance the manager is elected from among the members of the collective when competent personnel become available. This occurred, in particular, in the cotton plantations of Egypt. The principle of transforming expropriated lands into collective or state farms was most often applied in the case of foreign holdings, in Algeria and Tanzania for instance.

When the motives behind land reform were primarily or even exclusively political, the question of efficiency was somewhat neglected at first. On the whole, however, it has usually been possible to maintain or to restore the previous level of operation, and in a few cases even to exceed it. This has been achieved at considerable expense for the government and sometimes with external technical assistance.

Land reform is also essential if agriculture is to provide employment at least to part of the 400 million who will be added to the present agricultural population by 1985. From the point of view of employment, the impact of the *"Green Revolution,"* which has reduced the danger of catastrophic food shortages in developing countries, may not be favorable. The new high yielding cereals necessitate profound changes in traditional farm techniques. The changes require capital and technical skills which are more easily available to large landowners than to small farmers. One notes that in countries where the introduction of the new seeds has made rapid progress without radical land reform, such as West Pakistan, it has led to the adoption of capital-intensive techniques by large farmers and to the displacement of farm laborers by tractors. With the present scarcity of capital and the surplus of labor this is a waste of national resources, although it may be economical for the individual farm. The example of irrigated rice cultivation in Japan and Taiwan demonstrates on the contrary that agricultural modernization, which increases productivity per unit of land and unit of labor, can provide more employment per unit of land if excessive use of labor-saving machinery is avoided.[6] The production and harvesting of one acre planted with the "miracle" rice in Japan and Taiwan absorbs 170 man days, compared with 125 in India and 100 in the Philippines for the traditional varieties. On the other hand, the labor requirements per ton of "dwarf" wheat have been reduced by about 20 per cent.

According to Lester Brown, the impact of the Green Revolution

6. *Development Assistance Review, 1970,* Organization for Economic Cooperation and Development, Paris, 1970, p. 126.

on employment should be favorable.[7] He considers that a system of land tenure based on small farmers who work their land without the help of hired labor, and who are not interested therefore in economizing on the cost of wages, can best exploit the new varieties. The green revolution also opens up opportunities for substantial expansion in industrial production and employment to provide the necessary equipment and supplies: tube wells, pesticides, fertilizers. This depends, of course, on the extent to which it is possible to manufacture such items locally. Their production could normally be organized in all developing countries with a sufficiently large domestic market and a minimum of prerequisites for industrial development.

Gunnar Myrdal also thinks that the introduction of new techniques, of the "green revolution," can occur most favorably in a system of small-farm ownership.[8] In countries where large estates still exist, reform is essential therefore to increase both productivity and employment. There must be a direct relationship between the farmer and his land to provide incentives for increased effort and investment. Chile offers a striking example of the importance that the question of employment has assumed in the popular drive for land reform. There the number of workers employed on an estate taken over from a large landowner has gone from 5 to 25.[9]

But in spite of these relatively encouraging indications, FAO judges it unlikely that agricultural production will be able to absorb the large increase in the agrarian population.[10] The situation is particularly serious in southern Asia where the greatest concentration of population exists. There is not enough arable land still available. Labor-intensive techniques must be used with multiple cropping. Major public works programs and village industries must be developed, again, in particular, for processing agricultural commodities with maximum use of labor.

e. Problems of industrialization

Industrial development must obviously be an integral part of overall economic development, but there are different views on the kind of industries which should first be established. The question

7. Lester Brown, *Seeds of Change: The Green Revolution and Development in the 1970s*, Praeger, New York, 1970, pp. 80–104.
8. Gunnar Myrdal, *The Challenge of Poverty*, Pantheon, New York, 1970, p. 114.
9. *The New York Times*, 16 February 1971.
10. *Op. cit.*, p. 32.

also arises whether their output should be directed to the domestic market or to export.

There are quite valid reasons for giving priority to heavy capital goods industries in developing countries where there is a potentially vast domestic market and adequate natural resources. These industries can eventually operate on a scale that would permit them to be competitive. This would be possible in India, Pakistan, Brazil, Mexico, Nigeria, Algeria, to name only a few. When regional customs unions or common markets can create a sufficiently large interior market, heavy industry will be possible even in smaller countries.

Albert Hirschman in particular points out that heavy industries, notably iron and steel, have the greatest backward and forward linkages.[11] They encourage the development of sources of the raw materials which they require (coal and iron ore) and of processing plants which can use their products, such as the manufacturing of automobiles and machines. Thus they are a powerful stimulant to overall industrial development. But these industries make no immediate contribution to improving the standards of living, and as we have said before, they require vast capital backing without offering much opportunity for employment.

The more traditional approach to industrial development has been to start with industries of light consumer goods, for which a domestic market is immediately available. The production of beer and soft drinks is usually among the first to be established. These industries can operate economically even on a small scale and employ more labor and require less capital, both in absolute figures and per unit of output. They are therefore much easier to develop and provide immediate benefits. In so far as they can replace imports, they can prevent the expenditure of foreign exchange. When these industries are able to process domestic raw materials—for example, when they can manufacture cotton textiles in cotton-growing countries, their establishment can put an end to the exporting of raw materials and the importing of the finished products. This has been the traditional pattern of trade in developing countries and is both absurd and harmful.

It is true that such industries do not provide immediate incentives for the spread of industrialization to the same extent as the heavy industries. But in the long run they facilitate the accumulation of capital and the creation of entrepreneurial skills in the economy. Thus they open the way for larger and more sophisticated industrial enterprise. This is only a gradual process, however, and few if any of the

11. Albert Hirschman, *The Strategy of Economic Development*, Yale University Press, New Haven, 1958, pp. 98–110.

developing countries today would be satisfied with such a slow rate of development and would therefore agree to rely exclusively on light industries.

Another policy problem of industrial development is to select the market for the new products. Should they replace imports on the domestic scene, or attempt to penetrate and conquer foreign markets? Neither is necessarily mutually exclusive.

The natural tendency in developing countries is in favor of import replacement. This gives the impression of increasing the economic independence of the developing country by reducing its reliance on imports. National pride is bolstered by the prospect of eliminating the need for traditional suppliers in the developed industrial countries. The task seems relatively easy. The scope of the market is identified by the volume of imports. Thus it is possible to ascertain whether or not the market would justify the establishment of one or several industrial plants on a large enough scale to permit reasonably efficient operation. Tariff protection is always demanded and easily granted. The traditional argument of infant industry serves here. A new industry cannot be expected from the outset to be as efficient as its older and more established foreign competitors. It should therefore be protected until it has had time to gain experience, to acquire technical and commercial competence, and in general to meet all the conditions required to become fully competitive. This tariff protection is usually quite generous; it may even grant a practical monopoly to ensure high profits and to attract entrepreneurs. In some cases the foreign corporations, which had previously supplied most of the imports, now agree to establish local factories when they are faced with the danger of losing their export market. These new plants usually start off by assembling imported parts, but they gradually use an increasing proportion of locally manufactured components. This was the trend in several Latin American countries such as Brazil and Argentina, where the major American and European manufacturers have co-operated in the development of a local automobile industry.

This approach to industrial development has many advantages. It enables the developing countries to make use of the technical and financial resources of the large foreign corporations for their industrialization. But the problem is that tariff protection once granted is rarely abolished or even substantially reduced. The manufacturers and the workers who are employed, at wages generally well above those prevailing in other sectors of the economy, have vested interests in the policy. They are usually able to exert sufficient pressure to avoid such a contingency, which, they assert, would spell ruin to the industry as a whole. With tariff protection there is no longer a real incentive to reduce costs, or to improve efficiency. The developing country will thus have acquired an expensive, non-competitive industry which makes no positive contribution to economic development and even retards it. By raising the domestic price level, such an industry is a drain on the economy and an impediment to the progress of its export sector. This was the general experience in Latin America after World War II, as the reports of the Economic Commission for Latin America of the United Nations (ECLA) repeatedly stated.

There is obviously much room for industrial development through import replacement. But it should be the policy of the government to make sure that the new industries become competitive in a reasonable time. In particular, a government should refuse to provide assistance to enterprises which most likely will never be able to stand on their feet.

Import replacement makes an important contribution to reducing the need for foreign exchange and to improving the balance of payments. But it does have its natural limits. All industrial imports cannot be replaced even if the import-replacing industries were fully efficient. They alone therefore cannot bear the burden of industrial development.

Export industries have to be competitive in order to survive on the world market. There must exist from the outset a high standard of efficiency and an organization geared to make full use of their comparative advantage in low costs of labor. As a rule, therefore, they are labor-intensive. The manufacture of textiles, clothing, and shoes has usually been one of the first industries to be established. In recent years their scope has grown, and they now include such highly specialized activities as the manufacture of some electronic components, where labor-intensive methods have proved economical.

But there are other problems which export industries must resolve in order to be successful. An abundant supply of cheap labor, used to industrial work and its discipline, is not difficult to find in most developing countries. But these industries require entrepreneurs as well, who are capable of initiative and skillful management. They must attain a high level of sophistication in manufacturing and merchandising techniques and possess adequate financial resources.

Up to now these conditions have been met only in a limited number of developing countries. They exist in countries such as India, Mexico, and Brazil, which may be considered already semi-industrial. Most of the others which did manage in the '60's to expand considerably the exports of their manufactured products either already possessed a dynamic entrepreneurial class or were able to attract foreign capital and foreign entrepreneurs.

Thus Hong Kong, Singapore, and Taiwan benefited from the concentration of Chinese entrepreneurs who lacked neither skills nor resources. They were able to secure forign capital and, what proved even more important, contracts with United States importers and manufacturers who farmed out to them manufacturing assignments at certain stages of production, with guaranteed outlets for the finished product on the American market. The export industries of Jamaica and Puerto Rico were successful because of a policy of tax exemptions and other facilities which attracted foreign enterprise. The products were then sold primarily on the markets of the respective capital-exporting countries. Many other developing countries have tried to follow similar policies. But only in a few of them are there the pre-requisites for successful export industries which would be based chiefly on plentiful labor.

On the other hand, many developing countries should be able to develop industrial exports by establishing processing plants for their primary products. The processing of indigenous agricultural products remains still quite limited in scope, with the notable exception of the cotton goods industry, a major export activity now in India and Brazil. But even the processing of peanuts into peanut oil in Senegal and the manufacture of soluble coffee in Latin America and Africa can make a sizable contribution to both employment and export proceeds.

Mineral raw materials sometimes require large-scale processing plants and heavy capital investment. Such plants have been established by foreign corporations, in particular for the refining of copper in Chile and Zambia. In other developing countries governments have taken the initiative in co-operation with foreign companies. Among the most ambitious of these projects are the factories which are being built for the refining of aluminum in Ghana and the production of petrochemicals in Algeria and Iran. They should make an important contribution to the balance of payments and stimulate the establishment of ancillary industries to furnish the raw material and to transform their output further. This "export enclave" method seems therefore effective in promoting the industrialization and the general development of the country concerned.

The United Nations is emphasizing the necessity of expanding industrial exports and consider it the most feasible approach to bridge the rapidly growing gap in balance of payments for the Third World. Although not all developing countries will be able to carry it out successfully, this policy still seems the most promising for many of them.

f.   Problems of financing economic development

The financing of economic development raises not only technical but also major political questions. There is the problem of selecting an effective method of drawing out of the economy as much capital as possible for productive investment. By causing a minimum of inconvenience, meeting therefore the minimum of opposition, it should encourage the productive effort of the population. In the last analysis the basic decisions on sharing the financial burden and on meeting the recurrent cost of government are political in nature. They are determined by the balance of power within the individual country, as well as by the value system which dominates public opinion. Thus the switch from indirect to direct taxes, including the graduated income tax, which has taken place since the early part of this century in most Western developed countries, is undoubtedly due to the growing power of low-income groups and especially of labor unions. But one cannot ignore the extent to which the general public has been sympathetic to the practice of fiscal redistribution as a method of redressing social injustices.

As a general rule the financing of economic development is found in a combination of private savings and public savings derived from taxes. Economic development in the West was carried out principally by the private sector, the entrepreneurs, and was financed accordingly by them. The low prices paid for the imports of primary products from the underdeveloped countries, and the low wages paid to workers during most of industrial development, permitted the accumulation of private savings. Later, and most noticeably since the depression of the 1930's, public funds from the proceeds of direct taxes took on a greater importance.

In Japan the government mainly financed its share of the development program out of the proceeds of the land tax, thus at the expense of the peasants. But the greater part of development was financed through private savings which were available because of the strict adherence to a traditionally inexpensive standard of consumption by most Japanese.

In the socialist countries the public sector undertakes to carry out all economic development, and the national budget reflects the results of the economy as a whole. As we mentioned earlier, the capital needed for development is found in curtailing private consumer expenditure with a turnover tax applied even on foodstuffs, and in the profits of government enterprise. In the Soviet Union at the height of its industrialization in 1935, the turnover tax had accounted for 75 per cent of total revenue and the profits of government enterprise for 9 per cent; less than 4 per cent was obtained from direct taxes.[12] By 1960 pressure on the consumer had somewhat subsided: the turnover tax provided 40 per cent of revenue and government enterprise an additional 23 per cent, while the income from direct taxes had grown to 8 per cent. Similar methods are being used in other socialist countries; in 1969 taxes on the national economy, including both turnover tax and profits of government enterprise, provided 85 per cent of Czechoslovakia's total revenue, 78 per cent in Bulgaria, and 81 per cent in Poland.[13]

Private savings, however, are not completely dismissed in socialist countries; savings banks have been established and the practice of regular savings through payroll deductions is being encouraged. But the role of such private financing is very small. Still one notes that in recent years private savings have been increasingly mobilized in the USSR, with the sale of co-operative apartments to private individuals to pay for the construction of housing.

The developing countries which admit the existence of a private sector must apply a policy of taxation and encouragement of private savings which will maximize the total resources available for investment. Quite naturally they cannot jeopardize their political position by imposing too heavy sacrifices on the population, particularly on its most powerful groups.

The easiest and most natural targets, therefore, are the foreign corporations, notably those that operate mining concessions. They usually have made a heavy investment which they cannot abandon or withdraw. One assumes here that these corporations do not enjoy—as was frequently the case during the colonial or semi-colonial period—a position of such strength in the country that they are able to dominate the government and dictate terms. Since their profits derive from exports, an increase in their taxes would have the advantage of bringing not only additional revenue but also foreign exchange.

A drastic increase in the taxes of these companies, sometimes even

12. Abram Bergson, *The Economics of Soviet Planning*, Yale University Press, New Haven, 1964, p. 362.
13. *United Nations Statistical Yearbook, 1969*, United Nations, New York, 1970, Table 191.

actual nationalization—with varying degrees of compensation—would
not encounter domestic opposition.[14] On the contrary, it seems justified by public opinion in the developing countries which look upon
it as a fair exchange—or a revenge—for the excessive profits which the
companies reaped because of the previous inability of weak or corrupt
governments to defend adequately their national interest. There were
indeed many such abuses in the past. One of the most scandalous was
the secret clause in the concession contract of the former Anglo–Persian Oil Company which stipulated that all ships of the British navy
were to be supplied with oil at a reduced price. This clause was only
revealed when the concession was cancelled.

In general terms the level of taxation will depend on the relative
bargaining power of the governments versus the companies. On the
whole, in recent years the balance of power has shifted in favor of
developing nations with rich mineral deposits. Countries have also
begun to enter into agreements among themselves in order to present
a common front to the foreign companies. But conditions vary according to the different commodities. In the case of oil, the producing
countries are in a particularly strong position and have exacted a
spectacular raise in their share of the total value of the oil produced
and distributed. For other commodities the terms may be less favorable; prices cannot be increased beyond a certain point because of the
possibility of substitution, as for instance aluminum for copper.

An entirely different situation arises when governments wish to
attract foreign enterprise, in particular to establish new industries
when neither the necessary capital nor the technical skills are available in the domestic economy. In such a case fiscal policies can be
drawn up with this in mind. Normally this would involve a temporary
reduction or even a total exemption from taxes. This is usually granted
only if the new enterprise is expected to make a useful contribution
to the economic development of the country and export at least part of
its output. This is the case, for instance, in Puerto Rico and in the
former United Kingdom territories under the Pioneer Industries legislation.

Taxes on foreign trade, imports and exports, provide the developing countries with a substantial portion of their public revenues which
they spend for development, as well as for recurrent government expenses. Collecting these taxes presents fewer technical difficulties

14. No compensation whatsoever was paid for foreign capital expropriated
after the 1917 Revolution in Soviet Russia. On the other hand, some compensation
was paid for foreign property nationalized after World War II in the socialist
countries of Eastern Europe.

than do other forms of taxation, such as personal income taxes. This point is of particular importance for governments whose tax administration frequently is far from efficient. Foreign trade transactions, by and large, occur only in a few major ports. Even if one takes into account the rather extensive smuggling that goes on in some countries, they offer less scope for fraud and tax evasion.

From a political point of view, taxing the imports of goods, which are already, or which can be, locally manufactured has a character of protection or encouragement. The public response is bound to be favorable. Taxes on imported capital goods are actually very low, if they exist at all, in order not to raise the production costs of the industries that need them. Customs duties are levied on consumer goods which cannot be produced locally, for the time being, at least. This can and does encounter the opposition of groups whose vested interests are involved: low-income groups for the import of mass consumption items, such as sugar and cotton textiles, the upper and middle classes for consumer durables, such as automobiles and refrigerators, or for alcoholic beverages. To some extent their resistance may even bear fruit. But on the whole, governments have been able to rely on these taxes as very productive sources for a substantial part of their revenue. Moreover, the proceeds of these taxes grow at a more rapid rate than does the economy as a whole, at least in the early stages of development, when opportunities for import replacement are still limited.

In many cases governments have managed also to introduce an element of social justice. They set lower customs duties on mass consumption items than on luxury goods. In this way customs duties have become to some extent a substitute for the progressive income tax.

The taxation of exports also accounts for a substantial part of government revenues, particularly in countries at an early stage of development, where a few, or even a single, commodity furnishes the major part of total export proceeds. In such countries the production of the export crop is the most developed sector of the economy. The rest of agricultural production is usually at a subsistence level and the export sector therefore normally generates most of the money income in the country. Export taxes are easy to collect, but they fluctuate widely, reflecting the fluctuation in price and volume of exports sold on the world market. In some countries exports are taxed on a sliding scale, paralleling the rise of prices. Thus the government skims off at least part of the farmers' windfall when the world price rises, and eases the tax load when prices fall to cushion the blow.

A more effective system of taxing export crops exists in a number of former British territories, in Africa mainly, called Marketing Boards.

These are government agencies which enjoy the monopoly of purchasing the whole crop each year at a fixed price. This put an end to the common exploitation of farmers in the past by private traders or agents of international trading companies. The prices which the Boards paid were initially slightly below the level of world prices, to enable the Boards to maintain a stable purchase price if world prices fell, and thus ensure the stability of farmers' incomes. Because of the conservative policy of the Boards and the general rise in prices, since the start of their operation after World War II, they were able to accumulate very substantial reserves. The purchase prices paid to the farmers rose far less than world prices, but still remained quite attractive. They even stimulated a considerable expansion in the production of cocoa in Ghana and Nigeria, and of coffee in Nigeria and Kenya. After paying for the development costs of the export crops, the surpluses which the Boards accumulated could finance national development programs.

The farmers naturally objected strongly to this system, under which they were forced to make (what they considered to be) a disproportionate contribution to the financing of their country's development. These objections did not prevail. The Boards were established before independence on the initiative of British colonial officials; although they included representatives of the growers, their policy remained on the whole independent of local political pressures.

On the contrary, in some countries of Central America, such as Guatemala where there is an oligarchy of coffee planters, export taxes on coffee generate only a very small part of public revenues (see table V).

Indirect taxes levied on locally produced goods, such as the sales or the turnover tax, place a heavy burden on low-income groups. In order to create revenue, they must be imposed even on basic items of consumption. In some countries higher rates are devised for more expensive products of luxury consumption. But in view of the overall difficult financial position in which developing countries find themselves, they have been unable, even had they desired, to avoid reliance on these taxes generally for a substantial share of their total revenue.

In countries with a comparable social and economic structure, a study of the ratio between indirect taxes and taxes on income in the national budget throws light on the balance of power between different income groups. Thus in Costa Rica, with a system more democratic than that of Guatemala, the share of indirect taxes is lower in proportion to income tax (see Table V).

The graduated income tax is generally acknowledged as the most

democratic method of taxation. It represents the most equitable distribution of the total burden of public expenditure among taxpayers
of different income brackets. But although the desire for social justice
is one of the strongest motivating forces in the drive for social and
economic development, the income tax has actually played less of a
role in most developing countries than in the leading Western
democracies.

The reason for this is to a great extent political: the resistance of
high-income groups, who would naturally have to bear the heaviest
burden if an income tax were fairly assessed and its collection strictly
enforced. In countries where such groups are in control, they are
usually able in any event to avoid paying fair taxes by sending their
money illegally out of the country or by preventing a just assessment
of their property, in particular of their land.

There are also technical difficulties as well. The assessment and
the collection of income taxes are highly complex matters which
require a well organized and efficient system of financial administration; this exists in few if any of the developing countries. More important is the fact that in developing countries an income tax cannot
be levied on the majority of the population, as is the case in the United
States and the United Kingdom, where it is the main source of
revenue. The bulk of the population is simply too poor to be taxed
on an individual basis. An income tax can only apply, therefore, to a
relatively small minority. Thus, even in a country like India, with
strong equalitarian tendencies, it contributes only a small percentage
of the nation's total revenue.

But with a system of progressive income taxes the yield should
increase more rapidly than the overall national income. Eventually,
therefore, it can account for a major part of government revenue.

Inflation is a sort of invisible tax which reduces consumption by
increasing prices. The equivalent of this reduction becomes available
to the government for financing development. This is a very tempting
form of taxation; in its early stages it seems to hurt no influential
groups of people and encounters thus no opposition.

But a deliberate policy of allowing, or even furthering, inflation
is very dangerous for the developing countries. Because of the rigidity
of their economy, the fact that frequently a rise in demand cannot be
met by an immediate increase in production, and their inability to
apply effective price controls, there is always a latent inflationary
danger. Once started inflation easily gets out of hand. This can discourage productive savings, stimulate speculation, and throw off balance the elaboration of a systematic economic plan. Experience with

such inflationary developments in several Latin American countries in recent years (Argentina, Brazil, and especially Chile) has been quite convincing. The political consequences of runaway inflation are even more serious. Its worst effects are felt by the low-income groups, the urban wage earners who are unable to protect themselves through speculation. The feelings of resentment that result generate social and political tensions.

Table V provides some data on the contribution in percentages of the chief categories of taxes to the public revenues of selected developing countries in 1969.

Table V

	Taxes on Income and Wealth	*Taxes on Foreign Trade*			*Taxes on Consumption*
		Imports	*Exports*	*Total*	
		(in per cent of total public revenue)			
AFRICA					
Ghana	18	19	24	43	23
Kenya	31	26	1.5	27.5	14
Tanzania	25	5	31	36	19
LATIN AMERICA					
Guatemala	16	20	4	24	54
Costa Rica	25	25	1	26	39
ASIA					
Ceylon	15	20	12	32	45
India	14	13	—	13	30
Pakistan (1970)	13	23	—	23	31

Source: Calculated from data published in the *United Nations Statistical Yearbook, 1969*, United Nations, New York, 1970, table 191.

The method of encouraging private savings to make them available for investment is different for small-size savings deposited in savings institutions than it is for larger sums amassed by private capitalists, who lend them to the public sector or more commonly invest them in private undertakings.

Small savings are encouraged in all countries—including the socialist ones—through an extensive network of savings banks, often utilizing the facilities of the post office. These institutions pay interest at attractive rates and invest the funds in accordance with government regulations in fields that profit the public interest: government bonds and mortgages. Contrary to popular opinion, savings are accumulated even by the poorest segment of the population. But at the beginning of development their volume is relatively low; the value of encouraging savings is chiefly educational, to nurture along savings habits which may become at a later stage an important source of capital.

Large-scale private savings pose more complex problems. As we pointed out earlier, many large capital owners in developing countries invest their wealth in areas which are of little or no relevance to economic development: usurious money lending, speculative trading, luxury housing. It should be government policy, therefore, to dislodge them from these activities, while encouraging them to engage their energies and resources in fields where their contribution would be most useful—for example, in industrial development. Measures to this effect should guarantee security from expropriation without equitable compensation and the right to reasonable profits. Such measures might also apply, as in Taiwan, to the reinvestment of indemnities due land-owners whose estates had been expropriated as part of the land reform.

g. Degree of reliance on relations with developed countries: foreign trade, foreign private investment, external aid

No country has managed to attain economic development within the framework of our modern technological and industrial civilization without benefit of contact with more developed countries. Through these contacts came the capital goods, and the knowledge and experience needed, at the very least, to launch the development programs. As further proof one can point to the fact that countries with the least outside contacts, usually landlocked countries difficult to reach, are also the most backward in their respective regions: Nepal in Asia, Yemen in the Middle East, Ruanda and Burundi in Africa, and Paraguay in South America.

While this fact is generally recognized, there is a tendency throughout the Third World to reduce the rapport with, and reliance on, the outside, and in particular on the developed countries of the West. This trend can be explained by the well known fact that outside contact in the past visibly reflected the dominant position of the West over the colonial or semi-colonial developing countries.

It is therefore natural that for political and economic reasons alike, the developing countries aspire to strengthen their independence by putting the main emphasis on developing their domestic economy. They desire to reorganize their international relations with the developed countries on a basis of equality, with equal benefits to both sides.

In this common effort to improve the relationship with their traditional partners, one can see considerable differences in approach. These differences relect the political orientation of the respective country. The majority of developing countries are aware of their continued economic dependence on the West and are therefore interested in maintaining reasonably friendly relations. Though they exert maximum pressure to protect their interests, there is no feeling of deep hostility toward the West, toward the people—even toward those who were their former masters—or toward its system' of capitalism and political democracy. This attitude still prevails on the whole in Latin America and in the former colonies of Great Britain and France in Africa and Asia.

International relations with the West are viewed quite differently in countries where social revolution is the major objective. There is deep resentment not only because of the West's economic exploitation but because of its political and economic system. This has inspired drastic measures in countries such as Cuba, where the expropriation of all foreign investments leads inevitably to reprisals and rapidly to a total rupture in relations.

In international trade the traditional pattern is the exchange of primary goods from the developing countries for the manufactured goods of the developed ones. The terms favored the industrial countries, because of their overwhelming strength and the normally weak position of producers of agricultural primary products who cannot influence world prices by reducing their output. Prices of primary goods have remained low on the whole, especially when compared with the constant rise in prices of industrial products which the developing countries must import, and which reflect the inflationary trends in the Western countries.

Terms of trade for developing countries have changed only slightly during the decade of 1959 to 1969. The United Nations index of terms of trade of developing countries has dropped from 105 in 1959 (1963 is 100) to 102 in 1969. But if one excludes petroleum, the index has risen from 103 to 107 during the same period.[15] For individual countries the terms of trade have fluctuated widely from year to year, with changing conditions in developed countries. Since falling prices were usually due to a reduction in demand in the volume of exports, the proceeds of exports of developing countries have fluctuated even

15. *United Nations Statistical Bulletin*, January 1971, United Nations, New York, p. xviii.

more violently. It has caused serious difficulties in balance of payments, and has jeopardized the success of their development plans.

This has led the developing countries to make repeated demands
for international commodity agreements, ever since the period right
after World War II. These would stabilize world prices for primary
product exports and could set an average level of prices based on an
equilibrium between supply and demand. The developing countries,
moreover, emphasized the need for fixing equitable prices—i.e., at a
level satisfactory to the producers.

The argument of the developing countries is that their producers
of primary goods should be in the same position as the farmers in
developed countries. The farmers in all industrial countries receive
higher prices than those which they would have found on a free market. This preferential treatment has been justified explicitly in the
United States by the principle of parity between prices of farm
products and those of industrial products needed by agriculture. The
same principle should apply to the farmers of the Third World, but
up to now the developed countries have not accepted this theory and
only a few commodity agreements have been worked out to suit the
developing countries.

Even an improvement in terms of trade for primary products,
however, will not eliminate the increasingly dangerous deficit in the
balance of payments. The United Nations Conference on Trade and
Development (UNCTAD) has estimated that the trade gap of the
developing countries, the deficit which they have incurred in the flow
of goods and services, would amount in 1975 to $24 billion.[16] The
expansion of traditional exports, in particular agricultural products,
encounters increasing difficulties because in many cases they can be
replaced by synthetics. On the other hand, the value of trade in manufactured products which the developed countries are exporting is
growing rapidly. In great part this is due to the increase in the sale
of highly elaborated goods where the cost of raw materials is only
a small factor. As a consequence, the relative share of developing
countries in world trade is steadily decreasing.

In order to compensate for the stagnation of traditional exports,
many developing countries are trying, as we mentioned earlier, to
develop exports of industrial products mainly to the wealthy industrial countries. But in view of the powerful competition which their
infant industries must face from the old established industries of the

16. *Towards a Global Strategy of Development: Report of the Secretary-
General of the United Nations Conference on Trade and Development,* United
Nations, New York, 1968, p. 16.

industrialized countries, the developing countries demand preferential treatment—total or partial exemption from customs duties. Little concrete action has been taken as yet by the developed countries along those lines (see Part Three, Chapter 2).

The climate for foreign investments in most developing countries was quite unfavorable in the period after World War II, when many of them achieved their independence. They considered investments as ruthless exploitation of their natural resources, a view which was justified to a great extent, as we stated earlier. Foreign capital was blamed for having invested only in export activities, in mines and plantations, deliberately neglecting industries for the domestic market, in order to maintain the economic dependence of the developing countries on the West. Thus it was held responsible for the lopsided structure of the economy, where only the export sector was developed and efficient. In fact, foreign investment concentrated on export activities mainly because there was more money to be made on the world market than on the usually limited domestic markets of the developing countries.

But this approach led many developing countries to adopt a basically negative attitude to foreign investments. When they were not actually nationalized, with little if any compensation, they were subject to strict regulations. New investments were prohibited in areas essential to the national interest, or where foreign capital might influence domestic policies. In a number of countries foreign capital was excluded from the production of armaments, ownership of land, basic heavy industries, and public utilities. Even the exploitation of mineral deposits was in many cases barred to them, at least under the old system of concessions, where the foreign company could claim ownership of the minerals. Severe restrictions were placed on the rate of profit foreign investors could earn and transfer home, and on the repatriation of their capital. Finally, few if any guarantees were given against the danger of nationalization without appropriate compensation.

Such legislation was bound to make foreign investment most unattractive, and in adopting it the developing countries labored under a double misapprehension. On the one hand they overestimated their appeal to foreign capitalists, and on the other, the ability of the latter to realize high profits regardless of restrictions.

Their assumptions proved to be entirely unfounded. In the first decade after World War II there were ample opportunities for investment in the domestic market of the United States, then the only major capital-exporting country, and in Western Europe and Canada, where such political risks did not exist. Therefore, scarcely any foreign investments were made during that period in developing countries. Drilling for oil was the only major exception.

Gradually, however, the governments of developing countries, including those least inclined to private enterprise and particularly to foreign capital, became aware of the contribution that foreign investment could make to their economic development. It could supply capital and, more important, technical know-how, difficult to come by otherwise. New foreign investments were invited into certain fields by the governments, provided they adhered to general government policies. This general welcome included government guarantees for the security of these investments and for a reasonable return on capital at mutually satisfactory rates.

There are special laws in a number of developing countries regulating foreign investments. These laws, usually called Foreign Investment Codes, specify the terms under which foreign investment can be admitted, with provisions for security of the capital invested, the transfer of interest or profit at a given rate of return, the level of taxation, and the procedures to be applied in case of litigation.

Foreign aid for economic development is a relatively new approach to the economic relations of the developed countries with the Third World. It was introduced by President Truman as an important factor in international economic policy, and the United States became from the outset the principal donor country. The foreign aid programs of the other major Western countries, Great Britain and France, were essentially an extension of the assistance which they had previously granted to their former colonies. When the latter became independent, this aid was continued to some extent and grew in scope to include also other developing countries.

The usefulness of such aid cannot be denied, at least to the degree that it offered additional resources to finance economic development. In principle, therefore, it should have always been accepted with gratitude.

In practice, however, foreign aid raises delicate political problems for both donor and recipient countries, even when it is called economic assistance, and is really designed to be purely that. This is especially true when it comes from the superpowers with world-wide interests, such as the United States, the Soviet Union, and in recent years also China. It is difficult if not impossible to isolate economic aid from other aspects of international relations. Donor countries insist

that their aid has no strings attached, and is simply to promote economic development, consequently a greater equality among nations
and a better international order. Yet their governments will admit that
economic aid is a tool of their general foreign policy, particularly when
they must request the funds from their legislative bodies.

This concept of foreign economic aid as part and parcel of general
foreign policy is quite visible in the case of the two super powers: the
United States and the Soviet Union. Thus one can find striking similar-
ities in their attitude toward foreign aid. Both rejected the recommendation made by the United Nations of setting a target of 1 per
cent of the G.N.P. of donor countries to be given as aid to economic
development. The reasons for their refusal were nearly the same. The
United States argued against this recommendation, which had been
accepted by all the allies in the O.E.C.D., by stating, among other
reasons, that they carried a far heavier load than their partners for the
common defense and security of the Free World. During a seminar on
"Soviet aid to developing countries" which was held in Moscow in the
fall of 1969 and was attended by the author, the Soviet Union's refusal
to accept the 1 per cent target was justified in terms of the heavy
burden which it had to shoulder in defending peace and international
security.

The recipient countries fear therefore that their acceptance of
economic aid may imply at least tacit approval on their part of the
general policies of the donor country. Thus it may jeopardize their
own choice of policies. Such fears were not always unfounded, particularly during the Eisenhower administration, when Secretary of
State John Foster Dulles spared no effort to sign up countries all over
the world into regional security treaties.

This was a relatively minor problem for countries whose political
orientation was clearly defined. If they were in favor of the policies of
the donor country, for example the United States, they could have no
objections to economic aid. In any event it would be less substantial
than what they received as direct military aid or as "defense support,"
economic aid specifically to permit the country to bear the cost of its
military obligations. On the other hand, economic aid at that time
was seldom offered to countries whose policies were hostile to the
donor governments, and would not have been accepted. In ·recent
years, however, the policies of foreign aid have become more flexible
and sophisticated. The United States, for instance, provides some economic assistance to socialist countries like Poland, but this aid is
granted for political, not economic, motives.

The question becomes most delicate in the case of developing countries which are anxious to preserve their position of complete non-alignment. It has led Burma, for example, to refuse all bilateral economic aid.

Gradually, more developed countries have started to provide economic aid on a large scale, and the situation has become more complicated. The political intentions of the former colonial powers, Great Britain and France, are quite simple: they would like to maintain and consolidate their economic, political, and cultural spheres of influence. Countries like West Germany and Japan, without recent colonial connections, seem to be motivated to a great extent by a desire to build up their image in the Third World and to create the good will which would facilitate the expansion of their export markets. Smaller developed countries with no special axe to grind, such as the Scandinavian countries in particular, are more influenced by humanitarian ideals. Therefore, developing countries find bilateral aid from these countries easier to accept. The USSR entered the field of economic aid somewhat later than the major countries of the West, but it has been providing aid to a large number of developing countries whose governments sometimes show little sympathy for its system of government.

The proliferation of sources of foreign aid has led several developing countries to play one donor against the other, in order to obtain aid on the most favorable conditions. Their schemes have most often miscarried. But by accepting aid from all available sources, including both of the superpowers, they have managed to preserve their independence and their stand of non-alignment, while at the same time drawing maximum assistance for their economic development. India, Brazil, and Ethiopia are among the countries which accept aid without discrimination.

On the whole, bilateral economic aid is considered a useful contribution to economic development and the developing countries are pressing for more with better terms. But there is little gratitude if any at all for this assistance. The reaction often is that this aid is only long overdue, and perhaps inadequate compensation for the centuries of exploitation which they have had to endure. This feeling is particularly widespread in Africa with its recent memories of slavery. Because of their suspicion of the motives behind bilateral aid, they usually prefer multilateral aid provided by international organizations.

Chapter 6. *CERTAIN SPECIAL REGIONAL PROBLEMS*

THE PROBLEMS which we have just discussed are common to all developing countries. In the following chapter we would like to single out others which apply more specifically to certain regions in the Third World.

a. *Latin America*

The present situation in Latin America can be fully understood only when viewed in the perspective of its historical background.

Latin American countries won their independence from Spain and Portugal in the first quarter of the nineteenth century, more than a hundred years, that is, before the major developing countries of southern Asia and Africa. This early political independence should have given Latin America a head start in economic development and an opportunity to progress much further. This was not the case, however, to any great extent.

The wars of independence in Latin America were fought in order to liberate the dominant creole class of semi-feudal landowners from the colonial yoke. While they paid lip service to the principles of the French and the American revolutions, and introduced elected presidents and legislatures, they were no different from their cousins in the Iberian Peninsula, the most reactionary class of Europe. They maintained their monopoly of wealth and political power based on ownership of land. Their rule was absolute, particularly in countries where the lower classes were largely of non-European descent, mainly Indian peons, hereditary tenants whose status was similar to that of serfs and Negro slaves.

Economic development was introduced in Latin America through trade with the industrial countries. At first the trading partners were Western European countries, mainly Great Britain, but later the United States increasingly took over. They supplied Latin America with its imports of manufactures and absorbed its exports of primary products: raw materials and foodstuffs. They created and developed a

modern export sector in Latin America by investing in mines, plantations, and transport facilities such as railroads and harbors. This trade
was extremely profitable for the privileged few in Latin America, and
it became the basis for their solidarity and alliance with foreign capital.

The influence of powerful foreign holdings gradually dominated
the economies and even the domestic policies of Latin American countries, particularly in the smaller ones which were less able to resist
such pressures. For all practical purposes their dependence on the
United States—whose presence in Latin America had been unchallenged since the end of the First World War—paralleled that of the
colonies of Great Britain and France on the mother country. There
was, however, still an essential difference in their legal status. Although Latin America was a *de facto* American dependency, the
United States government took no responsibility for its administration,
or for the welfare of its inhabitants. Control was in the hands of private American interests. Public opinion in America therefore could
remain ignorant on the whole of this situation, without concerning
itself with its political implications. The average citizen in the United
States could thus proclaim in good faith at a later date his sympathies
with anti-colonial movements in other continents. American domination over Latin America was a clear case of authority without responsibility.

In the early period of development—up to World War II—the
greatest economic progress was made in the south: in Argentina, Uru-
guay, Chile, and the southern states of Brazil, where the temperate
climate had attracted a great number of immigrants from Europe. A
modern middle class and an urban proletariat developed in these
countries, established industry, and organized an efficient system of
agriculture and stock-breeding. The landed oligarchy there had somewhat less of a stranglehold than in most other countries of the continent.

On the whole, however, they dominated all of Latin America, and
in view of their close ties with American capital any opposition to the
oligarchy had to be directed against the United States as well.

But until World War II only one successful revolution occurred,
in Mexico, and we will describe the development of Mexico in Part
Four.

In a report entitled *Change and Development: Latin America's
Great Task,* the great Latin American economist, Raoul Prebisch,
names four problems which have prevented Latin America from
achieving the high rate of growth commensurate with its resources

since the end of World War II.[1] The first is an archaic and inefficient system of land tenure which hampers growth in agricultural production and limits the size of the labor force that can remain on the land. Because of the present inequality in land distribution, the rural masses are kept in a state of abject poverty; needless to say, this reduces their purchasing power and restricts the domestic market for industrial products.

Strenuous efforts have been made to create industries which would replace imports. But this has been tried only on the national level, and the national markets, taken singly, are too limited because of the lack of purchasing power of the rural population. The new industries are faced, therefore, with high costs which restrict their expansion and reduce their ability to absorb the additional workers who are no longer needed in agriculture. With the very high rate of population growth in Latin America, surplus workers are very numerous. It turns out that the proportion of industrial workers in non-agricultural work actually declined during the period of 1950 to 1965, instead of increasing, as would normally have happened after development. For Latin America as a whole it went down from 35 to 31.8 per cent; for Argentina from 41.2 to 41.0, and for Brazil from 31.6 to 24.3 per cent. Only in Mexico did it grow, from 36.2 to 40.2 per cent.[2]

The inability of industry to absorb the additional labor that moved into the cities—primarily because only there were available such social services as health insurance and unemployment relief—led to the employment of too many people in service occupations: public administration, transportation, and small crafts. Productivity is traditionally very low in these fields, and there is considerable under-employment. One can see this, for instance, in the proliferation of shoe-shine boys everywhere in the cities of Latin America. What has happened is that part of the unemployable labor force has shifted from the rural to the urban scene. Concentrated in the slums encircling the cities, the unemployed become an even greater albatross on the economy and force the government to make additional investments in urban services.

Raoul Prebisch's last point is that Latin America has had to make do with too few resources for investment. The net flow of external resources, through public aid and private loans, has been very small. Taking into account the cost of amortization and the transfer of interest and profits, the end result has even sometimes been on the wrong

1. Report to the Inter-American Development Bank, Washington, D.C., 1970, pp. 1–15.
2. *Op. cit.*, p. 33.

side of the ledger. Thus from 1966 to 1968, the gross inflow of capital averaged $3,825 million, amortization $2,274, and interest and profits $1,952, leaving a deficit balance of $401 million.[3] Too many foreign loans and credits had been proffered and accepted at rates of interest which imposed a crushing burden of debt on many of the countries of Latin America. The rate of domestic savings available for productive investment did not develop because of reluctance on the part of the potential investors and the flight of capital abroad. The government seems unable to increase public savings by putting through an effective fiscal reform and cannot prevent increasing luxury consumption by the wealthy classes.

There are various remedies which could be applied. Land reform would increase the productive capacity of agriculture and raise the purchasing power of the rural population. A drastic tax reform would press harder on the wealthy minority and increase domestic savings. (At present 5 per cent of the population receive 31 per cent of the total private income and pay on the average only 25 per cent of their income in taxes.) More investment would accelerate industrial development, particularly if it were made in conjunction with regional economic integration. This would enlarge the scope of the market, facilitate the utilization of economies of scale, improve the efficiency and competitiveness of the new industries, and stimulate their expansion. Latin America would be able gradually to absorb the pool of unemployed and underemployed in agriculture and the service industries.[4]

Any adoption of these policies would involve some basic changes in the social and economic structure of Latin America and would require considerable sacrifices from the wealthy ruling classes. If these policies are not adopted voluntarily, the only alternative seems to be the prospect of seeing them imposed by an authoritarian or totalitarian regime after violent change of government. Raoul Prebisch expressed this diplomatically in his report: "Concentration of political power might be the logical sequence of stubborn opposition to inescapable structural changes."[5]

b. Africa

"Black Africa," Africa south of the Sahara, was before colonization for the most part divided up among a multiplicity of usually small

3. *Op. cit.*, p. 107.
4. *Op. cit.*, p. 112.
5. *Op. cit.*, p. 212.

autonomous tribes and was not organized into states. Each tribe had its separate existence with its own system of government headed generally by local chiefs, its own language or dialect, and its own form of land tenure. When the various countries of Western Europe split up Africa at the Berlin Congress of 1885, no notice whatsoever was taken of tribal boundaries. Frontiers were determined on the basis of political, strategic, or economic criteria; sometimes the question was solved simply by drawing a line down the map. This can be seen in the fact that some of the boundaries between independent African countries which stemmed from former colonial empires follow surprisingly straight lines, usually in a north-south, or east-west direction. In many instances, the borders cut through tribal territories so that members of the same tribe found themselves subjects of different colonial powers, with different systems of administration and official languages. Most colonies included members of more than one tribe.

The sixty to eighty years under foreign domination were not sufficient to merge the different tribes of one colonial territory into a unified nation. Only the minority who had been educated in the sole common language of multitribal territories—that of the colonial power, English or French—were at all able to overcome their tribal loyalties. This common training gave them a certain understanding of the joint interests of all those who lived in the territory and evoked in them a sense of patriotism.

When this élite came to power, however, in the newly independent countries, this feeling of patriotism was still much weaker than the traditional bonds of tribal solidarity. Yet it would have been impossible to realign the frontiers in accordance with tribal boundaries. There would have been intertribal wars throughout the whole continent. Thus, in spite of their initially artificial character, the new states were faced with the major task of creating and consolidating their national unity within their existing borders. They had to overcome the pull of tribalism and develop a sense of attachment to the nation as a whole. In this respect they found themselves in a position similar to that of Western Europe when national states were first established. There, too, provincial and regional loyalties were stronger for several centuries at least than national patriotism.

In the developing countries of Africa tribalism is a major obstacle not only to national unity but also to the operation of good government and to the success of economic development. It is an unfortunate fact that tribalism is a source of power, that governments favor certain tribes over others, and that even where there is a coalition government, the head of a government agency may often call on members of his own tribe to fill all the posts under him. The effect of this tribal nepotism is naturally ruinous to the efficiency of public administration.

A former high official of the government-owned Eastern Nigeria Development Corporation discussed this problem in a Ph.D. dissertation which he submitted to New York University in 1971.[6] He provided significant data on the manner in which tribalism can pervert the operation of an agency which was founded in order to promote the economic development of a multitribal region. He shows that the operations of the Eastern Nigeria Development Corporation were all geared to further the interests of the Ibo tribe and that projects thus were created only in the Ibo areas, even when other locations might have been more appropriate. Only Ibos were employed and usually in excessive numbers, as all the projects were overstaffed. This policy created great financial deficits and had only disastrous results. Far from advancing the economic development of the country or even of the Eastern region, the Corporation drained its economy.

One can hope that the spread of education—in languages other than the local ones—the expansion of cities, and, in particular, the growth of new ones in the coastal areas, where members of different tribes can meet and mix, will contribute to the governments' efforts to subvert the corrupting influence of tribalism. Then modern nations could function, capable of economic development which will benefit their entire population. But this result will probably not come rapidly.

c. Asia

In Asia, and particularly in the very populous countries of southern Asia, one of the major obstacles in the path of economic development is the conflict between the traditional values of its ancient civilizations and the exigencies of modernization. Traditional Asian society was—and still is to a great extent—very rigidly structured. It is dominated by strict religious taboos and prohibitions, such as those which forbid in India the use of lifestock for practical purposes. Castes, classes, and religions effectively preclude any social mobility and the great majority of the rural population are tenant farmers or landless laborers at the bottom of the social ladder.

During the colonial administration no real change was made in the life of the great majority of the population, in so far as the main-

6. "The Organization and Management of Economic development in Developing Countries," Ph.D. dissertation submitted by James Thomas Daniell to New York University, 1971, unpublished.

tenance of law and order was not affected. Only the privileged upper classes were influenced by, and to some extent benefited from, the new values introduced by the West.

In his monumental study, *Asian Drama*, and in *The Challenge of World Poverty*,[7] Gunnar Myrdal analyzes the fact that since the countries of Asia have become independent, more than 25 years ago, there have again been too few basic changes made. The lofty statements embodied in their constitutions, and their laws, in many cases have only been partially carried out, if at all. Land reform has been a boon up to now mainly to the prosperous farmers. In spite of equalitarian phraseology, absentee landownership has not only not disappeared but is even spreading. The upper and middle classes, including professionals in the cities, and even government officials, are attracted to the traditionally safe and profitable practice of investing in land. The position of the rural masses, helpless, unable to voice their complaint and apathetic, is steadily deteriorating. The population explosion is separating them even further from the privileged classes. A decreasing proportion of workers are employed in the agricultural labor force and those that flee to the cities cannot be absorbed into industry; trade and services are already overcrowded.

The priority given to secondary and higher education serves the interests of the privileged classes. It prevents the bulk of the population from acquiring any degree of literacy and a minimum of equality. At the same time the academic orientation of the educational system does not correspond to the requirements of a modern economy. The result is a class of unemployed graduates. Lacking the dedication which might have inspired them to guide and assist the rural masses, they remain in the cities and feed on discontent and social disturbance. The absence of social and moral discipline, which can be seen in the government's failure to enforce its laws and regulations, is particularly dangerous in an economic structure that is supposed to reflect an ideal of social justice. The discrepancy between this ideal and the reality is especially alarming when only the rich and the powerful can obtain the administrative approval which is required for any important economic measure.

This desperate, nearly hopeless, situation could only be improved by drastic changes in the region which up to now neither the democratic nor the autocratic governments have been able and/or willing to make. These changes should include an effective land reform which

7. Gunnar Myrdal, *Asian Drama: An Inquiry into the Poverty of Nations,* Pantheon, New York, 1968; and *The Challenge of World Poverty*, Pantheon, New York, 1970.

would safeguard the right of farmers to the fruit of their own labor and lead to greater productivity in agriculture. There must be reform in education to establish universal literacy as rapidly as possible, and more efforts must be made in the area of family planning—actually the only field where in some countries at least a real start has already been made. Finally, the authority of the government must be strengthened to enable it to carry out its own laws and regulations and to consider the public interest as its first concern.

Chapter 7. WHY THE DEVELOPED COUNTRIES SHOULD CONTRIBUTE TO ECONOMIC DEVELOPMENT

THE IMPACT of economic development in the Third World on the industrialized countries should normally be a positive one. But in actual fact this will only be the case if the policies of the developed countries are indeed oriented to a mutually profitable co-operation which would further development. Placing obstacles in the path of development in order to protect their domestic vested interests will ultimately only backfire.

The economy of the developed countries must be sufficiently dynamic and flexible to adjust to changes in their traditional trading patterns. They should be in a position to take advantage of the opportunity for expansion of trade which will arise when economic development in the Third World increases the purchasing power and the need for imports.

Economic development will inevitably disturb vested interests in the developed countries of the West, and in particular their present foreign investments. To a great extent this has already occurred. There will be a difficult transition from the principle of investments based on domination by developed countries to a new formula whereby private foreign capital would make a useful and mutually profitable contribution to economic development.

Trade between developing and developed countries will require even greater adjustment. But if the problem can be solved, the new pattern of world trade will offer great opportunities to expand the international exchange of goods and services and the world economy, which will benefit both sides.

The pattern of trade in developing countries has been traditionally to exchange their agricultural and mineral primary products for the manufactured goods of the developed industrial countries. There was then the fear that economic development would deprive the industries of developed countries of their customary export markets as well as of their normal sources of supply. Rather than export them, the developing countries might process the raw materials themselves.

Economic development has already brought far reaching changes

Part Three

External Contribution to Development

It is generally acknowledged that economic development in the developing countries must come largely as a result of their own efforts and sacrifices. Development cannot be imposed on independent countries nor can it be imported from the outside.

In the past, however, as we pointed out in Part One, the initial development of the Third World was both imported from and imposed by the Western nations, which started it to suit their own interest. The political domination of the West extended over most developing countries, while its economic supremacy went unchallenged. Raoul Prebisch expressed this by drawing a circle with the developed countries at the center of the world economy and the underdeveloped countries on the periphery.

Freedom from such dependence, with its corollary of economic exploitation does not entail—at least for most of the Third World —a refusal to recognize or accept the interdependence of the industrialized and the developing countries within the framework of the world economy. The developing countries usually agree that active foreign co-operation can make an important contribution to their economic development. But this co-operation, in order to be acceptable and productive, must be based on an entirely new approach. The present political facts of life are such that there is no longer any room for the traditional attitude of superiority, the conscious or unconscious sense of paternalism. This would only revive their resentment of the West's former exploitation and eliminate any possibility for fruitful dialogue or constructive co-operation.

Only as equal partners can the developed countries make an effective contribution which would bring about increased production, greater purchasing power, and an improvement in the welfare of developing countries.

Two questions arise in this connection. What should induce the developed countries to adopt this new approach? What guidelines should their policies follow?

in this traditional pattern of trade. The developing countries have refused to continue as the "hewers of wood and porters of water" of the world economy. The progress of their development is altering and expanding both their import requirements and their available exports.

In keeping with their development programs, the developing countries have established consumer goods industries to replace the manufactured products which they previously imported. As we said earlier, they normally start off by taking advantage of their available resources of abundant and cheap labor. Their first import replacement industries are usually labor-intensive, such as the manufacture of cotton textiles, shoes, or beer, which will not drain their scarce capital. Inevitably this means a loss of export markets for the developed countries which used to supply these products.

On the other hand, economic development is bound to create new and rapidly expanding markets for capital equipment imported from the developed countries. This equipment will be needed both in the newly established industries and in the modernization of agriculture. The creation of import replacement industries to manufacture capital goods would require a high level of technology, vast resources of capital and skilled labor, and a large domestic market. With India and Brazil as the chief exceptions, these prerequisites will not be found for a long time to come in most developing countries.

Economic development will raise the purchasing power of consumers in the developing countries. They will be able to afford products of higher quality and greater sophistication than the inexpensive basic consumer items that alone were within their reach in the past. These far more complex and expensive consumer goods, especially the durables such as motor vehicles and electric appliances, can be bought only from the developed countries.

These new markets for industrial exports should more than compensate the developed countries for their losses in the export of cheap labor-intensive consumer goods. It is a well known fact that economic development and industrialization, far from reducing the proportion of manufactured goods in a country's total imports, on the contrary will increase it. To cite only one example, in Mexico, which has a record of very rapid economic and industrial expansion since the end of World War II, the total value of imports grew from 1948 to 1968 by 730 per cent. During that same period the share of manufactured goods in the total import rose from 77.8 to 86.5 per cent, and the share of machinery and transport equipment from 43.9 to 53.7 per cent.[1] As

1. *Yearbook of International Trade Statistics, 1969, United Nations, New York, 1970, pp. 568 and 569.*

development progresses, the import pattern of developing countries will resemble that of the developed countries. There the proportion of industrial products in their total imports is steadily increasing. Thus in the United States it went from 29.1 per cent in 1949 to 43.4 per cent in 1959 and to 58.8 per cent in 1968.[2]

The industrial products which the highly developed countries buy from one another are also those which the developing countries of today will increasingly be able to afford as their development progresses. They are quite different from the manufactured items imported in the past. Cheap mass-consumption goods are replaced by high quality consumer items, simple agricultural tools by complex and sophisticated equipment which is extremely capital-intensive and necessitates a high level technology. This exchange of manufactured goods among the industrialized countries is the most dynamic and rapidly growing sector of international trade. It offers the greatest scope for creative competitive management. Inventions and innovations at one stage permit a particular firm or country to expand its exports while in the next phase another competitor may take the lead. This occurred for instance after World War II in the international automobile industry, where the competitive advantage switched back and forth between America and Europe, and within Europe among the main producing countries and the big individual firms.

This kind of export trade is also the most profitable for the developed countries because it takes advantage of the factors of production which are their strong points: technological skills and capital. These industries have the highest rate of productivity and are able to pay the highest wages. Professor Walter W. Heller, then the chairman of the Council of Economic Advisors of the President, confirmed this in a lecture given at New York University on March 24, 1962, when he pointed out that two thirds of the major American export industries paid higher wages than those received by the average industrial worker. The opportunity of acquiring new markets for these products in the developing countries is therefore far more important for the industrialized countries than is the decline in their former exports to the countries of the Third World.

But in order to take full advantage of this growing market it is in the interest of the developed countries to increase the import capacity of the developing nations. To this end they would be well advised to open up their own markets and encourage the import of manufactured goods from the newly established industries of the Third World. These imports are the products of labor-intensive indus-

2. *Ibid.*, pp. 891–894.

tries and capitalize on the comparative advantage of ample cheap labor and shortage of capital resources. In the developed countries these imports compete with domestic industries which have not kept pace with the current state of labor and capital. These industries require so much labor that wages account for a major share of their overall production costs. Yet their productivity is low and they can only afford to pay wages lower than the national average. This is the state in which the American textile industry finds itself today, located essentially in the South where wages are the lowest in the nation. In 1969 the hourly wage in the textile industry was only 77 per cent of the average wage of non-agricultural workers.[3] Such industries require high tariff protection in order to survive in the competition with cheaper imports.

It is visibly in the interest of the developed countries to encourage when possible the move of capital and labor over to capital-intensive and technologically advanced industries where they have the maximum comparative advantage. The old and inefficient labor-intensive industries should be phased out. The gain would be twofold—a supply of cheap imports and a bigger market for their most lucratic exports.

Such a policy would only be effective, however, if two conditions are met. As we already suggested, the economy of the developed countries must be sufficiently flexible and dynamic to ensure that such a switch will be made without causing an excessive dislocation which would have serious economic and social repercussions. Equally important is the fact that the government and public opinion must be conscious of the need for such a switch and willing and able to withstand the pressure of vested interests which would be affected.

In the long run the import capacity of the Third World would also be increased if the developed countries would agree to more favorable prices for the exports of primary products. This would benefit both sides. Improvement in terms of trade for the exchange of these primary products would avoid the danger of a scarcity of raw materials from the developing countries which are essential to industries in the developed countries. At present the export of these raw materials is still the major source of foreign exchange for the Third World and necessary to its development. But the situation is bound to change. When the economies of these countries become more diversified and balanced, they will grow less dependent on the world market for their exports of non-processed raw materials. At that point

3. *Handbook of Labor Statistics, 1970*, US Department of Labor, Washington, D.C., 1970, table 100, pp. 203–205.

they will be processing their own raw materials and would be interested in producing additional quantities for export only if they were paid prices which would make such production at least as profitable as an alternative use of their resources in land, labor, and capital.

If policies such as those we have just outlined were adopted by the developed countries they should reap considerable advantages from the economic development of the Third World, with the ensuing expansion of world production and international trade. If this economic development were achieved through this sort of international co-operation, there might also be a general improvement in the climate of relations between the rich countries and those who will grow less poor at least as a result of this development.

Chapter 8. *WHAT THE DEVELOPED COUNTRIES SHOULD CONTRIBUTE TO ECONOMIC DEVELOPMENT*

THE DEVELOPING COUNTRIES need the co-operation and assistance of the developed countries, especially of the market economy countries, their main trading partners, in order to satisfy their rapidly growing import requirements. Economic development implies an enormous rise in imports. These imports include capital goods to establish the infrastructure of the economy, in particular transport and power, to modernize agricultural production, and to develop industries. Intermediate products, such as semi-manufactured goods; basic industrial materials, such as steel and chemicals; dyes for textiles; and fuel, which are not produced domestically in the early phase of development, must also be imported. We have already mentioned the rise in the imports of consumer goods which occurs when development improves consumer purchasing power.

The traditional export trade of primary products from the developing countries will not grow at the same rate, however, because of unsatisfactory terms of trade and because primary products no longer figure so importantly in overall world trade. The deficit between the imports and exports of developing countries inevitably is growing larger.

The developing countries are pressing for the stabilization of their primary export products at a satisfactory level of prices in order to improve the terms of trade. At the same time they ask that the products of their new industries, mainly labor-intensive consumer goods, be admitted on the markets of the developed countries. For the time being these industries are not fully competitive in international trade and should be granted special treatment to enable them to reach a significant export volume.

International trade is a two-way street, with the *quid pro quo* immediately at hand. Thus exports are the most convenient way of obtaining the imports which the developing countries require for their development program.

No reverse flow of resources which might endanger the balance of payments in future years should in theory be involved. But in actual fact the deficit in balance of payments is such that even an improvement in the terms of trade for primary products, and an expansion of the market for the new industrial products of developing countries, would not bridge the gap.

The developing countries badly need, therefore, a massive injection of what is officially called a "net flow of financial resources." The problem is that in most cases this transfer of resources from developed to developing countries goes both ways. Moneys leave the developing countries in the payment of profits and/or interest, and in the repatriation of capital. While they can bail out the recipient country on a short-term basis, these transfers can also become a source of difficulty for the future. Their overall impact on the balance of payments deficit needs to be studied carefully.

Usually this transferring of funds has come in the past through private investments, and has made a major contribution to whatever development has existed in the recipient countries. But under present conditions this sort of economic development is no longer considered desirable or effective. The role of foreign private investment, especially of direct investment, will most likely be more limited now. Other forms of capital import, such as private or public loans and credits, raise fewer objections but involve commitments which may impose a heavy responsibility in the future.

Since World War II foreign aid from developed countries has become a major source of capital. This implies no reverse flow or future financial burden. One must remember here, however, that only through grants do the developing countries actually receive the full amount as aid. There is the tendency in donor countries to list under their aid programs transactions whose character is mainly financial or commercial. Credits or loans represent aid only to the extent that they are made on concessional terms. The Pearson Report estimated that the grant element of all official aid in 1967 represented only 75 per cent.[1]

The present trend of these various transfers of resources to developing countries is not likely to solve the difficulties in balance of payments which have occurred in their development. If it continues there will be no relief on the horizon for the crushing burden of accumulated foreign debts which has already created a crisis situation in several developing countries which have not been able to meet their commitments in paying interest or repaying capital.

1. *Partners in Development, Report of the Commission on International Development,* Praeger, New York, 1969, p. 140.

The following chapter attempts to examine further these different aspects of the economic relations of the developed countries with the Third World, and to describe the prevailing trends, in particular as they concern the transfer of financial resources. It also tries to outline policies which developed countries should adopt in order to facilitate the solution of these problems in a mutually satisfactory manner and to consolidate international friendship through co-operation.

a. *International trade*

The participation of the developing countries in international trade consists principally still in their exports of primary products, mainly to their traditional trading partners, the developed Western market economies including Japan. These same countries are also the chief suppliers of their imports of manufactured items, and in particular of capital goods.

The socialist countries have not had a large share in the international trade of the developing countries, although the picture is somewhat changing. Of their total exports in 1968 only 5 per cent were sent to the socialist countries, as compared with 3 per cent in 1957.[2] Because of the policy of austerity which strictly limited consumption in socialist countries, and which is only being gradually relaxed, their imports and consumption of tropical foodstuffs and beverages are still far lower than that of the developed market economies. Thus the import per capita of coffee in 1968 for East Germany represented less than half of West Germany's import, 2.5 kilograms as compared with 5.2 kilos. The small number of passenger automobiles restricted the consumption of natural rubber. Finally the socialist countries of Europe, including the Soviet Union, are nearly self-sufficient in most of the mineral primary products, oil in particular, which the developing countries export. But the trade of some developing countries with the socialist countries is much more substantial. The reasons are usually political rather than economic. Thus the United Arab Republic sent 48.6 per cent of its exports to the socialist countries in 1968, and received from them 41 per cent of its imports.

The trade of the developing countries with each other, not counting those who share a socialist economy, has increased at a slower rate than that of their total international trade. Thus it has gone down proportionately from 24.4 per cent in 1957 to 19.9 per cent in 1968. The reason for this is that most of their primary products exports are

2. Calculated from data in the *Yearbook of International Trade Statistics, 1968*, United Nations, New York, 1970.

either industrial raw materials whose natural markets are found in the highly industrialized countries, or tropical foodstuffs and beverages consumed primarily in countries with a high purchasing power. Attempts have been made to expand the trade between developing countries by creating regional common markets, within which large-scale industries could be established which would use the raw materials produced in the member countries. Only in Central America and East Africa has any significant progress in this line been achieved.

The developed market economies are therefore the ones held responsible for the unfavorable terms of trade of these exports. The developing countries feel that they are entitled to an improvement in these terms of trade from their trading partners. As we have mentioned earlier, they are demanding international commodity agreements to stabilize world prices for the primary products they export. Such agreements would ensure a stable level of income for producers and adequate earnings of foreign exchange, which could pay for their imports, in particular for the capital goods which are required in their economic development.

Such agreements were recognized as an essential part of the future world economic order envisaged at the end of World War II. A provision dealing with these agreements was embodied in the draft charter of the International Trade Organization, prepared at the Havana Conference in 1948. Unfortunately this charter, which was drafted at the initiative of the United States government in order to devise an institutional framework for multilateral international trade, was never even submitted to Congress for ratification. The ITO has never been created.

The attitude of the United States and of most other industrialized countries has not been in favor of international commodity agreements, for theoretical as well as for practical reasons. It was argued, and not without good cause, that commodity agreements could become producers' cartels, which would impose exhorbitant prices prejudicial to consumers. By encouraging excessive production, especially on the part of outsiders who did not submit to the restrictions imposed on member states, such agreements might give rise to a total disequilibrium between supply and demand, and a catastrophic collapse of the market. This occurred in the 1920's, under the Stevenson Plan, which was an attempt to control the production and price of rubber. While it remained in effect, the extra cost of rubber purchased by the American tire manufacturers was on the order of $500 million a year. It has also been pointed out that the allocation of quotas among existing producers would in fact grant them a monopoly and prevent other countries that might be able to produce at lower costs from entering the field. But there are solutions to these problems, and they have been successfully applied. Recent commodity agreements have included the representatives of both consumers and producers, and have tried to establish a price level and a margin between minimum and maximum prices which would be fair to both sides. Arrangements have been made to admit new producers.

Even more important than these objections of principle were practical considerations. The Western industrial countries felt that these agreements might involve additional costs to their industries and consumers. They thought that with the operation of an open world market they would be able to purchase the primary products at lower prices on the average than under international commodity agreements.

Here one must note that at times when world prices did not favor the industrialized market economies, there was no hesitation on their part to intervene and establish monopsonic purchasers' cartels in order to prevent a rise in prices. This policy was pursued during World War II, when prices of all primary products purchased by the allied countries were set by the Combined Commodity Boards in Washington, which were also empowered to allocate the shipping required. The prices paid to the developing countries for their wartime sales were considerably below those which they might have obtained had a free market existed. Moreover, the developing countries at that time were unable to use the proceeds of these sales to purchase manufactured goods. There were no industrial goods available for export, as all production was concentrated in the war effort. The developing countries thus accumulated considerable foreign exchange reserves —mainly in dollars—which suddenly lost 40 per cent of their purchasing power when price controls were lifted in 1946 in the United States. The rise of United States prices caused an abrupt deterioration in the terms of trade of the developing countries for their wartime primary products exports, *a posteriori*. This created considerable discontent and resentment in the developing countries.

A somewhat similar policy of price restraints on primary products from the developing countries was adopted by the United States during the Korean War.

In a few instances developing countries have been able to exert sufficient pressure in order to obtain more favorable prices. The monopolistic cartel of the oil-producing countries was able to drive an extremely hard bargain with the international oil companies, and is the most striking example of the effective use of economic power by developing countries.

It is hardly surprising, as we have just shown, that the policies of developing and developed countries alike, in regard to prices of primary products, have been motivated up to now mainly by national interests. But the question arises whether such a policy, when viewed in a broader perspective, may not be shortsighted for the major developed countries, especially for the United States. These countries make substantial allocations in their budgets for aid to the developing countries that supply the primary products. A drop in the world price of a product which is the major export item of a given country (coffee for Brazil or Columbia, copper for Chile or Zambia) can cancel, and in many cases has more than erased, the total benefit derived from foreign aid during a particular year. Such a price drop may well have disastrous consequences for the whole economy, crippling its ability to import capital goods, even essential consumer items and food. It would cause a deterioration in international relations, in particular with the donor country.

This danger would be bypassed if world prices of primary products were stabilized at a level only slightly higher than the average of the fluctuating prices on the world market. At no cost to their budget and with relatively little additional expenditure for the industries and consumers of the donor countries, this would give the developing countries the equivalent of the foreign aid which they have received up to now. It has been calculated that an increase of one cent in the price of a cup of coffee in the United States would raise the proceeds of coffee exports of Brazil by over $100 million, more than the total cash value of aid provided annually to that country by the United States.

This "aid through trade," if it were applied to all primary products, thus benefiting all exporting developing countries, would relieve the donor governments to a great extent of the delicate problem of submitting their program of foreign economic aid each year to their legislative bodies. The discussions that occur at such times are usually far from conducive to good rapport between the donor and the recipient countries. The developing countries resent the inevitable criticism of their performance, or of their attitude, and are offended by the inferior position which the aid relationship attributes to them.

Aid through trade would not raise such difficulties in the legislatures, or in public opinion on either side. Although this approach would make economic aid seem less apparent and therefore less easy to attack, it would, however, make it harder to control, and for this reason it has been generally rejected. In the discussion of the United States Congress on the International Coffee Agreement, it was quite clear that this opposition emanated not only from a desire to protect consumers from excessive prices, but from the fear of relinquishing legislative control.

France is the only major developed country to have steadfastly defended the general stabilization of primary products at favorable prices. This policy was in line with her tradition of granting tariff protection to her former colonial territories in her domestic market. It was extremely advantageous at first to those exporters of primary products. But when their production had expanded to the point where it exceeded the absorptive capacity of the French market, problems naturally arose. Such difficulties, however, could be easily overcome by imposing quotas to restrict production, in accordance with the common practice of most commodity stabilization agreements.

In spite of their official refusal to grant "aid through trade" to all of the Third World, some Western developed countries, in particular the United States and the United Kingdom, are in fact providing such aid to certain developing countries by giving them preferential treatment. Thus Great Britain, under the Commonwealth Sugar Agreement, has set fixed quotas for the sugar she imports from the developing countries who are members of the Commonwealth. The United States also imports free of duty a specified amount of sugar, mainly from the Philippines and a number of countries in Latin America. These preferential quotas are extremely valuable, as the price of sugar on the American domestic market is considerably higher that the world price. The most important of these quotas was granted to Cuba before the Castro revolution.

With the exception of such instances of preferential treatment, it is the socialist countries who offer the developing nations outlets for their primary products at stable prices which may be higher than the world prices. These sales are negotiated under long-term trade agreements which also involve usually the import of capital goods manufactured in Soviet bloc countries. These are supplied on a credit basis, with their costs to be met by the sales of the traditional primary products. Both the quantities and the prices are set in advance. Another attractive feature of this trade for the developing countries is the fact that the socialist countries represent new markets for them and additional sales.

On the other hand, most of the developing countries, at least those that have free access to other markets and sources of supply, see to it, on the basis of recent experience, that their sales to socialist countries do not substantially exceed the quantities which these countries actually need for domestic consumption. Sales to socialist countries do not bring convertible currency. Their proceeds can be used only for purchases from the same country. It has happened that when a socialist country has imported primary products in excess of its requirements, the surplus has been sold on the world market. Thus the producing country is deprived of convertible currency and denied the possibility of using it to purchase its imports elsewhere. After the Suez crisis of 1956 Egypt sold most of its cotton to the Soviet Union, which then resold part of it on the world market and preempted Egypt's traditional markets in Western Europe.

The general reluctance of the developed market economy countries to accept price stabilization of primary products has been slowly fading away. The pressure of the developing countries, the growing awareness that this is a source of increasing hostility and resentment, possibly also an impetus to greater trade between the developing and the socialist countries, are at the root of this gradual shift in attitude.

In recent years a number of international agreements have been concluded which deal with the marketing and stabilizing of prices of primary commodities from developing countries. The United Nations Conference on Trade and Development—UNCTAD—since its creation in 1964, and FAO in the agricultural field, have played a leading role in this area.

By the end of 1971, however, only a few commodities were covered in comprehensive official international agreements. The first of such agreements to have been concluded, shortly after World War II, dealt with wheat exported mainly by developed rather than by developing countries. Other agreements have been made for coffee, sugar, olive oil, and tin. These agreements generally include provisions for maximum and minimum prices and quotas for the distribution of production among member countries. There is usually an executive body to set policies which will reduce price fluctuations. As the case may be, it can limit production to a certain percentage of each country's quota when prices are falling, or on the contrary abolish all quota restrictions when prices are rising. If there is a buffer stock, as in the tin agreement, purchases for the buffer stock are made when prices fall below the minimum level; when they rise above the maximum, sales would be made from the buffer stock.

It is difficult to ascertain the effect of these agreements on the fluctuation of prices, which are influenced by the special market conditions for each commodity. It would seem, however, that these agreements have had a stabilizing influence. But they definitely should not be considered as "aid through trade," and have been negotiated after hard bargaining on the part of both consuming and producing countries.

Informal agreements have also been concluded for hard fibers: sisal, henequen, and abaca, and for jute and kenaf. These agreements have no mandatory provisions; they only recommend measures to be taken by member countries.

FAO and UNCTAD have established study groups for a number of other commodities with special interest to developing countries: bananas, citrus fruit, cotton, oil seeds, oil and fats, rubber, and tea. Their function is to co-ordinate the policies of their member countries.

In the last decade one would be hard put to single out any one dominant trend in the price and volume of international trade in primary products. In general the increasingly high level of industrial activity in the developed market economies has expanded the demand for raw materials. Competition from synthetics has also increased, however, in the case of some of them, such as cotton, wool, sisal, abaca, jute, and rubber. Great efforts have been necessary to lower production costs. The effect of the Green Revolution has already begun to be felt in the increased production of wheat and especially rice in the main importing countries, and it has reduced the demand for these cereals and caused prices to drop.

Table VI indicates that on the whole the value of exports from the developing countries that concentrate mainly on primary products has risen during the period from 1953 to 1969. But the rate of increase has been inferior to that of the oil-producing countries, or of those few countries which export chiefly manufactured goods: India, Hong Kong, Taiwan, Israel, and South Korea. Since the exports of developing countries are still mainly primary products, foodstuffs, and raw materials, the expansion of their international trade cannot be considered at all satisfactory. They are disappointed that the introduction of a number of international commodity agreements has not significantly improved the level of prices, although it may have contributed to a certain stabilization in prices. Their exports have not kept up with those of the developed countries, so that in actual fact their share in the total value of world exports has shrunk constantly. It declined from 30 per cent in 1948 to 22.3 per cent in 1959 and to 18.5 per cent in 1968.[3]

The developing countries persist in their efforts to expand their exports of primary products. They demand the co-operation of the developed countries in facilitating admission to their markets. In

3. *Yearbook of International Trade Statistics, 1968,* United Nations, New York, 1969.

particular they insist on a reduction of the indirect taxes levied by
some major importing countries, such as those of West Germany on
coffee and tea, which undoubtedly have curtailed the consumption
and import of these products.

Table VI

VALUE OF EXPORTS FROM DEVELOPING COUNTRIES BY
MAIN COMMODITY GROUPS

(per cent change per annum)

Countries Exporting Mainly:

	Food and Raw Materials	*Fuels (oil)*	*Manufactures*
1953–55 to 1963–65	2.6	7.1	8.6
1964 to 1965	3.2	6.4	13.2
1965 to 1966	4.2	6.5	16.3
1966 to 1967	−2.2	9.7	9.8
1967 to 1968	7.0	11.5	16.0
1968 to 1969 (first 9 months)	9.5	7.0	19.0

Source: UNCTAD Commodity Survey 1968, United Nations, New
York, 1968, table 2, p. 2; UNCTAD International Action on Commodities in the Light of Recent Developments, *United Nations document TD/B/C1/94*, 1970, table 1, p. 2.

It is clear, however, with the growing need for more imports of
capital goods that the deteriorating situation in the balance of payments of developing countries will only improve if their production
of manufactured goods for export can be expanded further. The
volume of these exports has grown, although it is still small. From
1960 to 1968 the proportion of manufactured goods in the exports
of developing countries to the developed market economies—which
comprised 77 per cent in 1968 of the total exports of lesser developed
countries—went from 13.3 to 20.6 per cent. During that same period
food and raw materials other than fuels declined from 60.5 to 55 per
cent. Fuels increased from 26.2 to 34.4 per cent.

Those countries in the Third World which are not blessed with
rich oil resources must therefore undertake the arduous task of
building up their export industries for the world market. They ask
the developed market economies, which will remain at least in the
immediate future their chief trading partners, to assist their efforts
by granting preferential treatment to these products.

The main arguments in favor of this preferential treatment have been put forward by Raoul Prebisch, the first Secretary-General of UNCTAD.[4] Since its establishment in 1964 the adoption and general implementation of this policy has been one of the major objectives of that institution. Dr. Prebisch pointed out that since the end of World War II the policies which the non-communist countries have followed in order to restore and expand international trade have only benefited the industrialized countries. The general reduction of tariffs which was negotiated in the framework of the GATT (General Agreement on Tariffs and Trade), including the Kennedy Round, ruled out inequality in the admission of exports from all member countries. But this equal treatment was important only in the case of industrial products, the only ones essentially to be subject to customs duties. Industrial raw materials were admitted free. Tropical food-stuffs and beverages which did not compete with domestic products were subject only to fiscal duties. These duties were designed to bring in revenue and not to protect local producers or limit imports.

Imports of manufactured goods into the industrialized countries from the Third World are quite another matter. To establish equal terms for imports by applying the "most favoured nation" clause is justifiable for developed countries. It permits fair competition between well established and efficient industries. But as we have stated earlier, the industries of the developing countries are not yet able to compete on equal terms on the world market. Their only competitive advantage, their reduced costs of labor, is more than offset by the lower productivity of their labor force. Above all they have the drawback of operating in a relatively primitive and undiversified economy. Most of the ancillary services and facilities which could be taken for granted in developed countries are either non-existent there, or at least very poor. The shortage of skilled personnel obliges industry itself to set up training programs at its own expense. Inadequate supplies of public power, inefficient public services, in particular transport and communications, difficulties and delays in obtaining equipment and spare parts, lack of adequate banking services to provide necessary credit are only some of the many drawbacks in an underdeveloped society which prevent the export industries in the developing countries from competing on equal terms.

At the first conference of UNCTAD in 1964 there was a proposal that the developed market economies grant a unilateral preferential treatment to the industrial products of developing countries. Imports of these products would be free of customs duties; at the very least

4. *Towards a Global Strategy of Development,* Report by the Secretary-General of UNCTAD, United Nations, New York, 1968.

the rates would be substantially lower than those applied to similar imports from industrialized countries under the "most favored nation" clause. The proposal took into account the fact that these preferences would be granted only on a temporary basis, until the young industries had gotten off the ground.

Favoring this proposal was the argument that this expansion of industrial exports would be beneficial to the world economy as a whole, and even, at least in the long run, to the developed countries. On both sides better use would be made of their resources and their particular strengths. By exporting labor-intensive products, whose costs of production are far higher in the developed countries, the developing countries would offer new markets for the capital-intensive and technologically advanced goods which can best be manufactured in the West.

Several major developed countries are already granting this preferential treatment. But they do so only to nations with whom they have special relations of an economic and political nature. Reciprocity is also involved—that is, the developing countries granting preferential terms to the products of their developed trading partners. Great Britain has such agreements with developing countries in the Commonwealth, and the European Economic Community with those African nations that are associated with the Common Market. But these differential duties discriminate in fact against all other developing countries, and arouse considerable opposition and resentment, especially in the countries of Latin America.

Both in Latin America and in the United States there have been proposals to establish a regional preferential system with reciprocity for the Western Hemisphere, similar to the treaty of the Association of African Countries with the European Common Market. Under such an arrangement the United States would grant preferential treatment to industrial imports from Latin America and reap similar benefits for its own exports to Latin America. At the UNCTAD conference Dr. Prebisch argued that such regional North-South preferential blocs would be extremely undesirable. They would most likely jeopardize the further expansion of multilateral trade and thus the progress of the world economy. Even more dangerous might be the political repercussions of such agreements. New tensions would be created if it was thought that they consecrated a new colonialism, a return to the domination of the weaker and less developed countries by the powerful industrial nations. Yet without a general preference system for the industrial exports of developing countries on a non-discriminatory basis, there was a strong likelihood that competing regional blocs would indeed appear.

In his recommendations on the export trade of developing countries, Dr. Prebisch also made some requests to the developed socialist countries. Tariff rates, unlike customs duties, have little to do with the origin of their imports. Socialist countries would be unable therefore to grant preferential treatment to products from developing countries on the same order as market economies. On the other hand, they do import, usually under bilateral agreements, both primary products and manufactured goods from various developing countries. It should be possible for them to increase gradually their purchases in developing countries, both of primary products and of industrial consumer goods, and to integrate this expansion into their general economic plans. This increase in imports would meet the rapidly growing consumer demand in the socialist countries. Furthermore, this would enable the socialist countries whose industries have heretofore concentrated on capital goods to make consumer goods readily available on their domestic market without having to develop to the same extent their industrial capacity in this field.

Nonetheless, the most important steps had to be taken by the developed market economies, which are still the major trading partners of the Third World. But when the proposal for general preferential treatment of exports from developing countries was put forward at the UNCTAD Conference in 1964, the reception it got was far from favorable. The industrialized countries opposed it on the ground that such preferences would be contrary to the "most favored nation" clause, a basic principle of multilateral trade. Countries such as France and other member states of the European Economic Community argued that generalized preferences would be harmful to the African states associated with the Common Market, which include some of the poorest and most backward countries of the Third World.

Gradually, however, this outright opposition as a matter of principle to general preferences was abandoned. The political cost of this stand which provoked the resentment of developing countries was visibly too dear. With the continued expansion of international trade these exports would do little damage to the industries of the developed countries. Only a few developing countries would be able to establish significant export industries in the near future, and their exports would represent only a relatively small part of the total increase in the world trade of industrial goods. This would be in line with the trends observed up to now. Thus from 1953 to 1968 the value of industrial exports from developing countries to developed market economies nearly quintupled, from $1.33 billion to $6.52 billion. But in comparison to the total value of industrial exports from market economy countries, it declined from 7.7 to 7.0 per cent.[5]

At the second conference of UNCTAD in 1968 the principle of general preferences for the industrial exports of developing countries was unanimously accepted by all countries. In May of 1970, at the annual meeting of the Ministers of the Organisation for Economic Co-operation and Development, all the members, which included all the major developed market economies, agreed on the principle of such preferential treatment. This was an even more significant gesture. But no one at that point made a definite commitment on a date when the agreement would become effective. Up to now this agreement in principle has not been fully transformed into action because of bitter opposition on the part of vested interests, which stand to lose by the increase in imports from the developing countries.

Already industry in the developed countries has protested against the steadily growing flow of textiles and other labor-intensive consumer goods from the low-wage countries, and this without preferential treatment. Supported by labor in their campaign against imports, industry tried to win over public opinion by painting a desolate picture of unfair competition from countries which exploit their workers, paying only starvation wages, thus jeopardizing the fair pay standards enjoyed in the West. Their dire prediction was that imports would ultimately create mass unemployment and wreck havoc with the economy of the country. The pressure on governments and legislative bodies was very great to prohibit these imports, or at least to restrict their expansion with a strict quota system.

Export industries, import traders, and other groups interested in the overall expansion of international trade were unable to marshall such convincing arguments for their side. It was impossible to prove tangibly that present losses from the increase in imports would be more than offset in the future by the advantages of export expansion. In recent years in the traditional industrial countries of the West and especially in the United States, there has been a dramatic increase in the imports of industrial consumer goods. The spectacular expansion of industrial production and exports from Japan has contributed as much to this new situation as has the development of industrial exports from the Third World. But one can see from Table VII that manufactured goods, particularly for the three main types of consumer

5. *United Nations Statistical Yearbook, 1969*, United Nations, New York, 1970, table 12.

goods (textiles, clothing, and footwear), have been coming into the United States from developing countries in increasingly substantial quantities since 1964. The American industries are pressing the hardest for protection from developing countries through import quotas in these areas.

Table VII

UNITED STATES IMPORTS OF SELECTED CONSUMER GOODS
(in thousand dollars)

		1964	1967	1969	*Per cent of Increase of 1960 over 1964*
TEXTILES	Total	683,156	811,904	1,019,008	49
from Japan		174,450	213,358	284,937	63.5
from major developing countries		193,302	229,673	267,619	38.5
CLOTHING	Total	451,838	646,705	1,105,732	140
from Japan		113,413	160,476	254,685	125
from major developing countries		100,595	208,100	444,577	341
FOOTWEAR	Total	141,436	263,220	488,172	244
from Japan		50,365	61,813	84,458	67
from major developing countries		4,527	20,334	39,902	780

Source: Commodity Trade Statistics for 1964, 1967 and 1969, *Statistical Papers, Series D,* volumes XIV, XVII and XIX, United Nations, New York.

The imports of clothing especially have surged forward, along with some other industrial consumer goods because of labor-intensive production processes which were transferred to the developing countries by United States concerns. As we have mentioned earlier, those responsible were large distributors, such as department stores or discount chains, or even American manufacturers. This kind of production under contract offered guaranteed outlets to the industries in developing countries and enabled them to overcome the handicap of a weak marketing apparatus. Consequently it was feared by industry and especially labor in the United States.

The major spokesmen for developing countries, such as Dr. Prebisch, realize that it would be unrealistic to expect developed countries to apply the principle of general preferences for industrial exports from developing countries without considering their own

vital interest. In particular they could not allow an excessive increase
in imports to disrupt their domestic market. Certain limitations would
have to be imposed on the general preferential treatment. Preferences
would be granted only on a temporary basis, for a period of 10 to
12 years. Then the situation would need to be reviewed to determine
whether or not the need for preferences still existed. Industries which
from the outset were competitive on the world market should be excluded. Finally, the developed countries would be entitled to certain
protective measures, such as a safeguard clause—when the flow of
imports became excessive and threatened the equilibrium of their
economy—or tariff quotas. The latter would limit preferential treatment to a certain proportion of the consumption, the output, or the
total import volume of a particular product.

Both the safeguard clause and the quota for imports from low-
wage countries, which include Japan as well as the developing countries, have been a major subject of discussion in trade negotiations and
agreements. Several international agreements have been concluded
since the early 1960's under the auspices of GATT, in particular for
cotton textiles. Usually there were provisions for an orderly increase
of imports from developing countries whose role on the overall market
of the importing country would expand only gradually.

After protracted negotiations with Japan and other leading exporting countries of Asia, the United States was able to obtain a
"voluntary" agreement in October of 1971 which limited further increases in their exports of non-cotton textiles. The developing countries concerned, Hong Kong, Taiwan, and South Korea, consented to
a 7.5 per cent annual increase in order to avoid more drastic unilateral
restrictions of their sales by the United States.

Significant differences appear among developed countries in
their attitude toward industrial imports from low-wage countries.
Great Britain has adopted the most liberal policy and has allowed the
productive capacity of her cotton goods industry to be drastically
reduced. Imports from developing Commonwealth countries, such as
Hong Kong, have replaced domestic production. The European Common Market countries up to now have followed a much more pro-
tectionist policy. The generally liberal policy of the United States has
grown more restrictive since the start of the recession, as the example
quoted above would indicate. Obviously it is easier to embrace a
liberal attitude toward foreign trade when the economy is expanding
than in a period of economic difficulty and stagnation.

UNCTAD, in its Special Committee on Preferences, pursued its
negotiations on the preferential treatment of industrial exports from

developing countries. Hard bargaining went on during a number of sessions with representatives of the bloc of 77 developing countries which would benefit from the preferences, the socialist countries, and the developed market economy countries. Finally in October 1970, the Committee arrived at a set of mutually acceptable "Agreed Conclusions."[6]

Still there was no single system of preferences. The developed market economy countries were unable to agree on this point. Each one of the major countries, or each group of countries such as the European Common Market, submitted its own proposal for the preferences it might grant to developing countries. The proposals were obviously tailored to fit the structure of their domestic economies and took into account pressure from the vested interests which would be challenged. Still all the proposals offered roughly the same degree of preference. These arrangements were to be ratified as soon as possible by the legislative branch of each country and put into effect.

Each proposal included safeguard measures, such as those envisioned by Dr. Prebisch, to give the developed countries some control over the volume of imports generated by the new agreements. There were escape clauses which granted the right to change or even to withdraw the preferences if the state of the economy demanded it. These would be drastic measures to be applied only in exceptional cases, and provisions were made for consultations with the developing countries to protect the mutual interests of both parties.

Since preferences would apply to all the developing countries, the members of the Commonwealth and the African countries associated with the Common Market would no longer receive special treatment. But their loss would be compensated in the long run by easier access to the markets of all the developed countries. To protect their interests, however, this special preferential treatment would be phased out only gradually. There were no specific provisions for abolishing the reciprocal preferences which were granted to members of the Common Market by the associated African countries. The United States only agreed to include these last countries in the overall preferential treatment agreement if these reciprocal preferences were gradually removed.

As Dr. Prebisch had suggested, the generalized preferences would be granted for an initial period of ten years, with periodic reviews by UNCTAD to assess progress made in the increase of export earnings, the growth of industrialization, and economic development in the Third World.

6. United Nations documents, TD/B/329, Add. 1 to 6.

The socialist countries also pledged to take into account Dr. Prebisch's recommendations. Efforts would be made on their domestic markets to favor greater and more varied consumption of products imported from developing countries, to facilitate the establishment there of export industries, and to accept their products in repayment of credits which might have been granted for the construction of factories or the purchase of equipment.

The developing countries, while appreciating all this, pointed out that most of the proposals were far from comprehensive, and that some excluded products of vital importance to them. Cotton textiles, for instance, were left out because they fell under an earlier international agreement, which applied also to exports from other than the developing countries. Processed agricultural products—of special importance to the least developed countries, which obviously were those most in need of preferential treatment—and primary metals were excluded as well. Moreover, the developing countries feared that legislative approval of this agreement would be difficult and time consuming because of powerful domestic opposition.

Fortunately it appears that this agreement on general preferences will be put into effect by a number of developed countries rather promptly. One developed country had applied these preferences even before the Geneva agreement. That was Australia, which had introduced them unilaterally shortly after the 1968 UNCTAD conference, although the scope of the preferences she granted was relatively limited. In March of 1971, less than six months after the agreement, the Commission of the European Economic Community stated that it would enforce the generalized preferences by July. Shortly thereafter Switzerland set a date of January 1, 1972, and Japan declared itself ready to do the same.

Thus in spite of limitations and reservations, this agreement on the general preferential treatment of industrial imports from developing countries, which was reached in Geneva in October 1970, seems an important and decisive step forward. The developed countries have finally agreed to promote the industrialization of the Third World by opening up their markets to its industrial products. If this policy is followed and gradually expanded, the world economy as a whole will benefit, as well as the developing countries. International trade will be given an impetus and both the developed and the developing countries will be able to specialize and thus make effective use of their respective comparative advantage. One may even look forward to important political consequences. With greater equality in economic relations there might be an improvement in international political relations between the North and the South.

One must hope, however, that none of these possibilities will disappear in the rising tide of economic nationalism in the United States, which has been provoked by the crisis in their balance of payments. This new spirit of protectionism is reflected particularly in the quota restrictions on imports from low-wage countries described on page 104.

b. *Private foreign investment*

In the pre-independent past of most developing countries, it was private foreign capital, as we said earlier, which made the major contribution to any economic development that might have occurred. Foreign entrepreneurs had organized and financed the establishment of their export sector, producing primary products for sale to the developed countries of the Western World.

But today most of the developing countries consider that these foreign investments exploited their human and physical resources and that therefore they cannot be allowed to continue under the same conditions. Previous administrations, whether colonial or even theoretically independent, had been frequently unwilling, and in any case unable, to protect adequately the interests of the developing countries and those of their indigenous population.

The present governments of developing countries object particularly to the very favorable terms which were granted to foreign corporations, with only moderate royalties to be paid for very lucrative concessions. Most of these concessions exploited valuable mineral resources, a source of natural wealth which is not inexhaustible and which in some cases would vanish rapidly. Other concessions were for vast land areas planted wth export crops, this while indigenous farmers suffered from a scarcity of land. Moreover, foreign-owned plantations appropriated vast stretches of normally the most fertile land, which was thus unavailable for food production and raised the possibility of famine. Finally, the developing countries want to put an end to the dominating influence of powerful foreign countries over their domestic policies. Most visible in small and impoverished developing countries, this relationship made a mockery of their legal status as independent states. It is a well known fact that this occurred in several countries of Central America, the "banana republics," where the United Fruit Company was far more powerful than the local government. The former Belgian Congo was dominated for a long time by an international copper mining corporation.

It is quite understandable, therefore, that a drastic revision of the conditions under which foreign investments are made has been urged and that there is strong pressure frequently to cancel them altogether and to nationalize their properties.

The natural reaction of the foreign investors is to appeal to their own governments for protection in order to safeguard their investments or, at the very least, to obtain adequate compensation. The government of the capital-exporting country concerned finds itself in a very delicate position. On the one hand it is duty bound to protect its nationals and the desire to do so is particularly strong when powerful economic interests are involved. Yet even the traditionally great nations have come to realize that the age of gunboat diplomacy has definitely come to an end. It is no longer advisable, even for a superpower, to pressure a small and weak country into changing or abandoning policies which are within the normal jurisdiction of a sovereign state. Such attempts are contrary to international law and may lead to most unwelcome international publicity at the United Nations where an appeal can be lodged. Even the most hard-headed proponents of power politics feel that the risks involved with such a policy in today's world, with its precarious balance of power, would not be justified by future material benefits.

Yet attempts have been made, and in some cases even successfully right after World War II. A striking example of such an intervention was the revolution which ousted President Arbentz in Guatemala in 1954. It is common knowledge that it was engineered in order to safeguard the property of a foreign company whose plantations would have been nationalized under new legislation for land reform.[7]

The complete failure of such a policy can be seen in the attempt by Great Britain and France in 1956 to occupy the Suez Canal in reprisal against President Nasser's move to nationalize. The invasion had to be called off because of joint pressure from the United States and the Soviet Union. Its failure came as a shattering blow to the prestige of both countries and destroyed any illusions which they might have retained of having a policy independent of the superpowers.

Excessive government pressure to protect the interests of its own nationals in all likelihood is counter productive and will irritate the

7. Gunnar Myrdal, *The Challenge of World Poverty*, Pantheon, New York, 1970, p. 466.

government of the developing country to the extent that even more violent and hostile policies may be adopted. This is what occurred in Cuba, as we describe later in Part Four.

In recent years this protective policy has softened considerably. When there was a dispute over fishing rights between the United States and Ecuador, where the latter claimed control over territorial waters far beyond normal international usage and excluded foreign, in particular American, fishing boats, the United State government was not inclined to retaliate sharply.

On the contrary it reacted far more violently when the Allende government nationalized the properties of the American copper companies in Chile. Their right to compensation was recognized but the Chileans deducted from the amount due the super profits which they claimed these companies had made and had already transferred out of the country, which they therefore owed to the Chilean treasury. According to such calculations no compensation had to be paid at all. Washington not only stopped immediately all aid to Chile but refused even purely commercial credits. Predictably, this intransigent attitude proved counter productive: it won Allende the unanimous support of Chilean public opinion, including even from right-wing opponents, and drove him to look for credits and trade from the socialist countries.

What can a developed country do to protect its nationals and to find a solution which will be acceptable to the developing country and useful in its economic development? While seeking maximum compensation for lost investments, a developed country should take into account the ability of the debtor country to pay in foreign exchange, as well as the sum total of profits made and the rate at which they were previously transferred abroad. It might also be advisable to apply the same guarantees against political risks to existing investments which most developed countries have already granted to new investments in developing countries. This formula, however, would transfer a major portion of the cost of compensation to the capital-exporting country. France, for example, granted compensation to Frenchmen whose land and property were nationalized in Algeria and other former dependencies after independence. Such indemnification is authorized under the United States aid legislation and will probably be offered in the case of the Chilean copper mines.

Equally appropriate and mutually profitable would be provisions for reinvesting the proceeds of nationalization in other fields, such as manufacturing, where the developing country might want to attract foreign capital. Thus, following the nationalization of an American-owned telephone company, the government of Brazil indemnified the parent company, which then agreed to reinvest the proceeds of the compensation in a factory to produce telephone equipment.[8] A similar example was the case of an international trading corporation in West Africa, which invested the monies received after the expropriation of its plantations to establish local plants manufacturing the consumer goods which it used to import.

On the whole, opportunities for new private foreign investments have grown in recent years, in comparison to the period just after World War II. This is true despite the spectacular instances of nationalization, especially in mining and land. There appears to be a better understanding, both in the capital-exporting and in the capital-importing countries, of the potentially useful contribution that foreign investment can make to development, provided it is in fields where there is a real need, and that it accords with the policies of the recipient government.

Most developed countries with market economies are increasingly active in promoting private investment in developing countries. They have instituted investment guarantees against political risks, the nationalization of property without adequate compensation, and the prohibition against transferring profits or interest out of the country. The most important of such measures recently was the creation in 1970 of the United States Overseas Private Investment Corporation (OPIC), which took over the programs of the Agency for International Development (AID) in providing incentives to private investment. OPIC has the authority to offer guarantees which would cover 75 per cent of the value of private loans and equity investments up to $750 million in toto.

But of greater consequence for the development of foreign private investment has been the move to work out arrangements which would meet the need of investors for security and reasonable returns and the developing countries' desire to retain control of their natural resources and basic industries. Local public and private companies have begun to team up more with foreign concerns, which supply not only the capital but also the essential technical knowledge. Foreign industry has learned that this seems to be the only way to maintain and expand markets that might otherwise be lost with the introduction of tariff or quota restrictions. International manufacturing corporations, largely American-owned, are the major exceptions to the general trend on the part of industries investing in developing countries to abandon

8. Paul Alpert, *Economic Development: Objectives and Methods*, Free Press, New York, 1963, p. 244.

the practice of retaining full ownership, or at least majority control, of their subsidiaries.

Domestic and foreign interests are also often associated in licensing agreements, where technical knowledge comes from abroad and contributes little or no capital investment. The foreign manufacturer lends his patents in return for royalties on output or on profits or both. In addition there are technical service agreements under which technical information and the services of trained personnel are made available to enterprises in developing countries—engineering and construction agreements, for example, with the design and construction of a plant entrusted to a specialized foreign company, and management contracts, where a foreign concern manages for a specified period a newly established plant in an underdeveloped country. In many instances more than one such agreement is in effect at the same time and often they are negotiated in connection with loans for the purchase of equipment.

Contractual arrangements which separate management or technical expertise from ownership have the special advantage of allaying political fears in those industries such as oil where there is strong opposition to foreign control. Many underdeveloped countries have passed laws nationalizing all mineral deposits and granting all rights of exploitation to government-owned agencies. These laws are to prevent the abandonment of natural resources to foreign companies which own the minerals outright for the duration of the concession. Because of the absence of domestic capital and technical knowledge, the government agency still has no alternative but to invite a foreign company to provide capital, costly drilling equipment, and managerial and marketing skills. Under this arrangement the foreign company will finance a program of mineral exploration and development in return for a share in the production or in the profits. Such arrangements are in essence not very different from the concessions of the past. The distinction is a legal one and an important one: ownership of the mineral and the right of exploitation are vested in the state. The government uses the resources of foreign companies without violating the letter of the law or provoking popular anti-foreign sentiment.

But in reality, such arrangements are legalistic subterfuges which provide the shadow but not the substance of economic independence from foreign companies. Probably they will be only a temporary solution until the developing countries are in a stronger position, with more skills and financial resources, and can demand a share, perhaps even the principal one, in controlling the industry.

This has been the trend increasingly with oil rich countries, who are now insisting on a percentage of the proceeds not only from oil wells but also from the transport and the refining of crude oil. A typical example of co-operation between producing states and foreign companies is the agreement signed by the Algerian National Oil Company (Sonatrach) and the El Paso Gas Company. It is based on complete equality on both sides with full respect of national sovereignty and guaranteed long-term deliveries of natural gas to the American market.

In the spring of 1972, oil producing countries of the Middle East took another important step towards assuming control of their oil resources. They demanded and obtained from the Western oil companies a 20 per cent share in their properties. The oil producers make no secret of their intention to gain eventually a majority participation. One of them, Algeria, has already reached this goal, as will be described in Part Four.

The creation of public development corporations in some capital exporting countries can be useful for industries where the developing countries seek out private foreign investment as a means of providing capital resources, entrepreneurial and technical skills. These corporations finance private enterprises or joint public and private projects in developing countries by providing equity or loans. They act as intermediaries between investors and bankers and the local public and private sectors in developing countries.[9]

The largest of such corporations is the International Finance Corporation, an affiliate of the International Bank, which was established in 1950 in order mainly to promote the development of industry. In Great Britain and in France the government first set up financing agencies to operate in their former colonial territories. These have now also become development corporations: the Commonwealth Development Corporation and la Caisse Centrale de Coopération Economique. In West Germany, Denmark, and the Netherlands such corporations have been established specifically to function in developing countries. In the United States OPIC also works as a development corporation, but it is not authorized to participate in the share capital of the enterprises it promotes.

Another significant step in this direction has been the establishment of private multilateral corporations for each of the developing regions. These development corporations are intended to promote the development of the private sector, and particularly of manufacturing industries, by providing financial backing, skills, and when necessary

9. *The OECD Observer*, No. 50, February 1971, p. 32.

managerial and entrepreneurial talent. The Latin American Corporation, ADELA, has already been operating successfully since the early 1960's, and similar corporations exist for Asia and Africa.

Finally, some of the large banks in New York, London, Paris, and the other world financial centers have set up affiliated development corporations. These corporations explore the opportunities for investment and organize industrial enterprises in co-operation with local interests in the developing countries and firms in their own countries. These development corporations do not retain ownership of the enterprises they have helped. On the contrary, as soon as the operation becomes successful, they sell their share to local interests. Thus they realize their profits and can use the proceeds for new ventures. This policy appeals to developing countries because it prevents the permanent encroachment of foreign capital in their industries and seems to encourage local participation.

As shown in Table VIII below, the total amount of foreign private investments in developing countries has more than doubled during the period from 1960 to 1970. The investments were made by member countries of the Development Assistance Committee (DAC) of the Organization for Economic Co-operation and Development—that is, by all the major market economy countries. Long-term export credits— five years and above—are included in investments. The amortization and reimbursement of capital have been deducted from the net total but the payment of interests and profits have not been taken into consideration.

By far the most important concentration of foreign direct investment has been in the petroleum industry; it accounts on the average for about 40 per cent of all foreign investment in developing countries. The reason is the constant and rapid growth of the demand for oil and oil products on the world market, in spite of the high political risks involved, especially in the Middle East, which is the largest producing area in the Third World. Few areas are altogether free from risk, however, as was demonstrated by the nationalization in 1969 of an American oil company in Peru. No agreement on compensation had been reached as late as the fall of 1971. Increasing investments have also been made in oil refineries and processing plants, and in industries using oil or natural gas either as raw material or as cheap fuel in the oil-producing countries. For example, a major fertilizer plant was set up in Kuwait and an aluminum smelter in Bahrein.

Investment in metal mining was on a smaller scale because developing countries have less of the world's metal reserves than they do of oil. The major investments in this field have concentrated on

Table VIII

NET PRIVATE INVESTMENTS OF DAC[a] COUNTRIES IN DEVELOPING COUNTRIES
(in million US dollars)

	1960	1961	1962	1963	1964	1965	1966	1967	1968	1969	1970
Direct Investment	1,767	1,829	1,495	1,603	1,572	2,468	2,179	2,105	3,045	2,804	3,408
Bilateral Portfolio	633	614	147	327	837	655	480	800	972	1,277	809
Export Credits	546	573	572	660	859	751	1,194	1,007	1,596	1,978	2,174
Total	2,946	3,016	2,214	2,590	3,268	3,874	3,853	3,912	5,613	6,059	6,391

Source: 1971 Review Development Assistance, Organization for Economic Co-operation and Development, table 11-1, p. 34, Paris, 1971.
[a] All market economy countries with the exception of Finland, Iceland, Ireland, Luxembourg, New Zealand, and South Africa.

Africa—iron ore in Mauratania, Liberia and Gabon; manganese in Gabon; bauxite in Guinea; and processing plants to transform it into aluminum in Ghana. There have been considerable investments, however, in other areas as well: in copper mining in particular in Papua and New Guinea and also in Peru and Chile. In Chile these investments were made in association with the government, after the "Chileanization"—a partial nationalization—of the industry by ex-President Frei, and before their complete nationalization in 1971 by President Allende.

In manufacturing for the domestic market, private investment has had the greatest impact in Latin America, especially in the three big countries of Brazil, Mexico, and Argentina, where it focused on the rapidly growing, capital-intensive chemical, petrochemical, and automobile industries. But India, for instance, which is comparable in the size of her market to the largest countries of Latin America, has been unable to attract the same volume of foreign investment.

In export industries, foreign investments have been interested only in a few large-size projects for the processing of raw materials, mainly the metal ones already mentioned. There have been a far greater number of smaller-size investments in labor-intensive consumer goods industries whose goods are distributed in the capital exporting countries through the marketing apparatus of the respective investing firms. In many cases only the labor-intensive components are manufactured in the developing country. The production of other parts and their assembly takes place in the capital-exporting country. OECD explains the value of this procedure which provides additional employment, income, and a guaranteed market to the developing country, and which benefits the investing country as well, especially if it suffers from labor shortages.[10] Certainly for all parties concerned it is wiser to import components than to dislocate people on a temporary basis. During the 1960's, investments of this type were particularly important in Hong Kong, Taiwan, South Korea, Singapore, Jamaica, Mexico, and Malta.

Portfolio investments, usually in government bonds but sometimes also in the securities of private or public corporations, have varied widely from year to year because of conditions in the capital-exporting countries. The tightening of the capital markets in the United States in the second half of the decade of the 1960's has reduced American participation. There has been greater liquidity in the capital markets of Europe and especially in Western Germany, and thus more investments from those countries. These investments, which are re-

10. *Op. cit.*, p. 81.

flected generally in long-term loans or credits (securities issued by
the multilateral financial agencies on the capital markets are not included in the totals given in Table VIII on page 114), do not involve
investors in any form of control of decision-making. There is less
opposition to them, therefore, in the developing countries. But on the
other hand, they raise very serious problems for the balance of payments of the indebted country; interest and amortization will have to
be paid on schedule, regardless of the international financial position
of the country at the time. On the contrary, direct investments, when
successful, earn foreign exchange through exports, or save it through
import replacement. Moreover, if the project does not work out, there
are no profits to be transferred out of the country. The rise in interest
rates paid on portfolio investments has contributed to the burden of
the debtor countries.

Export credits for the sale of heavy equipment or, in many cases,
of complete factories, have expanded throughout the period. This
reflects the general growth of world trade and more directly the rapid
increase in the rate of industrial development and the intense competition for export orders among the countries that manufacture most
of the capital goods and guarantee most of the credits. As OECD
pointed out, this expansion of export credits is disturbing because it
severely taxes the ability of many developing countries to meet payments on their debts.[11] Outstanding export credits were estimated to
represent a total of $12 billion by the end of 1969.

There is no question that foreign private investment, especially
under its most important and dynamic though controversial aspect of
direct investment, is now generally recognized as potentially useful
in the economic development of the developing countries. But it is
just as apparent that it will have to play a more limited role than in
the past, when it was the dominant factor in economic development.
Under present economic and political conditions, foreign investment
can be effective only if it abides by the terms of the recipient government. These terms stem out of a concern to utilize the additional resources now made available in accordance with the priorities of the
country's development plan. Just as important is the desire to prevent
foreign capital from acquiring too powerful a position in the country's
economy.

Foreign investment, therefore, will probably not be involved to
any great extent in public utilities, transport, and communications.
In mining, where its financial backing and expertise are still essential,
the trend seems to limit foreign investment as far as possible to the

11. *Op. cit.*, p. 33.

role of a contracting partner with the national agency. Its services are remunerated, but it has no legal rights, either to the mine or to the minerals extracted. Even in industry, where foreign investment is most readily accepted, the developing countries stress the need for associating it with local interests. A typical example of this are the rules for foreign investment which were accepted by the Andean group countries (including Bolivia, Chile, Colombia, Ecuador, and Peru). In these countries majority ownership in any foreign-owned enterprise must pass to local interests within 15 years.[12]

With this in mind, the conviction of some capital-exporting countries, especially the United States, that foreign private investments should become the major source of external capital to developing countries, compensating thus for the reduction in public assistance, seems particularly misguided. This stand, which underestimates the determination of nearly all the developing countries to limit foreign investment, is reflected in the Rockefeller Report on Latin America. The report recommended that the "United States provide maximum encouragement for private investment in the Western Hemisphere." As Gunnar Myrdal pointed out, this advice shows total lack of understanding of the deep feeling in Latin America against the domination of its economy by American capital, which now controls 70 to 90 per cent of the exploitation of natural resources and about 50 per cent of industrial production.[13] In a more general statement OECD stressed that there should be no illusions about the extent to which private flows can replace official development assistance.[14]

The governments of the capital-exporting countries should cooperate rather with the developing countries in facilitating foreign investment but only to the extent and in the areas where the latter has requested it. As we mentioned earlier, they should also provide assistance in settling conflicts which arise in the liquidation of existing investments, with minimum damage done to the economic interests of both parties and to international relations. These investments may no longer be deemed appropriate by the governments of the host countries in light of present political or economic conditions. In this regard we look forward to the assistance of the International Bank, which is contemplating the organization of a multilateral insurance plan against the risk of expropriation. An International Center for Settlement of Investment Disputes has already been established by

12. *The New York Times*, 29 March 1971.
13. Gunnar Myrdal, *The Challenge of World Poverty*, Pantheon, New York, 1971, p. 471.
14. OECD Development Assistance 1971 Review, Paris 1971, p. 99.

the IBRD; by June 30, 1971, 62 states had ratified the Convention on settlement of such disputes and had accepted the jurisdiction of the Center in this field.[15]

c. *External aid*

External aid for economic development is a comparatively recent phenomenon. As we mentioned earlier, only since the end of World War II has it become an important aspect of international economic policy. Prior to then all external assistance had to be paid. Even in the dealings between colonies and the mother country the latter shouldered only the so-called sovereignty costs of foreign relations and defense. Expenditures for development, such as for the construction of railroads and harbors, were financed usually through loans serviced by the colonial budgets.

One needs here a precise definition of the term in order to assess properly the value of the aid which is actually being given. Economic aid implies a transfer of material resources without corresponding material advantage to the donor. If any benefit is reaped by the donor, then it must be deducted from the full amount of the aid given. In other words, the *net* amount of aid is equal to the sacrifice made by the donor.

According to this definition, only outright grants given without any *quid pro quo* can represent aid in the full amount. Loans offer aid only to the extent of their concessional terms: at rates lower than those of the capital market, and/or with a period of grace and repayment in a currency other than the one in which the loan was made. The real value of the aid in such loans can be determined in the difference between market rates and concessional terms. Loans made at the prevailing market rate, though they can be very necessary to developing countries, are purely financial transactions and include no element of aid.

The value of aid in kind cannot be judged by market prices. The most important example of such aid was the food aid program of the United States. The food came out initially of its surplus reserves which in fact were unsalable. Had they been offered on the world market they would have provoked a catastrophic crash. As long as this aid originated in these surpluses the real cost to the United States taxpayer was actually only the shipping, and from this expenditure one should have deducted the monies saved in dispensing with storage in the United States. Unfortunately all donor countries, including the United

15. World Bank, *Annual Report*, 1971, p. 35.

States, calculate their food aid in terms of its face value at market prices.

Technical assistance raises no such accounting problems. It is usually provided in grants and its cash value corresponds to the cost of the services rendered.

The rationale for bilateral economic aid to the developing countries is based on rather complex reasoning. Great importance is attributed to maintaining or consolidating political, economic, and cultural ties. But it would be unfair to deny the significant influence of less egoistic motives. When President Truman inaugurated the American foreign aid program in 1949, he emphasized the fact that the United States wanted to participate in the development of poor countries for humanitarian reasons. He also stated that improved conditions in these countries would facilitate world peace and the harmonious evolution of the world economy. Thus it would be fully in accord with the national interest of the United States.

These enlightened motives have certainly had an influence, especially in the field, on the policies of the donor governments when confronted directly with the needs of the recipient countries. On the other hand, the administration in the United States, which was the only country to provide aid on a world-wide basis, especially in the early period, and was contributing more than half of all bilateral aid, was justifying its request to Congress for funds by stressing direct national interest. Moreover, it generally neglected to point out that economic development is a complex long-term process and that the rapid and spectacular success achieved in Western Europe through the Marshall Plan would not be repeated here.

Because of this misrepresentation, both Congress and public opinion in America became increasingly disillusioned by the tangible results of foreign aid. Economic conditions were improving only slightly if at all in underdeveloped countries and their demands were growing more and more insistent. Furthermore, their attitude did not in the least reflect the proper gratitude for the aid they received. Most of them did not support United States policies and quite a number expressed outright hostility to American interests, usually to private investments and enterprises.

A particularly blunt and shocking expression for aid recipients of the conviction that acceptance of aid implies obedience to the donor country was the outcry in Congress after the vote in the United Nations that admitted Communist China and excluded Taiwan. Some senators demanded that aid be terminated to countries which had opposed the United States position.

Under these circumstances it is not surprising that the popular appeal of foreign aid gradually diminished. It became increasingly difficult for the administration to obtain congressional approval of foreign aid appropriations. The growing difficulties in balance of payments, the massive requirements of domestic anti-poverty programs which were strongly supported by public opinion, and the drain on the budget because of the Viet Nam War made the cause of foreign aid for development even less attractive. The traumatic experience of the Viet Nam War has led some of the most liberal members of Congress, those who had supported all forms of international co-operation, including economic aid, in the past, to become suspicious of any foreign entanglements. They fear that foreign aid will involve the United States in further undesirable commitments, especially in view of the fact that it is difficult to differentiate between purely economic development assistance and aid which is mainly politically motivated.

The coalition of these liberals and the traditional foes of international aid succeeded in October of 1971 in having the Senate reject the foreign aid bill altogether. The administration has obtained a temporary extension of the existing program and, at a later stage, has succeeded in securing approval by Congress of a foreign aid appropriation for 1972. It includes a new and drastic reduction in the amount of aid granted, a further hardening in terms, with fewer grants, and higher interest rates for loans.

Already during the last few years the total volume of United States economic aid has decreased steadily, apart from the support which does have definite political connotations, such as aid to the countries of Southeast Asia. The reduction can be seen in absolute figures, and even more clearly in the actual value when one takes into account the rise in prices. In comparison to the gross national product the reduction seems all the more serious, In addition, the terms on which United States assistance is granted have also already stiffened. loans are more common now than grants. Fewer loans are repayable in local currencies than must be reimbursed in dollars. Because of difficulties in balance of payments, United States aid has become subject to increasing procurement restrictions since 1959. At present American bilateral aid is virtually completely tied to procurement in the United States, the only significant exception being that procurement may be authorized in developing countries.[16]

The structure of United States aid is very complex and changes so frequently that it is difficult to compare the totals of successive

16. *Resources for the Developing World,* Organisation for Economic Co-operation and Development, Paris, 1970, p. 194.

years. But its main trend is reflected accurately in the size of the appropriations from Congress to its main organ, the Agency for International Development (AID). For fiscal 1961 to 1971 they represented:[17]

(in million $)

1961	2,631	1967	2,143
1962	2,314	1968	1,895
1963	2,574	1969	1,381
1964	2,000	1970	1,425
1965	2,195	1971	1,571
1966	2,463		

The latest appropriation for 1972, while again difficult to compare with those for previous years, clearly represents a drastic reduction in aid for economic development. The total for Development and Humanitarian Assistance has been kept on the same level as in 1971: $1,134 million,[18] compared with $1,137.8 million. However, in 1972 this total includes a new item: $200 million for South Asia Relief (refugees in East Pakistan and India). On the contrary, the sub-total AID Development Assistance has declined from $957.1 million to $715 million.

In addition to monies for economic development the budget of AID also must cover supporting assistance to countries receiving United States military aid. In 1969 such grants, mainly to the countries of Southeast Asia, amounted to $394 million.

According to the classification of United States foreign assistance found in the Report to the President by the "Task Force on International Development," bilateral aid for economic development in 1969 was broken down as follows:

(in million $)

Development loans	729
Technical assistance grants	340
Peace corps	101
Agricultural commodity credit sales	870
Food for work grants	62
Total	2,102

Loans from AID can be project loans which are granted to finance specific development projects; at the start of United States aid these

17. *Op. cit.*, p. 201.
18. Foreign Assistance Authorization and Appropriations, 1972.

loans took up most of the loan funds available. There are also program loans which are based on a comprehensive review of a country's development effort and which are intended to assist in supplying the foreign exchange resources necessary to carry it out. Sometimes they are made jointly with other bilateral donors and/or with multilateral agencies such as the International Bank. This kind of loan is now the most important. The third type of loan is the sector loan for programs which are given high priority by the United States authorities: agriculture, health, and education.

Technical assistance remains for the time being the only important aspect of the United States aid program to be financed solely through grants. It provides American experts and training facilities, on an individual basis through fellowships, for a group with special training courses or the establishment of institutions. More than other bilateral or particularly multilateral programs, American technical assistance utilizes private firms rather than individual consultants. It also takes advantage of services available in its educational and research institutions. This approach is generally well received and therefore more likely to be successful.

The United States Food Aid Program, "Food for Freedom," was initiated to make good use of the gigantic grain surpluses, accumulated as a result of the American policy of price support for agricultural products on the domestic market, for a worthy cause—aid to the poor nations. As we stated earlier, the donation of this food at that time did not require additional expenditures. The Americans were extremely eager to liquidate their stock which at one point had overflowed all storage facilities, and they granted very generous terms. A major portion of the food was given away in grants, and nearly all the rest in loans repayable in local currencies.

No precautions were taken to make sure that these grants would be used to make a real contribution to the economic development of the recipient country. Therefore, the results were sometimes quite disappointing. This was the case in India, by far the largest recipient of United States food aid. The prospect of meeting in this way a large part of their food requirements induced the Indian government to neglect its efforts to increase domestic agricultural production. When United States surpluses started to dwindle and food shipments to decline, India was suddenly faced with the danger of famine. The Indian government was forced then to change its agricultural policy.

In recent years United States policy has become less lenient in regard to food aid. The volume has gone down and terms have become harder, as can be seen in the table below:

BILATERAL FOOD FOR FREEDOM DISBURSEMENTS, 1962–1968
(in million $)

	1962	1966	1968
Local currency sales	857	727	391
Dollar sales	29	244	361
Donations	344	294	309
Total	1,230	1,265	1,061

Source: Resources for the Developing World, Organisation for Economic Co-operation and Development, Paris, 1970, p. 206.

The Peace Corps, which was created in 1961, is an organization of volunteers working in a variety of technical assistance programs, up to now mainly in primary education and community development. There has been greater emphasis recently on enlisting young technicians whose skills are particularly needed by the recipient countries, rather than liberal arts graduates.

Since its beginning the United States foreign aid program has undergone a number of reorganizations, usually with every new administration. The last major review was in 1969–1970, and the recommendations contained in the Peterson Report were supposed to be enforced in 1972. This report suggested that security assistance, including supporting assistance, be completely separated from economic development aid. The United States should make development a truly international effort by redesigning their policies, with the developing countries at the center of international development programs in charge of setting their own priorities. Development assistance, including United States bilateral aid, should be channeled mainly through multilateral lending institutions, and provided within the framework set by the international organizations.

The report envisaged a reorganization of AID into several agencies specialized in different aspects of foreign aid. One would be an International Development Bank, which would make capital loans and related technical assistance loans in certain countries for specific programs which the United States felt were of special interest. The fact of obtaining technical assistance on a loan basis instead of grants would represent the stiffening of terms set for United States aid. The second agency would be an International Development Institute, which would concentrate on applying science and technology to resources and processes critical to developing nations. It would deal with research, training, the problem of population, and the question of social and civic development. The work would be done largely through private organizations. Another agency listed in the report is the Overseas Private Investment Corporation (OPIC), which has already been established and facilitates the participation of American private capital and business skill in international development. The fourth, an International Development Council, would integrate aid to development within the general framework of United States policies and co-ordinate United States assistance with the work of international organizations.

The report recommended that the United States reverse its course in decreasing assistance, and that on the contrary additional resources be granted, primarily in support of international lending institutions. Its emphasis on private development efforts and private investment and the slighting, if not actual phasing out, of public bilateral aid, may be in accord with the domestic political situation in the United States, but seems out of line with present trends in developing countries.

The foreign aid budget for fiscal 1971–72, as submitted to Congress, fully reflected the recommendations of the Peterson report. As stated above, the changes in the allocation of funds make it difficult to compare the total figure with that of previous years, but the budget as submitted would have already undoubtedly resulted in a new net reduction of overall American development aid. The appropriation finally approved by Congress was, as usual, even smaller than the Administration's request. In particular, apart from reducing bilateral aid, Congress refused to go along with the recommendation for an increase in US contributions to multilateral aid agencies and agreed only very reluctantly to maintain them at their previous level.

Next in size is the French foreign aid program since the independence of her former colonies. In proportion to her national income, France has consistently been the most generous of all donor countries, especially in so far as grants are concerned. This is due to the origin of French foreign aid, which stemmed from previous appropriations out of the metropolitan budget for the development of French dependent territories. Education usually was emphasized as well as the economic, social, and administrative infrastructure. In addition to this massive aid program, which took up previous responsibilities in former French colonies, some minor assistance is also being granted to other developing areas, mainly in the cultural and technical fields.

The overall size of French public aid has remained more or less the same.

Nearly all French official aid is provided through grants. In 1968, the last year for which a breakdown is available, loans accounted for only 11.2 per cent of the total. The largest component of French aid

FRENCH OFFICIAL DEVELOPMENT ASSISTANCE
(in million $)

1960	1963	1966	1968	1969
847.3	851.7	744.8	855.2	965

Source: Resources for the Developing World, Organisation for Economic Co-operation and Development, Paris, 1970, p. 241.

is technical and cultural assistance and represented, in 1968, 48.9 per cent of all allocations. A large number of experts and teachers in particular has been provided—in 1967, 32,717 teachers out of a total of 46,363 experts. Grants for economic and financial support have been given, usually to the poorest of the newly independent states of the Franc area in order to help them maintain their essential services. This is gradually being reduced, although in 1968 it still represented 12 per cent of total aid. Finally, capital development projects are financed largely through grants (22.2 per cent of total aid) and to a smaller extent through loans. For the countries of the Franc area these loans are made on concessional terms, most of them at rates below 4 per cent. The concentration of French aid in countries of the Franc area has declined slightly; in 1968 they still received 87 per cent of total technical assistance, compared with 92 per cent in 1962.

The foreign aid program of the United Kingdom also originated in programs of budgetary support and project assistance granted to her dependencies during the colonial era. In 1958 loan programs were started both for independent Commonwealth countries and other Third World nations. But in 1968 more than 90 per cent of bilateral British aid was still being given to Commonwealth countries.

UNITED KINGDOM OFFICIAL DEVELOPMENT ASSISTANCE
(in million $)

1960	1963	1966	1968	1969
407.0	414.5	525.9	428.3	431

Source: Resources for the Developing World, Organisation for Economic Co-operation and Development, Paris, 1970, p. 241.

While the United Kingdom in principle provides assistance through loans, its policies do take into account the financial position of recipient countries. Since the financial situation of most of them would not permit them to entertain loans at commercial rates, nearly 90 per cent of British aid is actually given in grants or interest-free loans. In 1968,

27 per cent of total aid went for budgetary support; program aid to finance the purchase of British goods and services took up another 20 per cent; project aid and technical assistance absorbed, respectively, 16 and 20 per cent, mainly in the fields of education and public administration.

The Federal Republic of Germany did not start until 1960 to provide official aid for development, but the amounts have increased rapidly. From a low of $237.4 million in 1960, the total rose to $392.8 million in 1963, and to $595 million in 1969. Grants are reserved for the financing of technical assistance and accounted in 1968 for 19 per cent of total German aid. The emphasis is on development loans which are made either directly for specific projects or to local development banks and are granted for the most part on relatively concessional terms. German aid distinguishes itself from French or British aid by not concentrating on a particular area. It is closely connected with the flow of private capital, in particular of export credits.

Various organs of the United Nations have set targets for the volume of aid from the developed to the developing countries. In 1960 the United Nations General Assembly adopted a resolution calling on the developed countries to transfer 1 per cent of their national income through grants or loans. But in spite of universal agreement on this goal, only a few of the developed market economy countries reached this target during the decade of the 1960's. Moreover, there seems to have been some confusion on defining the aid that would be involved. It was thought to cover all net flow of resources, both public and private, to developing countries, with allowances made for the reimbursement of capital, but not for the transfer of interests or profits. Thus, in addition to grants and loans on concessional terms, there were included transfers to developing countries of resources obtained through loans on commercial terms or private investments. As we discussed earlier, however, these transactions should in no way be considered aid.

At UNCTAD's second conference in 1968, the target for net transfers to developing countries was increased to represent 1 per cent of gross national product (the latter, which includes the cost of indirect taxes and amortization at market prices, is about 25 per cent higher than national income). Again all the major donor market economy countries who were members of OECD accepted this recommendation.[19]

19. *Partners in Development, Report of the Commission on International Development,* Praeger, New York, 1969, p. 152.

UNCTAD clarified the situation by setting a target for *real* aid and by recommending that official development assistance through grants or public loans reach 0.7 per cent of G.N.P. This was strongly endorsed in the Pearson Report of the Commission on International Development to the President of the International Bank, which stated that total net flow of resources to developing countries should reach 1 per cent of G.N.P. by 1975, and official development assistance 0.7 per cent of G.N.P., if possible, by 1975, and not later than 1980.

Table IX shows the pattern of net transfers of resources to developing countries from the members of the OECD and its Development Assistance Committee (DAC) in ratio to their G.N.P.

The total G.N.P. of the DAC countries came to about $2,000 billion in 1970, so that the difference between net transfer of financial resources and the 1 per cent target hovered around $5.5 billion. Within this ratio, however, there was a great discrepancy between the contributions of various donor countries. The highest ratio of G.N.P. to flow of resources was from the Netherlands: 1.46, followed by France, 1.24. In the United Kingdom the ratio was 1.04, in Japan 0.93, in Germany 0.80, and only 0.55 in the United States.

The Pearson Report points out that if the DAC countries reached the 1 per cent target in 1975 and that if one assumed economic growth to proceed at the same rate, total net transfers to developing countries would come to $23 billion. This would make a major contribution to solving the difficulties in balance of payments of developing countries, and remove from their path a serious obstacle to their economic development. For the DAC countries it would mean increasing net transfers to developing countries by as little as 4 per cent of the annual addition to their own G.N.P.

One must remember here, however, that the net effect of this is substantially reduced by the reverse flow to developed countries of dividends and interest generated by the "non-aid" component. So the most important element in this overall flow of resources to developing countries is the percentage of public assistance.

Table X on page 130 shows that official development assistance from all the DAC member countries in 1970 was slightly less than half of the net transfers of financial resources. Its rate of increase was far slower, only 19 per cent between 1964 and 1970; by the end of that period the average figure for DAC countries as a whole was only 0.34 per cent, far below the target of 0.7 per cent, and about one third less than the 1961 ratio of 0.52 of G.N.P.: O.E.C.D. points out[20] that during the same period the G.N.P. of its member countries grew by 105 per cent and their per capita income increased in the average by $1,470.

20. OECD, *Development Assistance, 1971* Review, Paris, 1971, p. 28.

Table IX

NET FLOW OF FINANCIAL RESOURCES FROM DAC COUNTRIES

(in million $)

	1960	1961	1962	1963	1964	1965	1966	1967	1968	1969	1970
Total flow	8,115	9,249	8,487	8,632	9,142	10,420	10,348	11,310	13,113	13,670	14,701
Per cent of G.N.P.	0.89	0.96	0.81	0.77	0.75	0.78	0.72	0.73	0.78	0.75	0.74

Source: OECD, *Resources for the Developing World,* Paris, 1970.
OECD, *Development Assistance, 1970 Review,* Paris, 1970.
OECD, *Development Assistance, 1971 Review,* Paris, 1971, p. 34.

Again there are great variations among the member countries. France was in 1970 the leading DAC country in the ratio of official development assistance: 0.65 per cent, only slightly lower than the target of 0.7 per cent; the Netherlands was next with 0.63 per cent, while the other major donor countries were well below: the United Kingdom and Sweden at 0.37, Germany at 0.32, and the United States at 0.31 per cent.

The prospects in the immediate future for a substantial increase in bilateral aid by the developed market economies are rather dim. It seems unlikely, if the present trend continues without a basic change in the attitude of donor countries, that the target of 1 per cent for net financial transfer and the even more important goal of 0.7 per cent for development assistance will be reached. The United States, the most important donor, is largely responsible for this unfavorable prognosis. Its contribution to development, which it initiated on its own 20 years ago in a new policy of foreign aid, has declined in recent years in absolute figures and even more in relation to the total aid provided by the DAC countries. While the G.N.P. of the United States was 52.5 per cent in 1968 of the total G.N.P. of the DAC bloc, its share of official development assistance went from 57 per cent in 1960 to 51.5 in 1968, to 47.2 per cent in 1969, and to 44.8 in 1970. All the signs seem to indicate an even greater decrease during the next few years. In accordance with the Peterson Report the plan is to phase out United States bilateral aid altogether. Even if their participation in multilateral aid is substantially increased, the total volume of United States public assistance would still continue to drop.

The prospects in most other major donor countries are considerably better. The United Kingdom, Germany, Japan, and Canada in particular have promised substantial increases in public aid to 1975, while Sweden intends to reach 1 per cent of her G.N.P. for public assistance alone by that date. But as one must take into consideration the reduced participation of the United States, even this increase on the part of the other DAC members will probably not expand very much the total flow of public aid from the developed market economies.

Foreign aid from the socialist countries to the Third World—that is, to those developing countries which are outside their own bloc— started in 1954, somewhat later than the program of the United States. On a global basis it is still a relatively minor part of all aid to the developing countries, even though some of them have received an important volume of aid from this source.

Table X
Official Development Assistance
The Net Flow of Official Development Assistance to Less Developed Countries and Multilateral Agencies, 1960–1970
(in million U.S. dollars)

Countries	1960	1961	1962	1963	1964	1965	1966	1967	1968	1969	1970
Australia	59	71	74	96	100	119	126	157	160	175	203
Austria	0.1	3	7	2	12	31	32	26	23	15	19
Belgium	101	92	70	80	71	102	76	89	88	116	120
Canada	75	61	35	64	78	96	187	198	175	245	346
Denmark	5	8	7	9	10	13	21	26	29	54	59
France	823	903	945	820	828	752	745	826	853	955	951
Germany	223	366	405	389	459	456	419	509	557	579	599
Italy	77	60	80	70	48	60	78	155	146	130	147
Japan	105	108	85	137	116	244	283	384	356	436	458
Netherlands	35	56	65	38	49	70	94	113	123	143	196
Norway	5	7	7	10	9	11	14	14	27	30	37
Portugal	37	46	36	45	50	22	20	25	27	58	29
Sweden	7	8	19	23	33	38	57	60	71	121	117
Switzerland	4	8	5	6	9	12	13	13	24	30	29
United Kingdom	407	457	421	414	493	472	486	485	415	431	447
United States	2,702	2,943	3,181	3,567	3,592	3,418	3,349	3,472	3,242	3,092	3,050
Total DAC countries	4,665	5,197	5,442	5,770	5,957	5,916	6,001	6,552	6,316	6,610	6,808

Source: OECD, *Development Assistance, 1971 Review,* Paris, 1971, p. 165.

Table XI

BILATERAL ECONOMIC AID OF THE SOCIALIST COUNTRIES (1954–1969)
(commitments in million $ equivalent)
(cumulative total)

	1954–67	*1968*	*1969*	*Total*
Total commitments	8,623	758	537	9,918
Individual donors				
U.S.S.R.	5,217	368	247	5,832
China	841	42	—	883
Bulgaria	92	35	20	147
Czechoslovakia	929	200	5	1,134
Eastern Germany	542	8	98	648
Hungary	314	40	10	364
Poland	479	20	25	524
Romania	199	45	132	376

Source: "Financing of Economic Development of Developing Countries in 1969," *United Nations Document E/4873,* United Nations, New York, 1971.

From 1954 to 1969 the countries receiving the most aid have been: India, $1,830 million; the UAR., $1,741 million; Indonesia, $794 million; Iran, $864 million; Algeria, $468 million; Afghanistan, $399 million; Ghana, $169 million; Argentina, $159 million; Guinea, $122 million; and Mali, $112 million.

Official figures on monies actually paid out by the socialist countries are not available. According to United Nations calculations, the annual gross amount went from $563 million in 1960 to $957 million in 1968.[21] But repayments have also increased rapidly, reaching a maximum of $765 million in 1962; net transfers went down by 1968 to their 1960 level of around $560 million. On the average, therefore, the aid provided by the socialist economies represented about 5 per cent of net transfers of financial resources, and about 10 per cent of official development assistance from the DAC countries.

The socialist countries usually grant aid for specific projects, preferably for large-scale industrial plants or hydroelectric dams—the biggest project to be financed by socialist aid was the Aswan High Dam in the UAR. Grants do not figure prominently in their programs. They are given only for scholarships and for some social welfare projects such as hospitals. With these exceptions, the aid of socialist countries comes in the form of loans bearing low interest rates, usually 2.5 to 3 per cent, for a period of 8 to 12 years. Repayment in many cases can

21. *The External Financing of Economic Development, 1964–1968,* United Nations, New York, 1970, p. 48.

be made in kind, either the primary export products of the specific country, or the goods manufactured in plants built with socialist aid. In recent years socialist countries have been granting more aid through trade credits. These apply to the purchase of machinery rather than to the construction of complete projects; carry higher interest rates, 3 to 5 per cent; and are made for a shorter period of 3 to 10 years.

China provides aid on terms more lenient than those of the USSR and the socialist countries of Eastern Europe, and gives interest-free loans or grants. Her aid program is more diversified and includes small-scale projects in agriculture and light industries, and larger undertakings such as the Zambia–Tanzania railroad.

Relatively little information is available on aid from the USSR and other developed socialist countries to the developing nations in their bloc—including, in past years, China. OECD estimates that the aid within the socialist bloc must be double the amount given to non-socialist countries, which is equivalent to only 0.1 per cent of their G.N.P.[22] Counting the aid to both socialist and non-socialist developing countries, their total contribution to development represents only about 0.3 per cent of their national product.

In the last two decades bilateral foreign aid has undoubtedly made a major contribution to whatever economic development has occurred in the developing countries. In particular it has made available substantial resources in foreign exchange which could be invested in development projects. But as we indicated earlier, bilateral aid raises serious problems in developing countries. There are the political hazards of accepting foreign aid from the superpowers, which we already have discussed. In addition, by its very nature, bilateral aid is donor-oriented. It is the donor who determines the volume, the composition, and the destination of bilateral aid, its general objectives as well as the specific projects which will be assisted. These decisions can be motivated by self-interest on the part of the donor, both political and economic. There was the attempt of the United States Congress to prohibit the use of aid funds in establishing industries which might be competitive with American products. Although this may be an extreme example, bilateral aid will naturally reflect the views of the donor country on goals and policies of development.

However reasonable they might be, these views may not coincide with those of the recipient country. The United States, for instance, has been reluctant to encourage the establishment of heavy industries,

22. *Resources for the Developing World,* Organisation for Economic Co-operation and Development, Paris, 1970, p. 296.

such as steel, in developing countries. They are even more opposed when such industries will be government-owned. When India decided to create a state-owned steel industry, the government had to apply for aid to other bilateral programs, to those of the Soviet Union, the United Kingdom, and West Germany. In contrast, the USSR is particularly interested in assisting such industries, and particularly, if not exclusively, when they are government-owned. The smaller bilateral programs also have their own areas of preference and concentration. Thus Sweden is extremely interested in providing aid for family planning and has initiated international programs in this field. In most cases there is no deliberate intention to interfere in the development policies of the recipient country. But the very fact that aid is available in certain fields and not in others may cause a significant deviation from the national plan in the pattern of development.

Since bilateral aid can and indeed does influence the policy of recipient governments, the question arises whether or not donor countries should try to use their aid as leverage to impose changes in policy. One assumes here that national self-interest of the donor would not come into play, that the only motivation for these changes would be a desire to improve the impact of aid on economic development and on the welfare of the common people. In fact it would be extremely useful if certain reforms were considered prerequisites for economic assistance in a number of developing countries where the government is dominated by a small privileged class which shows little if any concern for its fellow citizen.

Unfortunately, experience shows that such a course of action would encounter great difficulties. It would arouse the bitter antagonism of the ruling oligarchy whose interests are hurt by effective land reform or fiscal reform which would put an end to their flagrant evasion of taxes and to their sending capital out of the country. This ruling "oligarchia" turns constantly to the donor country to protect its interest and privileges. But should this same donor come to demand domestic reforms, they would wave the banner of national independence madly about and protest bitterly against the scandalous violation of their national sovereignty.

This attitude was a major factor in the failure of the "Alliance for Progress," President Kennedy's attempt to establish a comprehensive 10-year plan for economic and social reform in Latin America. It was to have joined the efforts of the Latin American countries and of the United States, which had agreed to provide substantial capital assistance on a long-term basis. But the allocation of this aid depended on the willingness of each country to submit a comprehensive plan of economic and social development which would incorporate the basic principles of the Alliance. These plans had to be approved by a group of high-level experts, only one of whom would be a United States citizen, in order to avoid, or to minimize any outcry, against "Yankee interference." Even with this precaution, there have been delays in the submission of these plans. In one country of Central America, dominated by the oligarchia, the government finally submitted a plan which included some required reforms. Soon after it was approved and United States aid was allocated, the government was overthrown in a military coup. The new military regime, in fact, represented the same ruling class as its predecessor and immediately cast aside the planned reforms. Even without resorting to such drastic subterfuges, recipient governments have generally managed to prevent the implementation of the principles of the Alliance. They use the bogey of communism as their main argument in demanding immediate grants of aid. If aid is not proffered at once, without waiting for reforms, the government will collapse and the communists will take over. In the early part of the 1960's, these arguments were not well received in Washington. Since President Kennedy's death, however, his preference in dealing with democratic and progressive governments in Latin America has been gradually shunted aside. Reforms are no longer a prerequisite for aid.

It was pointed out to the author, at a meeting at the Economic Commission for Latin America in the spring of 1968, that as a consequence, land reform has nearly been dropped as a goal of development. When the Presidents of Latin American countries met together in 1961, land reform was given high priority on the list of objectives. At the next such meeting which took place in 1967, the topic was not even mentioned. Since then the events which have occurred in Chile and Peru ought to have shown the oligarchia in other countries on the continent that it is not in their best interest to oppose completely all reform. In Peru, where the oligarchia prevented any effective land reform, when the military took over in 1969 one of their first moves was to expropriate all the big estates. In Chile the same class of big landowners resisted former President Frei's attempts to impose more than a very limited program of land reform; at that the plan was being carried out only very slowly and with great reluctance. The disappointment of the landless farm workers contributed to the victory of a more radical administration, thus to a more drastic program of land expropriation.

Thus in spite of the political hazards involved in such a course, it seems perfectly proper for a donor country to insist that domestic policies in a recipient country strengthen rather than blunt the favorable impact of the aid given. There are fewer political implications for countries with smaller bilateral aid programs when they impose such conditions. Thus Sweden has stated that she will grant aid in particular to progressive countries with policies aimed at improving the welfare of the people. But because of the relatively small scope of the Swedish aid program, it will probably not be a strong incentive for developing countries to adopt appropriate domestic policies.

The political difficulties which are inevitably connected with bilateral aid, and especially the heavy criticism which United States foreign aid has received both at home and abroad, are obviously major reasons for the present trend to emphasize more participation in multilateral aid. There are few if any political overtones to multilateral aid. It would be a healthy move if it did not at the same time imply a reduction in total United States commitment to aid.

Multilateral aid is channeled mainly through the United Nations family of organizations, including the regional development banks. Its major components of technical assistance and financial loan aid are quite distinct and are handled through different institutions, according to different policies and procedures.

Technical assistance was first started on a small scale by the specialized agencies of the United Nations which were established after World War II. Each of them provided assistance in its own field of competence: FAO in developing agricultural production, WHO (World Health Organization) in eradicating epidemics and organizing medical services, UNESCO in education. The United Nations also began to furnish assistance in the fields that were not covered by specialized agencies, such as economic planning and social welfare.

Technical assistance became a major aspect of international economic policy when President Truman, in his inaugural address on January 20, 1949, emphazised the importance of sharing technical knowledge with the developing countries. He called for international co-operation and pledged a major United States contribution in this field. His initiative was met with the enthusiastic response of both the developed and the developing countries. It would enable the developing countries to bridge the gap which separated them from the more advanced countries and provide a short cut to economic development.

While financial aid costs the donor whatever the sums the developing country would receive, the expense of providing technical knowledge would be minimal for the donor in comparison to the real benefits that it would offer. Heralded as a co-operative effort in sharing skills, technical assistance was free from the stigma of paternalism. It was only natural therefore that since its inception in 1950, the United Nations Programme of Technical Assistance has constantly grown in scope, depth, and volume. Unfortunately, however, its financial resources have not expanded at the rate which was initially envisaged, and have not kept pace with the needs of recipient governments.

The program is financed by annual voluntary donations of governments. At first the United States contributed more than half of the total budget, but its share dropped in 1971 to 35.1 per cent. Other major donors with large bilateral aid programs have also fallen behind. This is the case of France and especially of the Soviet Union. The latter did not make its first contribution to the program until 1954. At that time, with the death of Stalin, there was a general shift in the Soviet approach to international problems. It was becoming obvious then that the lack of Soviet participation was enhancing the reputation of the United States, which was basking in the success of the program it had initiated. Since then, however, the USSR contribution has still been extremely small. On the contrary, several smaller countries that grant little bilateral aid are rapidly increasing their contributions. Canada, and especially Sweden, now the second largest contributor, are the most striking examples.

At first the scarcity of funds limited the activity of the program to providing experts on a short-term basis, and training through individual fellowships. In 1959 its scope was expanded to include more comprehensive surveys such as pre-investment feasibility analyses and studies and the establishment of local or regional training and research institutions.

The United Nations Technical Assistance operates under the authority of the Administrator of the United Nations Development Programme (UNDP), a central co-ordinating body which allocates

Table XII

PLEDGES TO THE UNITED NATIONS DEVELOPMENT PROGRAMME
(in million $)

	USA	UK	France	USSR	Ger-many	Sweden	Can-ada	Total
1950–58	108.7	15.6	10.6	6.0	2.3	4.3	11.1	204.5
1959	22.0	3.2	2.6	2.0	1.7	3.0	4.0	55.2
1971	86.3	14.4	5.0	3.0	13.1	23.0	16.0	240.1
1972	86.3	19.2	5.6	3.0	14.4	26.0	18.0	

Source: United Nations Development Programme Statements.

funds for country programs and individual projects. Resident Directors of the program in the recipient countries handle the negotiations with the governments and co-ordinate all United Nations technical assistance operations. The actual implementation of the projects is carried out by the various specialized agencies in their respective fields of competence.

The most important difference between United Nations assistance and bilateral aid is the fact that the former is not donor- but recipient-oriented. Within the limits of the program's total budget, it is the government of the recipient country that makes the final decision as to the kind of assistance which will be provided, its distribution in the various special fields, and the individual projects. Paul Hoffman, the first Administrator of UNDP, liked to emphasize that his team was only a junior partner of the recipient government, responsible for providing assistance in technical knowledge and skills required to carry out their national development projects. United Nations technical assistance, therefore, has to be integrated within the general development plan of the recipient country.

The only absolute prerequisite for United Nations technical assistance is the active participation of the recipient government, its willingness to support the project and to provide all the local resources and facilities required to ensure its success. This would include, in particular, finding a suitable counterpart for the United Nations expert who would assist and be able to replace him after his departure. In view of the fact, of course, that recipient countries are by definition underdeveloped, they are not always able to meet these requirements.

The absence of any strings, of any political condition, explicit or even implied, seems to be the most important aspect of United Nations technical assistance. Both developing and developed countries, capitalist or socialist, are represented on the Governing Council of UNDP. In accordance with the principle of equality, which operates also in the General Assembly of the United Nations, each member country regardless of the size of its contribution has only one vote. Assistance is granted to all developing countries under the same terms and rules, be they members of the United Nations or only of one of its specialized agencies. Since the latter are non-political, they have been able to admit countries such as West Germany, a major donor, and South Korea and South Viet Nam, which are recipients.

The international character of United Nations technical assistance enables it to take advantage of the experience of specialists from various countries. It offers a wide choice of candidates to the recipient countries which are free to accept or reject them, or to express their preferences in background or nationality. Developing countries, too, are increasingly providing experts to the United Nations program, which thus merits its description, "the sharing of skills." In some cases the experience of such experts may be more applicable to conditions in the less developed countries of the Third World than that of experts from more advanced countries.

United Nations technical assistance undeniably has its own drawbacks and difficulties. First of all, its procedures are cumbersome and time consuming. It must give all donor countries equal opportunity to submit candidates, which involves considerable delays. Moreover, the decentralization of United Nations assistance makes it difficult to coordinate. Working hand in hand with their counterpart in the recipient government—FAO with the Ministry of Agriculture, for example—each one of the specialized agencies lobbies to obtain the biggest share of the entire allocation for a given country for projects in its own field. This kind of pressure may influence the source of development contrary to the national plan. A study has been made on the United Nations capacity to handle an increased flow of aid, and recent changes in procedures should improve this situation. The authority of the Resident Director of UNDP will be strengthened in the recipient country. He will negotiate with the government a comprehensive program of technical assistance geared to meet the highest priority requirements of the country on the basis of its own development plan.

A more important drawback of United Nations assistance is the fact that it does not include capital aid. Defined as a program to transfer skills, and restricted by its limited resources, it is unable to provide investment capital. Thus it cannot offer much in the way of equipment, usually only for training purposes or for pilot projects. This can create considerable difficulties, when technical assistance projects must be followed up by capital investments. A feasibility study of a hydroelectric dam, for instance, should come with funds to finance its construction. In bilateral programs this separation between technical and financial aid does not exist. One can usually assume that if a bilateral donor agrees to undertake a technical study of a development project, and if the outcome is favorable, eventually the donor will also provide the capital required for the actual construction. There is a danger, then, that efforts and recources deployed in pre-investment surveys in particular will be wasted when "follow up" funds are not forthcoming.

To avoid this, UNDP does maintain close relations with major sources of financing, both public and private, and, of course, with multilateral agencies, such as the World Bank. The latter is always consulted in pre-investment surveys. Thus financial prospects are explored before a study is undertaken. Nevertheless, this uncertainty about the eventual financing of projects is a serious shortcoming of the United Nations program. Rapid progress has been made in developing new skills and trained personnel, the result possibly of a successful program of technical assistance. A greater number of developing countries now are capable of making good use of investment capital, and UNDP's shortcoming in this area is more serious than in the past.

The developing countries have often asked the United Nations General Assembly to establish a Capital Development Fund. In addition to ensuring the follow up of projects, such a fund would be a source of investment capital free from political strings of any sort and available to all developing countries.

The potential contributors, both the market economy and the socialist countries, were not very receptive, however, to this proposal, not a surprising reaction on their part given the political facts of life on the international scene. They have already agreed to donate sizable sums for United Nations technical assistance which the United Nations alone allocates in accordance with its principles. These contributions represent a significant sacrifice on their part since they as donors derive no direct benefits. One could have predicted that they would be unwilling under these circumstances to hand over the even larger amounts which would be needed to establish such a fund, a fund that would be controlled by the developing countries—i.e., the borrowers.

The fact that the developing countries command a majority in the United Nations General Assembly has given them the voting power to override the opposition and to pass a resolution calling for the creation of a United Nations Capital Development Fund. This Fund would be financed through voluntary contributions from all member countries, in the same way as UNDP. But so far the sums received have been insignificant, and most of them have been offered in non-convertible currencies. Therefore, the Fund has not yet been able to start its operations.

The International Bank for Reconstruction and Development (IBRD), also called the World Bank, does provide international financial assistance on a large scale. Although it is part of the United Nations family, the IBRD has a different structure and relationship with its members. In July of 1944 an international monetary and financial conference was held at Bretton Woods to discuss the establishment of institutions after the end of the war which would maintain the economic stability and ensure the progress of less developed countries. The great British economist, John Maynard Keynes, and the Under-Secretary of the United States Treasury, Paul White, confronted each other on opposite sides of the table. Keynes, representing the United Kingdom, wanted to establish a single powerful international financial institution with functions similar to those of a World Reserve Bank. This body would regulate the course of world economy, ensure the stabilization of prices of primary products, and promote economic development, in particular through long-term loans. But White's views prevailed, principally because of the overwhelming strength of the United States at that point. He argued in favor of two separate and less powerful institutions: the International Monetary Fund (IMF) to ensure international monetary stability and provide short-term credits to make up temporary deficits in the balance of payments; and the World Bank to promote through loans the reconstruction of the war-devastated countries and the development of the Third World. According to its statutes the Bank cannot accept as a member any country which has not joined the IMF. This requirement is probably the main reason for the refusal of the USSR to join the Bank and to benefit from the loans to which it undoubtedly would have been entitled for the reconstruction of its war-devastated regions. The members of the Fund are required to supply all data dealing with their balance of payments and their monetary situation, including gold and foreign exchange reserves. This data has traditionally been considered a state secret in the Soviet Union, and after World War II, in the heyday of Stalin, this secrecy was even more strictly enforced than at present.

The Bank obtains the resources for its loan operations from the "paid in" capital and from the bonds which it issues on private capital markets. The authorized capital of the Bank has been increased several times from the initial amount of $10 billion to $27 billion by the end of 1971. Only 20 per cent of this total is paid in, 2 per cent in gold or dollars and the remaining 18 per cent in the currencies of the member countries. At first only the fraction paid in gold or dollars was available for lending. Gradually, however, as the currencies of other major subscribers became convertible, their governments agreed to make the total of their paid-in subscription available to the Bank. The 80 per cent not called in constitutes a potential reserve fund which serves as a guarantee for the Bank's obligations.

While only governments can subscribe to the capital of the Bank and be shareholders, the distribution of voting power is more akin to that of a private corporation than an international organization. With

Table XIII
MAJOR SHAREHOLDERS OF THE INTERNATIONAL BANK
BY THE END OF 1971

Country	Value of Shares (in million $)	Share in Voting Power (in per cent)
United States	63,500	23.81
United Kingdom	26,000	9.81
Federal Republic of Germany	13,653	5.19
France	10,500	4.02
Japan	10,230	3.92
Canada	7,920	3.05

only the very minor reservation that each member has a minimum of 250 votes, the number of votes is proportional to the number of shares held. The wealthy developed countries, first and foremost the United States, have the power, therefore, to influence the Bank's policy and in particular to prevent any loans which would be contrary to its national interest.

United States control over the Bank was quite obvious in the early days of its operations. At that time the United States not only provided most of the paid-in capital available for lending but had also the only capital market on which the Bank could raise funds. The question of a loan to Poland was a striking example of political intervention in the lending policies of the Bank. Poland, as well as Czechoslovakia and Yugoslavia, had joined both the Bank and the Fund expecting to obtain funds for reconstruction. In 1947 Poland applied for a loan to rebuild and expand her coal mines. In view of the fact that there was a desperate coal shortage in the whole of Europe at that time, this loan would have benefited not only Poland but the economy of the whole continent. There could have been a cheaper and more convenient alternative to the massive import of coal from the United States. Yet in spite of a favorable recommendation from the surveying team sent to Poland by the Bank, the loan was never granted. Poland accordingly resigned as a member of the Bank. Yugoslavia remained a member and after its break with the Soviet Union in 1948 started to receive loans.

The political influence of the United States on the Bank's policies gradually has declined. New members such as Germany and Japan have reduced the American share in IBRD's capital (see Table XIII, this page, on the present distribution of voting strength). Moreover, most of the Bank's bond issues are now floated in Europe. International economic policies have also become more flexible; it is no longer common practice to prevent loans and prohibit trade for strategic and political reasons. Reliable sources report that informal exploratory discussions have recently been held to consider possible membership of several socialist countries. Obviously, if they joined, they would be given the assurance of obtaining loans.

Finally, the professional management of the Bank has grown increasingly independent of the day-to-day policy of even the most important member country. This is true not only of Robert McNamara, the present head of the IBRD, but also of his predecessors, who have always been American citizens. The officials of the Bank, just as their colleagues in other international agencies for economic development, all believe that active co-operation between the rich and the poor nations of the world is in everyone's best interest.

In spite of this growing independence, and the general recognition of the Bank's important contribution to the financing of economic development, the developing countries have not given up their request for a United Nations financial agency. This may be due to the fact that the Bank is even more independent of its clients. It has rejected projects dear to the heart of requesting governments in selecting only those projects to finance which will make the best use of the funds available. Their objective criteria for these projects are maximum efficiency and the greatest possible impact on economic development. Often the pet projects of governments are politically motivated rather than economically sound. Thus the Bank refused to assist the financing of the Zambia–Tanzania railroad. While its decision, as we describe in Part Four, was motivated by technical considerations, predictably it was not well received by many African countries. Naturally the IBRD has to take some notice of political facts of life and attempt as fair a geographical distribution of its loans as possible among the different regions and even major countries of the Third World. On the whole, however, the Bank has managed to avoid political involvement and has abided by its objective criteria. It has been very strict in supervising the execution of the projects which it assists, and in checking that governments meet all the terms of the loan contracts. In particular, it has insisted on local contributions to costs and an adherence to international bidding procedures.

The Bank's firmness has not endeared it to some governments which are reluctant to abide by the regulations. In requesting a financing agency under United Nations auspices, developing countries feel that such an agency would give more weight to their views and put less emphasis on technical and economic considerations. In these circumstances it is not surprising that—as we have mentioned earlier —none of the major developed countries—not even the Soviet Union, which certainly holds no brief for the IBRD—have agreed to contribute to the United Nations Capital Development Fund.

The initial plan called for loans from the Bank for only those projects which would have a maximum development impact on the economy of the borrower. Great care was taken to ensure that the project, either directly or indirectly in its impact on the economy as a whole, would generate additional income and foreign exchange. Thus it would guarantee the payment of interest and the amortization of the loan. When projects of this kind were involved, borrowing countries could certainly afford to pay interest at rates commensurate with those that the Bank had to pay itself on the capital market.

But it became evident gradually that financing was also urgently needed for essential projects which would not produce any income at all. They were indispensable in shoring up the economy, in many cases in preparing the ground work for other directly productive projects. Developing countries could not afford for such projects the rates which the IBRD charged for its normal loans; they had to have more lenient terms.

The major developed market economies agreed to establish an agency specifically empowered to make such soft loans. But instead of setting it up under the authority of the United Nations, as the developing countries requested, they associated it with the IBRD and created the International Development Association (IDA). For all practical purposes IDA, which has the same management and staff as the Bank, is simply the IBRD's soft-loan window.

The nature of the project and the economic and financial position of the recipient country decide if the financing will come through a regular IBRD loan or a soft IDA credit. As a general rule, only countries with a per capita G.N.P. of less than $300 are eligible for IDA credits.

IDA obtains its resources from voluntary contributions of member governments. It is therefore able to make interest-free loans for a duration of 50 years, charging only a service commission of ¾ per cent. The IBRD has had to raise the interest rate to 7 per cent in 1971 because of the tight money situation in the main capital markets. While this rate is considered exhorbitant by the borrowing countries, it does not even reflect fully the net cost to the Bank, as it uses also for lending its own capital and accumulated profits.

The initial resources of IDA amounted to $1 billion, which it expected to disburse in five years. But this annual rate of $200 million for soft loans proved inadequate in light of the great demand for such financing, and new funds had to be paid in on several occasions. The delay in obtaining the consent of the major contributors, in particular of the United States, to additional subscriptions, obliged IDA at one point to stop giving new credits. These difficulties were eventually overcome, and for the period of 1970 to 1974 IDA has been assured an annual allocation of $800 million. In addition, the IBRD now transfers part of its profits to IDA; by the end of 1971 this came to an additional $595 million.

The creation of IDA has allowed the management of the Bank to adopt more flexible lending policies than in the past. Not only can it now finance non-income producing projects, but it is able to set terms specifically tailored to the particular requirements of projects and borrowers. Thus a major undertaking such as a dam can be financed partly by a loan on IBRD terms—covering the cost of producing the electric power—and partly by IDA credits, which would pay for the non-income producing functions of the dam, such as flood control. The Bank has also extended the scope of its lending to areas such as agriculture and education. Previously these had been ruled out because of the overly general nature of their impact on economic development. In 1970 IBRD entered the field of family planning, which Robert McNamara considers of vital importance in order to avert the danger of catastrophic overpopulation, and in 1971 it granted a first loan for pollution control.

Table XIV
LOANS AND CREDITS OF THE WORLD BANK GROUP
(in million $)

Year	IBRD Loans	IDA Credits
1960–61	610	101
1961–62	882	134
1962–63	449	260
1963–64	810	283
1964–65	1,023	309
1965–66	839	284
1966–67	877	354
1967–68	847	107
1968–69	1,399	385
1969–70	1,680	606
1970–71	1,896	584

The distribution of IBRD loans and IDA credits in the major sectors was as follows:

Table XV
(in million $)

Purpose	IBRD Loans	IDA Credits
Electric power	5,010.6	273.4
Transportation	4,958.3	918.5
Agriculture	1,497.4	850.2
Industry	2,413.2	104.0
Education	212.7	211.7
General development and imports	637.7	680.0
Development finance	1,291.9	646.0

Source: Annual Report of the International Bank for 1971.

In recent years the Bank has considerably expanded its loans in the field of industry. It has even granted loans to establish government-owned plants, in contrast to its earlier wariness of such projects. In addition to direct loans for industrial development, it has also financed the import of industrial materials in the case of countries with severe problems in balance of payments—for example, India. Substantial assistance has been given to national development corporations, the agencies which are best equipped to promote the development of small and medium-sized industries.

Finally, another organization of the Bank's group, the International Finance Corporation, which we mentioned earlier, is actively promoting private industry in developing countries by offering both loans and equity capital. In 1971 the IFC had invested $598 million in industrial ventures and had managed to attract over $3 billion in outside capital to these industries.

Robert McNamara inaugurated in 1969 a program to expand the Bank's assistance to development and to double the volume of IBRD loans and IDA credits in the next five years. The plan was to raise the total of $12 billion. Taking into consideration the monies provided by local governments in conjunction with these loans, the total additional investment generated by the Bank would amount to $30 billion. Already in the first year of the program the Bank group made new loans totaling approximately $2.3 billion, nearly reaching the target set for the increased annual rate of lending; in the second year its new commitments exceeded the target and rose to $2.58 billion.

Thus the World Bank complex has become the largest single source of development financing. In volume it has now outstripped the United States' bilateral program, which from its inception right up to now had been the major donor of financial assistance. Moreover, it also surpasses all other aid programs in quality. Based on objective technical and economic criteria, and involving careful supervision of projects, the Bank's programs have had greater impact on development than their size alone would have warranted.

In order to raise the efficiency of its aid, the Bank is assisting the developing countries through its country missions in formulating their overall development strategies. The existence of a clearly defined plan should enable donor countries and agencies to channel their technical and financial assistance in as productive a manner as possible. Thus one sees that the scope of the Bank's operations is not limited to its lending activities. While the World Bank may not always be popular among developing countries, it has gained the respect of both donor and recipient nations and its advice carries considerable weight. As the leader in the field of financial aid, the World Bank is usually called upon to chair consortia or consultative groups of donor governments and multilateral agencies in co-ordinate aid. These bodies are formed to assist recipient governments in obtaining the external resources required for their development plans.

Multilateral financial aid is also being provided on a regional basis by Regional Development Banks in Latin America, Asia and Africa.

The Inter-American Development Bank (IADB) was established in 1959 when the United States government decided to increase its aid to economic development in order to improve the political and social climate in Latin America, and above all to prevent a deterioration in their relationship with their neighbor to the North. This step was taken a few months after Castro's revolution in Cuba, which may or may not have been pure coincidence. At the present the United States furnishes the major part of IADB's resources: $1,174 million out of a regular capital of $3,150 million, and $1,800 million out of the $2,328 million in the Fund for Special Operations. This Fund is equivalent to IDA in that it finances soft loans. Symbolic of its dependence on the United States is the fact that IADB's headquarters are in Washington, but there is a question of transferring it to some capital in Latin America.

In the first decade, 1960 to 1970, IADB emerged as the greatest single source of external financing in Latin America, and has provided loans totaling $3,430 million. It operates on somewhat the same lines as the World Bank, although the size of the loans is smaller to some extent. The allocation of funds in the various sectors of the economy reflects the specific needs of the continent. Agriculture has the highest proportion: 24.3 per cent; industry and mining: 16.8 per cent; transportation: 15.2 per cent; electric power: 13.9 per cent. The IADB makes a special effort to promote regional integration by financing projects which benefit an entire region or at least more than one country.

The Asian Development Bank was created in 1966 and started its operations the following year with an authorized capital of $1 billion, half of which was to be paid in. Its headquarters are in Manila, and as a precautionary measure against the domination of developed countries from outside the region, its charter stipulates that 60 per cent of the capital must be held by countries within the region. The major shareholders are Japan and the United States, with $200 million each. In addition to its regular capital which is lent out on IBRD terms together with monies raised on private capital markets, there are also special funds for soft-term lending. The contributions to these Special Funds come from Japan and several countries of Western Europe, where most of the bonds are floated. In the first three years, the Asian Bank had made loans on commercial terms totaling $304.6 million, $211.9 million in 1970 alone; soft loans from Special Funds came to $55.7 million, with $33.7 million in 1970.

The African Development Bank was established as early as 1963 with headquarters in Abidjan, Ivory Coast. Its limited resources have made it very difficult to launch any large-scale operations. In order to avoid any pressure from non-African developed countries on lending policies, its membership is restricted to African countries (South Africa, however, is not a member). They must furnish all its ordinary authorized capital of $250 million, and by the end of 1969 had pledged $217.8 million of it, although only $13.6 million actually was lent out on commercial terms. Countries outside the region can contribute to its Special Loan Fund, the African Development Fund which lends on soft terms, but up to now the major capital exporting countries have not proved very generous.

The resources of the developed countries, $\%_{10}$ of which came from the market economies as we have indicated, have made a considerable contribution to the economic development of the developing countries. Foreign aid alone has financed about 10 per cent of all investments. This 10 per cent, as the Pearson Report stated, can mean the difference between staying ahead of population growth, while at the same time improving public services, and barely keeping up.[23] External aid

23. *Partners in Development: Report of the Commission on International Development*, Praeger, New York, 1969, p. 48.

therefore may have enabled the Third World to come very close to
its target of an annual rate of growth of 5 per cent in national income,
which was set for the First Development Decade during the 1960's.

But in spite of this achievement, the position of developing countries in regard to balance of payments, with the exception of the major
oil producers and exporters, is quite serious. If the present trend continues, it may lead to a major crisis impeding further development
and resulting in a disastrous economic and political breakdown.

The need of developing countries for external resources to build
up their industries and infrastructure is growing rapidly. The World
Bank has pointed out that as infrastructure projects which were
initiated earlier come to fruition, they are able increasingly to use new
public and private capital productively.[24] By itself this expansion in
their absorptive capacity is a most encouraging sign. But the volume
of public external aid has recently been leveling off, and foreign loans
come with stiffer terms because of the rise in interest rates on the
main capital markets. Thus in order to find the necessary capital, the
developing countries are availing themselves more and more of export
credits, which are very expensive and given only on a relatively short-
term basis, for not more than 10 or 15 years, in many cases only for
5 years. They impose a heavy burden in payments of interest and
amortization of capital. The foreign debt of developing countries has
grown by leaps and bounds and stood at $43 billion at the end of
1968, twice what it had been in 1960.[25] In 1968 it took about 10 per
cent of all export earnings of developing countries to keep up with
the obligations of this debt. These debt service payments have been
increasing at an annual rate of 17 per cent, compared with a 6 per cent
growth rate for export earnings.[26]

The net flow of capital to the developing countries, after deduc-
tion of interest payments and profits on private investments which
are returned to the capital exporting countries, has declined rapidly.
According to United Nations data for 67 developing countries, in 1968
this net flow amounted only to $1,040 million, against $1,990 million in
1967.[27] These figures are misleading, however. There are great differences among the various groups of countries. The eight oil-exporting
countries have a considerable net outflow of capital, $2,386 million in
1968 compared with $2,053 million in 1967. But they can well afford

24. *Annual Report of the World Bank for 1970,* Washington, 1970, p. 7.
25. *The External Financing of Economic Development,* United Nations,
New York, 1970, p. 94.
26. Robert S. McNamara, "Address to the Board of Governors of the World
Bank," Copenhagen, September 21, 1970, IBRD, 1970, pp. 4 and 5.
27. *Op. cit.,* p. 92.

it and they have no problems whatsoever in balance of payments. The 59 remaining countries in 1968 still had a substantial net inflow of $3,426 million in external resources, but the figure had dropped by 15 per cent from a total of $4,043 million in 1967. Moreover, this surplus will rapidly disappear if the present trend continues. The projections quoted in the Pearson Report would indicate that if the gross flow of new loans remains the same as in the period from 1965 to 1967, by 1977 debt service payments would exceed new lending in all developing regions with the exception of Southern Asia and the Middle East.[28] There the inflow of new funds would equal the outflow.

With the exception of those blessed with rich oil resources, the export earnings of the developing countries will probably remain for some time insufficient to pay for the imports required for their industrial development and for their consumer needs. This imbalance in foreign trade will further complicate the problem of meeting payments owed to the rich creditor nations.

Ghana, India, and Indonesia are already facing crises in balance of payments because of an improvident policy which allowed debts to accumulate far beyond their ability to repay. Temporarily at least the creditors, headed by the World Bank, have agreed to bail them out by consolidating and rescheduling their claims. It is interesting to note in the case of Indonesia that the Soviet Union, one of their main creditors, did not participate directly in the joint rescue operation of the other creditors but still co-operated indirectly by postponing the repayment of its own claims. But such maneuvers, as was pointed out in the Pearson Report, do not offer a final solution to these difficulties.[29]

It will be impossible to provide even such temporary and partial relief when the problem of balance of payments becomes more widespread and arises, at the same time, in most if not all developing countries. Then most likely there will be a general suspension of all debt payments, a demand on the part of developing countries to cancel all debts, and a breakdown in financial transfers to developing countries. Their shortages then in essential import goods may well lead to serious economic, social, and political difficulties, as well as dangerously tense international relations between the rich and the poor countries.

What can, and what should the developed countries do to avert such a danger? Without question the consequences would be scarcely less serious for them than for the developing countries.

As we have said earlier, the effort which the rich developed coun-

28. *Op. cit.*, p. 74.
29. *Op. cit.*, p. 157.

tries are asked to make is relatively minor. They would almost as-suredly not affect their own progress or endanger their balance of pay-ments. The Pearson Report, which we have quoted already, points out that by 1975 the DAC member countries could reach the target of 1 per cent for the net flow of financial resources to developing coun-tries, going from $13 billion to $23 billion, simply by earmarking 4 per cent of the expected annual increment in their G.N.P. for this purpose. This additional $10 billion would go a long way in easing or even solving the expected balance of payments crisis of the developing countries and their demand for additional foreign exchange.

Together with an increase in volume, what is needed, and is in-deed possible, is an improvement in the terms of transfer of external resources. A first step in this direction would be to raise the annual amount made available to IDA for soft credits, from its present level of $800 million to $1,500 million, as the Pearson Report recommended. This is entirely feasible in view of the great respect enjoyed by the World Bank in the main donor countries and especially in the United States. The Pearson Report also advises bilateral donors to enable the World Bank to reduce the interest rate on loans to those develop-ing countries that are too poor to afford its regular rates, but not poor enough to be entitled to soft IDA credits. This could be achieved if the donor countries made available to the World Bank half of the interest payments on their own bilateral loans. The subsidy would reduce the rate of IBRD loans to such countries from a present rate of 7 per cent to possibly 3 per cent.

Part Four

Different Types of Development

Chapter 9. *CONCRETE EXAMPLES*

WE INTEND in this chapter to examine several examples of different types of economic development which have been tried in countries of the Third World. There may be some general conclusions to be drawn from a comparison of the goals they have set, the policies they have followed, and the results they have had.

Africa

ALGERIA: AN EXPERIMENT IN SOCIALIST NATIONALISM

The changes which have taken place in Algeria since 1962, in the first decade of her independence, are probably more extensive than any that have taken place in other developing countries. For more than a century Algeria was not a French colony but a part of France herself. She had a dual population as well as a dual economy. The number of French settlers in 1962 comprised over 10 per cent of the total population. Before World War II and the population explosion among the Arabs, the percentage of Europeans had gone as high as 15, only slightly less proportionally than the white population in South Africa. Europeans, moreover, were to be found in all classes and income groups. They made up a substantial part of the industrial proletariat in the biggest cities of Algiers and Oran as well as the majority of the wealthy upper class, the large farm owners and the urban bourgeoisie. In contrast, about 90 per cent of Arabs lived in rural areas. But there was a rapidly growing urban population of mainly unskilled workers, and a small Arab middle class which had been educated in French schools and universities.

The dual character of the population was reflected in an inequality of status which violated the French equalitarian tradition. French citizenship could be enjoyed only by Europeans and the few Arabs who had agreed to be ruled by French law and to relinquish the personal status traditionally conferred upon them by the Koran. (This

included, for example, the right of polygamy.) The great majority
of Arabs, therefore, had only limited voting rights, both in national
elections for the French Parliament, and more important, for the
Algerian legislature. They were only scantily represented in local
government, and Europeans dominated Algeria both politically and
economically. Most of the modern efficient farms and nearly all the
factories, mines, and trading establishments were under European
management and ownership.

Initially the Arab opposition demanded only equality with the
Europeans and full citizenship, not Algerian independence. The weak-
ness of nationalist sentiment can be explained in part by the fact that
in contrast to her neighbors, such as Morocco, with an old tradition
of independence, Algeria had not been a unified nation prior to the
French conquest. In a statement typical of the views of many Algerian
Arabs in the 1930's, Ferhat Abbas, then the leader of the main Arab
party, the *Parti du Manifeste Algerien*, declared: "There is no Algerian nation. We simply want to be full fledged French citizens." He
was later to become the head of the Provisional Government before
independence, and the first President of the Algerian National Assembly.

It is futile to wonder whether the Arab population would have
been content to remain as part of the French state if these demands
had been met at that point in history. The chances are that political
equality would not have been sufficient without a fundamental improvement in economic conditions, and in particular a drastic land reform. On the question of relations between Europeans and Arabs,
Algeria faced a situation somewhat similar to that of the Central
Asian provinces in the former Russian empire. There, too, a European minority dominated a native Moslem majority. The Soviet Union
appears to have solved this problem, and consolidated its hold on the
native population, by granting cultural autonomy and complete political and economic equality, in addition to using force in the early
stages. Equality is naturally easier to arrange in an economy which
allows no private property.

On several occasions—when the liberals prevailed in Paris—
the central government and parliament made attempts to grant full
equality to the Arab population. But these were always thwarted
and sabotaged by the obstinate resistance of the *pieds noirs*, the local
Europeans. When finally de Gaulle proclaimed solemnly the equality
of all Algerians, and pronounced them all full-fledged Frenchmen,
Français à part entière, the nationalist revolution was already in full
swing, and scornfully rejected his offer. It was a case of too little too
late.

The dominant role of Europeans in the economy of pre-independent Algeria can be seen from the following figures for 1955, the first year of the war of independence.

Table XVI

	Moslem	European
Population (in thousands)	8,449	984
Per cent of total population	89.5	10.5
Per cent of total national income	53	47
Agriculture		
Number of farms (in thousands)	630	22
Total area (in thousand hectares)	7,300	2,700
Average area per farm (in hectares)	11.5	127

European agriculture had taken over most of the fertile land, including 75 per cent of all irrigated areas, and was largely responsible for the major cash crops: wheat, fruits and vegetables, and, above all, wine for export to France. Arab agriculture was mainly devoted to traditional crops such as durum wheat, barley, and sheep raising.

Europeans owned and managed the mines of iron ore (1,762,000 tons in 1954) and phosphates (619,000).

The discrepancy in income between Arabs and Europeans was particularly striking within the various segments of the urban labor force, as shown in the table below:

Table XVII

DISTRIBUTION AND INCOME OF THE URBAN LABOR FORCE IN 1955

	Total Number (in thousands)		Average Income (in thousand francs)	
	Moslems	Europeans	Moslems	Europeans
Wage earners	225	88	150	400
Salaried employees	90	80	270	530
Small businessmen and supervisory staff	135	110	270	1,150
Owners and managers	8	27	1,250	3,000
General average income			230	950

Source: Samir Amin, *Economie du Maghreb,* Editions de Minuit, Paris, 1965, pp. 155–157.

When de Gaulle proclaimed equal political rights for Moslems and Europeans, he initiated at the same time a program of economic development on a large scale. Its main objective was the rapid improvement in the standards of living of the Moslem population. This was the *Plan de Constantine*," for the period of 1959 to 1963. It included a massive effort to expand light industries, mainly for the domestic market, and to establish basic heavy industry for steel, chemicals, fertilizers, and oil refining. In agriculture, although there was no attempt to redistribute the land and European farming was left alone, major improvements were to be made on Moslem farms through irrigation, reclamation, reforestation, and increased water supply. To a great extent French public aid would finance the Plan. The hope was that an early end to the war would permit the transfer of considerable public resources from the military budget to development projects. Naturally the impetus of development would also stimulate a rapid increase in private investment.

But the main assumption of the *Plan de Constantine* was that the war would end rapidly. When it proved unfounded, the Plan as a whole could not be carried out. It was completely abandoned on the day of independence. Still, a very considerable program of public investment had already been started under this Plan with French government grants, and was active during the years from 1959 to 1962. The result was a substantial expansion in the economic and social infrastructure—which was already quite extensive, at least in comparison to that of most other developing countries. This was one of the legacies which Algeria inherited when she became independent.

The efforts of France to develop oil resources in the Algerian Sahara had an even greater and more durable impact on the subsequent development of the new nation. The French government after World War II undertook the exploration of oil in the Sahara in order to avoid having to rely on oil imports. All the preliminary geological research and exploration was financed by the government. When considerable deposits of oil and natural gas were indeed found, concessions were granted to French companies, most of them fully or at least partly government-owned. Production on a large scale started only shortly before independence and increased rapidly. In 1960 it represented 8,632,000 tons of oil and 1,383 million cubic meters of natural gas; in 1961, 15,664,000 tons and 3,357 million cubic meters.[1]

Under the Evian Agreement of March 1962 independent Algeria was to retain her close economic ties with France. The premise for this assumption was that a strong French minority would remain in Algeria and would be entitled to choose within three years' time between

1. *United Nations Statistical Yearbook, 1969,* United Nations, New York, 1970.

French and Algerian citizenship. Their property rights were guaranteed against expropriation without equitable compensation. At the same time Algerian workers retained the right to emigrate to France as before. The oil concessions of French companies would continue under the same terms. Algeria would remain a member of the Franc area and would enjoy preferential treatment with reciprocity. France undertook to provide large-scale technical and cultural assistance, as well as considerable financial aid. For the first three years, the financing would be kept at the pre-independence level.

In the spring of 1962, however, and before the independence of Algeria became finalized, the Evian Agreement received a fatal blow. Exasperated by the surrender of their homeland to the Arabs, the OAS (*Organisation de l'Armée Secrète*), an extremist organization of the Algerian French, not only refused to accept the independence of Algeria but made a desperate effort to sabotage its success. They engaged in a campaign of indiscriminate murder and arson, directed against harbor installations, factories, even against French facilities which were being transferred to Algeria, such as the library of the University. This created a climate of explosive hatred between the two communities and led to the wholesale exodus of the French population. Abandoning their farms, factories, shops, and homes, more than 800,000 Europeans fled to France. By the end of 1962 scarcely 150,000 of them remained out of a million in the preceding year.

With the sudden departure of most managers, technicians, foremen, and even skilled workers, the Algerian government was confronted with the possibility of total collapse in the most productive sectors of the economy. In order to avert this danger, an immediate decision had to be made. This gave the government its first real opportunity to assert its socialist orientation.

Although the FLN (Front of National Liberation) fought against French capitalism, as well as against colonialist oppression, at the outset its ideology had not been completely socialist. It was essentially a nationalist movement, and this can be seen in the fact that the first head of its Provisional Government was Ferhat Abbas, a moderate liberal. But the "colons," and the French government, too, accused the FLN of being communist, and they justified their opposition to independence as a struggle against a communist takeover. As the war went on, more radical trends did prevail in the FLN. The strong support of communist countries—while the capitalist world remained indifferent, or gave at best only moral sympathy, such as that expressed by John F. Kennedy, a United States Senator at the time— inclined the FLN further to socialism. One could even say that by raising the bogey of communism the French created a real danger out of what had been only a figment of their imagination at first.

In the spring of 1962, before the FLN took over the government, they adopted the Program of Tripoli, which spelled out in general terms the socialist character of the "Popular and Democratic Republic of Algeria." But in specific terms they referred only to the imperative need for land reform which directly affected the vast majority of the population. Faced with the consequence of the flight of European owners shortly after assuming power, the government had to decide how to operate the abandoned estates and urban enterprises. There were several alternatives. One was to sell European holdings to private Arab farmers, entrepreneurs, or simply speculators. Many such highly profitable transactions had already taken place. But this solution was considered totally foreign to the spirit of the revolution. Moreover, it would have been bitterly resisted by the labor force, especially by the agricultural workers. Another was to nationalize them and let them be administered by government representatives. This was not feasible in the absence of competent personnel. The third possibility was to transfer ownership to the workers and have the plantations and factories managed by their elected representatives. The leaders of the government, in particular its head, Ahmed Ben Bella, considered this last to be most in line with the ideals of Algerian socialism. Allowing the workers to participate in the management and profits of the enterprises which employed them would erase the sense of alienation that comes from "wage slavery"; this even government ownership could not accomplish. To a great extent the government's decision to adopt this course only put the final legal seal on a situation which already existed. Farm workers and factory employees had already taken matters into their own hands by and large and were running the enterprises that had been abandoned by European owners and managers.[2] The decrees of October 1962 legalized the take-over of all "vacant properties" which were administered under the principle of "self management." Self-management in agriculture was extended in September of 1963 when the government expropriated all remaining European farms which were still operated by their owners.

The main objective of the Algerian revolution, as the Tripoli program and later statements made clear, was to free the country of any political or economic dependence. Great importance was attached to Arab nationalism and to a belief in Islam. In fact, the Moslem faith was made Algeria's official religion, although basically the society and economy was socialist.

2. Hervé Bourgès, *L'Algerie a l'epreuve du Pouvoir*, Editions Grasset, Paris, 1967, pp. 69–72.

The policies which Algeria has followed since independence have not deviated from these goals, and have combined socialism with traditional nationalism. But there have been some changes in emphasis. The tendency in the early years was to stress the kinship with other similar revolutionary movements in developing countries. On the domestic front the proliferation of self-management policies shows clearly that action by the people as a whole was given highest priority. When Colonel Boumedienne became the head of state in 1965, the point of focus shifted to the country's own national interest and power. This switch in attitude was inevitable when the new, essentially military regime condemned previous policies as wasteful and inefficient. With the great concern over efficiency, technocratic officials —whose approach was pragmatic rather than ideological—gained control at the expense of politicians. They set up government-owned and managed plants, rather than self-managed enterprises, to expand the socialist economy and promote industrial development in particular.

To what extent did government policies after independence achieve the objectives of the revolution? It seems clear that the happiest results were obtained when both nationalist and socialist motives combined to reinforce each other. The goal of establishing the nation's independence could be reached by throwing out all foreign capitalist enterprises, a move which seemed to remove as well the last vestiges of colonialism. The Algerians have pursued this policy of "economic liberation" with complete determination and ruthlessness. Short shrift is made of any agreement previously signed when it no longer serves their interests. They make no bones about their approach. An editorial in Algeria's official newspaper put it very plainly: "The commitments into which we enter are only considered valid so long as they do not harm in the least the interests of our country."[3] This was already the approach of the Tripoli program, which voiced serious reservations about the "neo-colonialist" provisions in the Evian Agreement, particularly those which guaranteed the protection of French rights and interests.

The first step in this direction was to permit the takeover of properties abandoned by French owners, and to refuse compensation. Further nationalizations of industrial and mining enterprises were usually introduced at politically opportune moments, when difficulties arose in the relations between Algeria and the country of the investors. Thus, for example, the properties of the American oil companies, which were relatively minor in size, were nationalized in 1967 during the Arab-Israeli War, when Algeria broke off diplomatic

3. *El Moudjahid* of June 2, 1967.

relations with the United States. Compensation was paid only in a few instances, when it was to the advantage of Algeria to do so. This was the case when the need remained for further technical co-operation with the foreign company concerned, or when it seemed wise not to jeopardize prospects for future co-operation.

By far the most important, and most typical, example of this economic liberation was the gradual but methodical elimination of any French influence in oil mining. The preservation of French interests in the Sahara oil fields had been one of the basic tenets of de Gaulle's Algerian policy; it was essentially the *quid pro quo* for the massive aid—without precedent as to size and generosity of terms—which France had agreed to provide. De Gaulle had claimed, and not without some justification, that the French policy of granting aid for development on a large scale, immediately after a fiercely fought war, was a unique example of friendly co-operation between a former colonial power and its now emancipated dependency. It is a fact that temporarily at least this policy considerably raised the prestige of both France and de Gaulle personally in many countries of the Third World. Although they took full advantage of the benefits which could be derived from French co-operation, the Algerian leaders were not distracted, however, from their resolve to assert their control over oil, the country's most important natural resource. By the middle of 1971 this goal had nearly been reached.

In 1965 the terms of the Evian Agreement dealing with oil were revised in a Franco–Algerian treaty of co-operation which provided for the joint exploration and exploitation of oil resources in the Sahara for a period of 15 years. The financial arrangements which revolved around the payment of royalties by French companies to Algeria were among the most favorable at that time. The most significant and original aspect of the treaty was the creation of two joint bodies. The first was ASCOOP, which would direct the exploration and extraction of oil. Both countries would share on an equal basis in the costs and profits; France, however, would advance 60 per cent of Algeria's share of the expenses. The second was OCI (Organization for Industrial Co-operation), to be in charge of the study, preparation, and financing of industrial projects submitted by the Algerian government. France agreed to allocate 200 million francs in grants and 1.8 billion francs in long-term loans for this purpose over a period of five years.

This ambitious and comprehensive attempt at Franco–Algerian co-operation proved a complete failure, mainly because of a conflict in the objectives and policies of the two partners. The Algerians considered French aid to be a sort of compensation for previous colonial exploitation.[4] They demanded that their interests alone be regarded in any use of proceeds from French aid, and took little if any care to encourage further co-operation with France. Created in 1964, the Algerian National Oil Company (SONATRACH) pursued an aggressive policy of overall expansion. It drew from various sources of technical assistance, from France as well as from the USSR—both countries set up training institutes for petroleum engineers and technicians—and used as well the services of American consulting firms. The technical competence of its managers thus approached rapidly their political adroitness. In a few years SONATRACH had developed its own production of crude oil and increased it in 1967 when some minor foreign companies were nationalized. It owns refineries and pipelines, both for oil and natural gas. Since the nationalization of all foreign-owned distribution facilities, it enjoys a monopoly on the domestic market. Yet the government still continued to harass systematically the foreign companies, including those of its French partner, by steadily increasing taxes and restrictions on the repatriation of capital and profits.

It is not surprising, therefore, that French companies were reluctant to make new investments in the costly prospecting of deposits when they were very unsure of being allowed to operate the mines. Naturally, the French also were not eager to provide capital on preferential terms for plans such as petrochemical factories. On the one hand, the Algerians demanded that the output of their plants be granted free access to the French market and on the other, refused to co-ordinate them with similar industries in France. Unfortunately, as Viratelle points out, the French showed a lack of political astuteness by insisting on the letter of the agreements, and even more by delaying negotiations on a rise in the base price of crude oil.[5] In view of the general rise in world prices at the time, this increase was more than due.

The final blow to Franco–Algerian co-operation in this area occurred in February of 1971 with the nationalization of 51 per cent of the properties of the two French oil mining companies, *Compagnie Français des Pétroles* (CFP) and ERAP. This unilateral decision clearly violated the Franco–Algerian treaty and in fact amounted to its revocation. At the same time, the Algerian government also unilaterally and retroactively raised the base price of crude oil. The

4. Gerard Viratelle, *L'Algérie Algerienne,* Editions Economie et Humanisme, Paris, 1971, p. 91.

5. Viratelle, *op. cit.,* p. 113.

indemnity which it offered to pay to the two companies was practically wiped out by their claim for back payments.

The companies refused to comply, stopped all purchases of Algerian oil, and requested all international oil companies to do the same. The serious crisis in Franco-Algerian relations which resulted lasted for several months. Finally the Algerians were faced with the considerable problem of finding alternative markets for their oil; more than half of it had previously been purchased by France. In the end they agreed to modify their claims somewhat. During the summer and fall of 1971 they worked out an agreement with the two major French companies which provided some compensation and promised not to take undue advantage of their position as majority stockholders.

For the time being the French retain sizable interests in Algerian oil and have guaranteed its outlets on the French market. But the power of decision is now firmly in Algerian hands. De Gaulle's grand design of Franco–Algerian friendship and co-operation has come to an end. His successor, Georges Pompidou, formally admitted this when he said that from now on only national interests would determine French policy on Algeria and that this would include aid to development.

Algeria is the first developing country to have gained so rapidly— in less than a decade since independence—complete control over her oil and natural gas resources. Thus she can draw maximum benefits, both in foreign exchange earnings and in cheap fuel and raw materials for her industries, especially petrochemicals.

She accepts the minority participation of foreign companies in order to involve them in the heavy risks and costs of oil exploration, and to use the highly specialized equipment and skills which are still not available locally. Increasingly, however, Algeria acts as an independent agent on the world market through her national company SONATRACH. This can be seen in the agreement between SONA-TRACH and the El Paso Gas Company which calls for the yearly purchase of 10 billion cubic meters of liquefied natural gas for a period of 25 years. In order to fulfill this contract SONATRACH will have to make substantial investments in liquefying plants and pipelines. She plans to finance this investment independently, with only a few international loans.

After economic independence, the major objectives of the Algerian revolution have been to modernize and expand the economy. Political as much as economic motives have determined the priorities within these overall goals.

The leading sector of the Algerian economy before independence . was large-scale export agriculture run by Europeans. It accounted for a major portion of the savings generated by the economy, most of which were invested locally. The Arab agriculture, as we said earlier, was mainly subsistence farming. The profits of the relatively small mining industry were largely transferred out of the country as dividends to French shareholders. Shortly before independence, the *Plan de Constantine* took into account the newly discovered oil resources and emphasized both industrialization and the modernization of Arab agriculture to improve rapidly conditions for the rural population.

When the Algerian government was in a position to plan the country's economic development, considerable changes had already taken place. The exodus of the European settlers had dislocated export agriculture, and the Arab agriculture had been a major casualty of the war. Livestock had been substantially reduced, and far less land was under cultivation. The new oil and natural gas production, however, had opened up new opportunities for industrialization, and was providing rapidly growing resources of foreign exchange for its financing.

The Algerian government decided to give absolute priority to industrialization and to put the main emphasis on the creation of heavy industries. This policy represented an endeavor to imitate the Soviet pattern of development, whose success in establishing a basis for both economic and military power made it particularly attractive to a country guided by socialist as well as nationalist aspirations. There were also valid economic reasons in the existence of abundant raw materials: iron ore, phosphates for the production of fertilizers, above all oil and natural gas for the petrochemical industry. Furthermore, in an economy where all industrial investment adheres strictly to government plans, heavy industries would logically lead to secondary plants for the utilization and further processing of their output. Thus the production of iron and steel should encourage domestic manufacture of machinery and motor vehicles. The availability of petrochemicals should give rise to the manufacture of the numerous products made out of plastics. Finally, heavy industry should facilitate the modernization of agriculture by supplying it with fertilizers and farm machinery.

Heavy industry, as we know, is capital-intensive, and its initial cost of construction is particularly high. On the other hand, the complex high level technology which it requires provides a challenge and meets the aspirations of ambitious young Algerian managers. They are anxious to prove to themselves and to the world that they can create and operate the most sophisticated industry, that they can compete with the traditional industrial countries.

In making their choice the Algerians knew all the drawbacks of the new heavy industries. It would be a while before they could benefit the mass of the people and raise their standard of living; at the very least, no improvement could take place until ancillary consumer goods industries were developed. On the contrary, the concentration of investment on heavy industry would probably retard such progress. Furthermore, the capacity of the new plants, initially at any rate, would be in excess of the domestic demand. A substantial part of their output would have to be exported to the highly competitive world market, and this would reduce if not completely offset their profitability. Thus in 1969, at the start, the pig iron plant in Annaba had to sell part of its output to Japan, one of the world's greatest producers. Finally, heavy industry creates little employment. This is particularly serious for a country like Algeria with a rapidly growing surplus of labor. By the time it reaches its planned capacity of 1.4 million tons, the iron and steel industry will offer only 1,400 jobs, and the phosphate fertilizer plant, 450.

The first comprehensive development plan for Algeria covered the period from 1970 to 1973 and allocated 45 per cent of investments to industry, including oil. Most of the new enterprises and all large-scale ones are state-owned, national companies. They enjoy a large degree of autonomy and are operated nearly single-handedly by government-appointed managers. There are a few cases of joint companies where the foreign partner is limited to a minority share. In most cases, however, the national companies simply purchase the machinery abroad, or even import fully equipped plants. Great care is taken to diversify sources of supply and avoid excessive reliance on any one country. Thus the iron and steel plant at Annaba was supplied with equipment for pig iron from France, for raw steel from the Soviet Union, for rolled steel from Italy, and for tubes from West Germany.

Although industry may ultimately determine Algeria's future, the country at present is still very much dependent on agriculture. In 1969 it provided 63 per cent of total employment. Yet agriculture has considerably deteriorated. Both production and income have declined in comparison to the level reached just before the war of independence.

Traditional Arab agriculture covers about 75 per cent of all arable land and employs nearly 80 per cent of the rural labor force (over 1 million in 1966). It has more or less recovered from the losses incurred during the war, especially in the number of livestock. But its methods of production have remained primitive. The government has provided aid mainly through increased farm credit, with little or no technical guidance. As yet it has not succeeded in stimulating production. About half of the output of this sector does not appear on the market but is consumed by the peasants and their families, in many cases "extended families" which include uncles and cousins. The traditional character of agriculture thus ensures the subsistence of a large number of disguised unemployed or under-employed.

The socialist agriculture which was established on large modern farms previously owned by the French settlers, enlarged somewhat later with the addition of all other foreign-owned land, faced from the outset serious problems of organization and management. Under the principle of self-management the administration of the farms was entrusted to a committee and a president elected by all the workers. This system is applied in Yugoslavia, mainly in the industrial sector, and appears not to have impaired efficient operation there; actually, it seems to have been even reasonably successful. But the level of general and technical education among Arab farm workers in Algeria was far too low to provide competent leadership from the rank and file. To resolve this difficulty the government appointed directors for the 2,200 farms (whose number had been reduced by mergers). Conflicts of competence and personality frequently arose between the directors and the elected presidents. Further complicating the problem was the fact that all the socialist farms were subordinated to a central body, the Office for Land Reform. It gave out general directives, established programs of cultivation, and regulated the supply of fertilizers, seeds, and other necessities.

The combination of over-centralization and local incompetence and disorganization produced catastrophic results. The volume of output declined and its quality deteriorated. This was particularly damaging to export products which had to remain competitive on European markets. It was estimated that the gross product of the socialist sector declined from 2.2 billion francs in 1961 to 900 million in 1967.[6] Although it was highly profitable in the past, it became a drain on the economy. By the end of 1968 the public treasury had to forgo payment of 1 billion dinars (more than $200 million) which represented credits made to these estates. Most of them were unable even to cover current expenditures out of their receipts. There were no resources left for investment or adequate maintenance, so that equipment deteriorated, could not be replaced, all this reducing the net value of previous investments. In the absence of profits, the income of workers could not rise, and it remained more or less the same as before independence. With such negative results the first popular enthusiasm for self-management began to wane, resulting in lack of interest and absenteeism.

Although less committed to self-management than its predecessor,

6. Viratelle, *op. cit.*, p. 134.

the Boumedienne government could not accept the failure of an institution which had been considered a major achievement of the Algerian revolution. In February of 1969 major changes were introduced. The centralized direction of agriculture was abolished and a co-operative organization for the sale of produce and for accounting was introduced. The workers were granted social security and were given the right to own small individual plots which they could farm for their own use. But they would forfeit these plots if they did not fulfill their obligations to the estate.

A major problem for socialist agriculture was the danger of losing the entire French market for its most important product: wine. Algeria's vineyards had all been developed originally to satisfy consumers in France, and under the Evian treaty France had agreed to purchase large quantities of wine at a guaranteed high price. But this provision was part and parcel of the general preferential trading relationship. When the oil treaty was broken, there was less incentive for France to favor Algerian wine. Pressure from the French wine growers built up against further imports. They asserted with some reason that France had now also become independent of Algeria, not only Algeria of France.

Nonetheless, the most serious agricultural problem is the fact that food production up to now has scarcely managed to attain its pre-war level. In 1968, 1,532,000 tons of wheat were produced, in comparison with 1,505,000 tons in 1960.[7] But in the meantime the population increased by over 25 per cent, in spite of the European exodus. Food imports are therefore an increasing drain on the balance of payments. In 1959, agricultural exports paid for 89 per cent of imports of food and supplies for agriculture. In 1969, agricultural exports covered only 72 per cent of these imports. Only an intensive program to spur farm production could bring about any improvement, and it is not likely to happen as long as agriculture receives only a small fraction of all anticipated investments—15 per cent for 1970 to 1973.[8]

As we mentioned earlier, the most serious drawback of a development policy based on heavy industry is its low employment record. Unemployment is already extremely high in Algeria, and will inevitably grow. The census of 1966 revealed that out of 2,832,000 in the labor force only 1,652,000—including workers abroad—were employed.[9] This is a ratio of 40 per cent full-time or part-time unem-

7. *United Nations Statistical Yearbook, 1969,* United Nations, New York, 1970, table 43.

8. Viratelle, *op. cit.,* p. 193.

9. Viratelle, *op. cit.,* p. 193.

ployment. From 1960 to 1966 the volume of employment remained static. The ranks of the unemployed during that period swelled in direct proportion to the growth in the labor force. At present the yearly rate of growth is 100,000 and is expected to reach 150,000 in a few years. The estimated number of additional jobs which could be created in the economy is 30,000. This leaves a staggering increase in unemployment of at least 70,000. Moreover, this does not even take into account the fact that the present labor force is over 90 per cent male. Should women enter the job market, the numbers would be much larger.

The government expects confidently that employment in industry will double from 1970 to 1975. In 1966 it amounted only to 160,000. The hope is that the establishment of heavy industries will have a multiplier effect, with the development of other widely diversified industries and the modernization of agriculture. This would indeed create an enormous demand for labor. According to some official statements, Algeria could easily support in 1980 a population of 20 million, going from 12.1 million in 1966, to 13.7 million in 1970, and might even then have a shortage of labor.

These forecasts seem highly optimistic in light of present levels of employment and the projections for the next decade. It appears unlikely that the yearly increase in the labor force, together with existing unemployment, could be absorbed into the economy by that time.

The emigration of workers to France has partially relieved this situation. It started before independence, when there were no restrictions on the movement of workers between Algeria and France. Under the Evian Agreement the right of Algerians to enter France was guaranteed, but certain regulations were introduced to prevent a mass influx. At present 35,000 new workers are admitted each year; the actual figure may vary, however, subject to the requirements of the French economy. In 1970, the total number of Algerians in France was estimated at 600,000, with 400,000 employed as workers. What they sent back to their families in Algeria came to 1.2 billion francs in 1969, or about 8 per cent of the country's gross national product. These remittances are the main support of innumerable households that cannot subsist on their earnings from traditional agriculture. With this additional income they can remain in their villages and not join the ranks of the urban unemployed.

The vital importance of this emigration to Algeria as an outlet for surplus labor and a major source of income is forging a new dependence on France. It gives the latter some leverage in negotiating Franco–Algerian agreements, although one must remember that it is profitable to both countries. It is a handy source of unskilled labor which is as much in short supply in France as in other countries of Western Europe.

The extremely high rate of population growth is responsible for this increase in the labor force. Earlier marriages have caused the birth rate to shoot upward since independence. In 1969 it was estimated at 4.7 to 4.8 per cent. With a death rate of 1.6 to 1.7 per cent, this brings the rate of net population growth to 3.2 per cent, one of the highest in the world. The impact of this population explosion has been to increase unemployment, as well as the minimum requirements for food, housing, education, and other services. This has put a heavy burden on the Algerian economy, and has retarded its development.

Viratelle has found little opposition to birth control among the Algerian population, including even the Moslem clergy. The spread of birth control has been prevented largely by the shortage of contraceptives and the ignorance of the women, who are generally illiterate. The government itself at first was rather hesitant on the matter. In June of 1969, however, Colonel Boumedienne formally opposed birth control as a false answer to Algeria's population problem, which development will resolve. His attitude reflects the traditional nationalist approach of the military and the conviction that maximum numbers are a basic element of military strength. It gives little thought to the economic and social aspects of development.

In summary we can say that the Algerian revolution, with its combined nationalist and socialist objectives, has been markedly successful in fulfilling its patriotic aspiration of economic independence and of establishing a powerful national state.

Its success in establishing a socialist economy depends on the kind of socialism one has in mind. There has been a considerable change in emphasis. It was thought at first that Algerian socialism would have a spontaneous and popular character, along Castroist lines. Self-management was the best expression of this ideal. With Boumedienne there was a switch to managerial socialism, which its opponents call state capitalism; this can be seen in the national companies which direct industrial development. The emphasis on equalitarianism, on active popular participiation, has diminished. The private sector in trade and small industry not only survives but prospers. Boumedienne has stated that he has no intention of expropriating Algerian-owned enterprises, as opposed to foreign-owned holdings.[10]

10. Viratelle, *op. cit.*

The concentration on heavy industry has accelerated the expansion of the economy but postponed major improvements in the standard of living of the rural population. This is particularly true for the overwhelming majority who subsist on traditional agriculture. While no official data have been published, reports indicate that the real per capita income has hardly, if at all, increased since independence. The rejection of family planning has postponed even further any prospect of substantial improvement in the rural areas, particularly since they essentially must bear the cost of the rapidly growing disguised unemployed.

Up to now no effort has been made, as in China, to mobilize this idle manpower for productive labor-intensive tasks. A major program of land improvement has been recommended by many experts and is long overdue. It would provide useful employment and augment the productivity of traditional agriculture. But it would also necessitate extensive reform in land tenure which the government for political reasons does not seem ready yet to undertake.

Despite these drawbacks, and with a strong and competent government, Algeria in the long run will most probably achieve economic and social development within a state socialist framework. The spread of industrialization and the massive campaign which has been undertaken in education and training should raise the living standard of the population. The sacrifices will not be equally shared during the transitional period, which may extend over several decades. But by appealing to nationalist and religious feelings the government will most likely succeed in winning active support, or at least passive acceptance, for its policies, even from those who must shoulder the main burden of the official doctrine of socialist austerity.

IVORY COAST: AN EXAMPLE OF SUCCESSFUL CAPITALIST DEVELOPMENT

The economic development of the Ivory Coast started only around 1950 with the opening of the deep sea harbor of Abidjan. This made it possible to export the output of fertile agricultural lands in the country's southeast region. In the last decade of French colonial rule, from 1950 to 1960, the economy made quite rapid progress, with a rate of growth in gross domestic product of 7 to 8 per cent (measured at constant prices). Since independence the pace has even accelerated; between 1960 and 1965, according to the estimates of Samir Amin, the annual rate was as high as 11 to 12 per cent.

The economic policy of the Ivory Coast is based on private enterprise; national planning, as in France, is of a purely indicative nature. Public investment provides mainly a framework, and an economic and social infrastructure, for the development of private businesses. Foreign investment is encouraged in fields such as manufacturing, lumbering, and export crops. The investment code is liberal, with no limitations on the transfer of profits or the repatriation of invested capital. The Ivory Coast has maintained close economic relations with its former metropolitan country. It receives from France substantial technical and financial aid, as well as the bulk of its private investment capital. It is also associated with the European Economic Community.

The progress achieved by the Ivory Coast is illustrated in the table below which shows the increase in per capita and in the total Gross National Product.

Table XVIII

	G.N.P. (in million $)	Per Capita G.N.P. (in $)
1958	439	142
1963	764	208
1965	924	241
1966	1,005	256
1967	1,079	269
1968	1,248	304

Source: United Nations Statistical Yearbook, 1969, United Nations, New York, 1970, table 183.

This impressive growth is the result of a high and rapidly increasing rate of investment, and of the great effectiveness of these investments. Samir Amin, whose study is the most detailed analysis of progress in the Ivory Coast, estimates that the gross rate of investment went from 14.7 per cent in 1950—already quite substantial for a developing country—to 18.6 per cent in 1965.[11] The capital output ratio dropped at the same time from 2.5 to 1.7, accelerating thus the rate of growth of the G.N.P. from 7.5 per cent between 1950 and 1960 to 11.5 per cent in the next five years that followed.

The structure and nature of the investments have undergone considerable changes. At the beginning, that is from 1950 to 1955, public investment comprised 60 per cent of the sum total. It was used mainly to develop the infrastructure (transport), the administrative and social services, electric power, and agriculture. Gradually private

11. Samir Amin, *Le developpement du capitalism en Côte d'Ivoire*, Editions du Seuil, Paris, 1967, p. 229.

investments grew in importance and since 1960 have taken over 60 per cent. Industry, which received only 12 per cent of all investments in the first decade, was allocated 25 per cent in the next five years, from 1960 to 1965. The direct yield of investments in the infrastructure is quite low; expanding the area under cultivation—where the main expenditure is for clearing the land—is far more profitable. Light consumer goods industries have also been able to make good use of the resources invested.

Public investment before independence was largely financed by the French treasury under the Development Plan for French Overseas Territories. Since 1960, the Ivory Coast has managed to finance 65 per cent of its public investment program with local resources, budget surpluses, and domestic loans. More than half of the remaining 35 per cent comes from French and Common Market grants and the rest in foreign loans. Foreign private investment—including reinvestment by foreign-owned companies—has remained at the same level, about 20 per cent of total investment from 1960 to 1965.

The development plan for 1966 to 1970 gave top priority to agriculture and education. In agriculture the emphasis was placed on food crops to cover rapidly growing consumption needs, and on industrial crops through intensive cultivation and greater use of fertilizer and reforestation. The prime objective of educational development was to broaden the base of primary education. The proportion of children who went to school varied widely from 65 per cent in Abidjan to only 15 per cent in the North, the least developed and populated area. But the most urgent need was to train local personnel who could replace in the near future expatriate managers, technicians, administrators, and foremen in industry, trade, and large-scale agriculture. In 1965 nationals of the Ivory Coast filled only 20 per cent of the managerial and 10 per cent of the technical posts.

At the start of economic development export agriculture was the leading sector in the economy. Coffee and cocoa had been pushed during the 1950's to meet the demand of the French market, and enjoyed high tariff protection. By the end of the colonial period the total production of the Ivory Coast and other French territories had outgrown the needs of the metropolitan market, posing a considerable problem. It had to be sold in other countries, and the difference made up by the French treasury. Since independence, however, the Ivory Coast has enjoyed preferential treatment from the European Economic Community for coffee and cocoa exports.

The production of coffee went from a yearly average of 75,000 tons between 1952 and 1956 to 267,000 for 1967 and 1968. The Ivory Coast is the world's largest producer, after Brazil and Colombia. Limited by quotas under the International Coffee Agreement, the output is not expected to expand further. The United States has become a major market, in addition to the Common Market countries, especially since the increased use of instant coffee; the beans grown in the Ivory Coast have been found particularly suitable for that purpose. The production of cocoa grew from 64,680 tons between 1952 and 1956 to 139,300 tons in 1967 and 1968. Plans to expand it further are under consideration today.

Bananas, another traditional export product, has encountered increasing difficulties since 1964 because of stiffer competition in the Common Market countries. Great efforts have been made to diversify agricultural exports, and significant progress has already been made with pineapples, palm oil, and rubber. The production of cotton is also advancing rapidly, but it is intended mainly to cover the needs of the domestic industry.

The most spectacular results have been obtained in the exploitation of forests and the sale of lumber, which became the most important export in 1969. In 1954 only 292,000 cubic meters of logs were produced, but by 1965 the total had risen to 2,600,000. An increasing portion of all lumber is being processed for export into sawn timber and plywood.

The development of export agriculture was made possible to a great extent by the mass immigration of farm workers from neighboring countries, who provide most of the extra labor required. Another positive element was the fact that expanded cultivation of traditional food crops, such as root crops and tubers in particular, did not necessitate much extra labor. As the population increased, however, and as the country's purchasing power grew, there was a corresponding rise in the consumption of cereals, of rice especially, and a demand for imports. Systematic programs are under way, therefore, to develop rice production; so far it has increased from a yearly average of 109,000 tons between 1952 and 1956 to 365,000 in 1968, and the hope is that it will take care of all consumer needs by 1970.

As yet no important mineral resources of either metal ores or fuel have been discovered in the Ivory Coast.

Hydropower resources do exist but they are not of a size to meet the needs of power-intensive industries such as metal refining. But power has become more readily available and has gone from 67 to 440 million kwh. Plants are under construction now to produce much more thermic and hydropower in particular.

Industrialization has made great strides, especially since 1960. The total value of industrial production has quadrupled from 1960 to 1966. Up to now industrial development has concentrated mainly on light consumer goods industries. These would include processing domestic goods largely for export, producing sawn lumber, plywood, instant coffee, canned pineapples, palm oil, and more recently cotton fabrics. Light industry is also involved in the final stage of manufacturing, assembling and packaging imported products in the Ivory Coast, such as assembling passenger cars and trucks, bicycles, agricultural tools, producing flour and biscuits.

The plan now is to continue the industrialization of the Ivory Coast more or less along these lines, and to establish also a few heavy industries: a steel rolling mill (capacity 12,000 tons), a chemical fertilizer factory (capacity 61,000), a glass factory, and plants for the manufacture of electric batteries and air conditioners. The textile industry will have the most important increase in industrial capacity in weaving cotton fabrics, printing, and dyeing. Other significant projects in light industries include a sugar factory, a plant for manufacturing livestock feed, and wood pulp and furniture factories.

The foreign trade of the Ivory Coast has grown very fast, both in exports and imports. Nearly 80 per cent of all exports still consist of the traditional raw materials, and can be broken down as follows:

Table XIX
SHARE OF TOTAL EXPORTS
(in per cent)

	1967	1968	1969
Coffee	31.7	34.2	25.5
Cocoa	17.3	18.5	22.3
Lumber	27.1	24.6	29.7
Bananas	3.2	3.0	2.5

Source: Bulletin Statistique de la Côte d'Ivoire, mai 1970.

Bulletin de l'Afrique Noire: Mémento de l'économie et de la planification africaines 1968, Paris, 1969, p. 145.

Increasingly the major exports are being processed before shipping, although up to now this has only represented a small fraction of all exports. Of greater significance is the sale of cotton yarn and fabrics to neighboring countries of Africa, which has recently gotten under way.

The proportion of capital goods in imports rose from 29 to 35 per cent between 1950 and 1965. Intermediate goods, including fuel, increased from 12 to 21 per cent; consumer goods, including foods, declined from 59 to 44 per cent. The most important import items are motor vehicles, machinery, cotton fabrics, and petroleum products.

Throughout the whole period from 1960 to 1969, the balance of trade remained very satisfactory, as the table below would indicate.

Table XX
FOREIGN TRADE
(in million francs CFA)

Year	Exports	Imports	Surplus	Ratio of Surplus to Exports (per cent)
1960	37,229	29,611	7,618	20.8
1962	47,693	38,534	9,159	19.2
1963	56,818	41,908	14,910	26.2
1964	74,501	58,873	15,628	20.9
1965	68,418	58,343	10,075	14.7
1966	76,659	63,612	13,047	17.0
1967	80,263	65,050	15,213	18.9
1968	104,890	77,627	27,263	26.0
1969	118,223	86,284	31,939	27.0

Source: Bulletin de l'Afrique Noir: Mémento de l'economie et de la planification africaines 1968, Paris, 1969.

Bulletin Statistique de la Côte d'Ivoire, mai 1970.

The rapid economic development of the Ivory Coast had a visibly favorable impact on the income and the standard of living of the African population. This is reflected in the mass immigration of workers from neighboring countries in search of employment and higher wages and in the increased mass consumption of higher priced and quality foodstuffs such as cereals, rice, and bread, as well as industrial consumer goods. Samir Amin estimates that the rural per capita income grew by 35 per cent between 1960 and 1965. In spite of considerable expansion in housing, slums still surround the capital of Abidjan. But there is less abject poverty among the urban population than in other African capitals, and unemployment is also considerably lower.

Samir Amin, who has little sympathy for this capitalist type of development, recognizes nonetheless that up to now it has been quite successful. It has shown that export agriculture can be a starting point at least for rapid economic growth. With skillful leadership from private foreign enterprises, projects for investment have been selected with rational criteria. Competent management has ensured smooth operation. The Ivory Coast has been able to avoid the mistakes which so often are made in a planned economy, where in the absence of trained personnel and direct responsibility resources are wasted and opportunities thrown away. An efficient light industry has been created, an achievement which no African state has been able to match in a socialist pattern of development.

This type of development has serious drawbacks, however, according to Samir Amin. The obvious one is that such a development must soon reach its upper limits. The extensive cultivation of export crops cannot expand forever but must be restricted to the arable land available. World markets for most primary products are shrinking, and terms of trade will deteriorate. Import-replacing industries cannot develop beyond the saturation point of a small domestic market. This has occurred already under similar circumstances in other African countries. Only heavy industry can furnish the impetus for self-perpetuating economic growth, but it requires a domestic market which is much larger than that of a small country such as the Ivory Coast. As development slows down in the Ivory Coast, the flow of foreign capital into the country will cease, and the problem of transferring profits abroad may cause increasing difficulty. Even more important, from Samir Amin's point of view, is the fact that the existing pattern of development perpetuates the dominant role of foreign capital in the Ivory Coast. It is the chief motor and therefore the chief beneficiary of any progress there. The participation of European income in the non-agricultural sector of the economy has remained constant throughout 1950 to 1965, but since this sector has grown more rapidly than the rest of the economy, the European share overall has increased substantially. The gross profit of foreign corporations has risen from 7 to 14 per cent of the country's G.N.P. In spite of progress made, the country remains entirely dependent on foreign capital. According to Samir Amin it has had economic growth but no real development. The latter implies structural changes and the achievement in particular of economic independence.

Many of Samir Amin's points are well taken. One cannot dispute the fact that the Ivory Coast as yet does not stand on her own economically, and that the present course of development cannot be pursued indefinitely. But was there a better alternative? In the absence of ample mineral and energy resources, as in Ghana or Guinea, it was obviously impossible to base economic development on heavy industry. This would have necessitated an even greater reliance on foreign capital. Furthermore, there would have had to be a large regional market. The political situation in Africa today would not encourage optimism on that score for the near future.

It seems clear, in any event, that the government does recognize the limitations of its present policies and is trying to modify them somewhat. Thus in the field of education most programs are designed to replace gradually expatriate personnel; this would reduce the European presence and their share of the national income. Public assistance is being given to small and medium-scale industry to stimulate African entrepreneurship. The government is becoming a partner in large-scale enterprises, along with foreign and domestic private capital. Thus, for instance, it acquired recently a majority participation in the country's biggest rubber plantation company.

At present the government is stressing above all greater diversification in the economy and the establishment of basic industries. As we said earlier, some progress has already been made in this area. With the rapid growth of public revenues, from 15 per cent in 1950 to 20 per cent of the national income in 1965, public savings have also greatly increased, and can now cover most public investment expenditures. Private domestic savings have risen, too, so that more and more investments can be financed out of domestic resources. Samir Amin calculated that of the total investment program, 74 per cent was locally financed by 1965. If this trend persists, there should be less pressure on the balance of payments from the transferring abroad of profits on foreign investments.

There are unquestionably drawbacks and limitations in this kind of economic development. But in our view, the Ivory Coast does prove that development can be successfully launched along traditionally capitalist lines by making full use of existing resources.

TANZANIA: RURAL AFRICAN SOCIALISM

Nearly all of the countries in Africa, especially those that have recently become independent, have espoused the socialist philosophy. One of the few exceptions is, as we have just seen, the Ivory Coast. Several have followed more or less strictly the Soviet model of organization and government, with centralized planning and direct control over every facet of the economy. But in most of the other countries the socialist ideology reveals itself primarily in a fierce opposition to foreign capitalism. It does not necessarily bring forth an equalitarian society, nor in many cases does it prevent a new indigenous ruling class from stepping into the shoes of their former colonial masters, when they see that political power opens the door to wealth.

In Tanzania, on the contrary, we see an attempt to introduce an authentic socialist society which is unique and totally independent of any existing pattern. It draws its inspiration from the traditional African village communities, emphasizes rural development rather than industrialization, and relies on persuasion, not coercion.

This experiment is the brain child of one man, Julius Nyerere, who created the Tanganyikan African National Union (TANU) in 1954 and became Tanzania's President after her independence in 1961. Nyerere's Arusha Declaration in February of 1967 described for the first time in detail the tenets of Tanzanian socialism and their practical implications. But all government policies have been guided by this philosophy since Tanzania's independence.

The basis of Nyerere's ideology is in his rejection of both capitalism, which permits the exploitation of man by man, and the Marxist dogma, which stresses that class struggle is needed to bring about a classless socialist society. He considers that there existed already a classless society in Africa in the traditional extended family and village community, although in a very primitive form.[12] There it was founded on mutual respect, on the obligation of all who could to work and on a fair distribution of the fruits of this labor. His goal thus is to revive and modernize these socialist *ujamaa* communities and to bring about the economic and social development of the country within this framework.

Nyerere realizes that a *ujamaa* type of development will probably evolve more slowly than its capitalist counterpart. Beginnings of capitalism can already be seen in Tanzania, not only in the cities but also in the rural areas. Some particularly energetic farmers have tried to expand their cultivation of cash crops by hiring less successful neighbours as wage laborers. Thus one finds that entrepreneurial aspirations can lead to exploitative practices and are starting to destroy the fabric of the traditional society with its sense of fraternal equality. At the risk even of slowing down progress in the standard of living, of cutting back on the production of material goods, Nyerere thinks it essential to preserve the "quality of life."[13]

He has therefore urged farmers to come forward of their own free

12. Julius Nyerere, *Freedom and Socialism*, Oxford University Press, London, p. 338.

13. There was only one other similar attempt to revive traditional pre-capitalist rural institutions as a basis for a socialist transformation of society. It occurred in pre-revolutionary Russia. There the populist socialists, the *narodniki* propagated the revival of the old village communities, the *mir*. The *narodniki* had a considerable following among the peasantry, but were wiped out during the October Revolution.

will and participate in *ujamaa* village communities by joining their lands together. Initially the members might contribute only a portion of their individual plots to the common pool which they would then farm as a group, dividing the proceeds in proportion to the amount of work done. Provisions would be made for taxes, for investment, and for the needs of the aged and the sick who could not work. The community would be administered by elected officers, but all major decisions—on crops to be planted, on public works of interest to all the members, such as roads, schools, and wells, which would be carried out by them—would have to be approved in a village assembly by everyone in the community. Government agricultural and community development services should give only limited guidance and technical assistance.

The Arusha Declaration spells out the policies and the rules which the members of the TANU party must follow. Under the present one-party system, TANU has grave responsibilities and must therefore abide by a particularly strict code of conduct. The Executive Committee of TANU has approved the Declaration which defines socialism in terms of an obligation to work on the part of all those capable of doing so without the use of exploitative or coercive tactics. It implies, further, public control of all major means of production and exchange, including land, natural resources such as water and minerals, public utilities, the news media, banks, insurance, exports, imports, and wholesale trade. All large-scale industries which employ a great number of workers, and all large plantations, are nationalized. The Declaration points out that Tanzanian socialism is democratic, and that this represents not only an economic system of public ownership, but above all a sincere commitment to the socialist ideal.

Strong emphasis is put on the need for self-reliance. Man and not money must be at the center of development. In the reverse a poor country like Tanzania would have no chance of developing. One should not rely on foreign aid or investment. Both can be useful, but can also jeopardize a country's independence if they take on too great a role in the economy. There should be less accent placed on industrialization while domestic financial resources are still scarce, because this involves heavy investment. More attention should be given to the condition of the rural population. There is an acknowledgement here that most investments in the past financed projects such as roads, utilities, schools, and hospitals, which all profited the cities for the most part, although the proceeds of taxes levied principally on peasants paid for them. The Arusha Declaration makes it quite clear that the country's biggest effort must focus on agriculture, which will continue to support the majority of the population for a long time. Along with food for domestic consumption, agriculture also provides foreign exchange essential for development through the proceeds of agricultural exports. Production can be increased at relatively little expense by working harder and improving methods of cultivation.

Finally, the Declaration of Arusha anticipates the possibility that high government or TANU officials may move away from the pure socialist ideal, and forbids them to hold directorships, or even own shares, in private companies. They cannot own houses rented out to other persons, or receive more than one salary. Presumably, therefore, it would be impossible for them to amass a private fortune.

Has Nyerere's experiment worked? Is Tanzania progressing on the road to economic development and a gradual, peaceable transformation into a socialist society? Again it is far too soon to draw definite conclusions. The evolutionary process which Nyerere has launched by definition must be very slow. The expected changes can only gradually become apparent. Too, one must remember that for the most part since independence Nyerere's philosophy has been invoked only in Tanzania's general policy. There were no clear guidelines before the Arusha Declaration for concrete matters such as industrialization, ownership of enterprises, foreign aid, and investment. Thus one can see a significant change in emphasis in the Second Five-Year Plan, which is not philosophical but the result of the experience with the First Five-Year Plan.

The absence of tribal tensions has facilitated economic as well as political progress in Tanzania. The country is made up of a large number of small tribes. Tribal loyalties, therefore, have presented less of an obstacle to nationhood than has been the case in several African countries, where conflict between a few major tribes has impeded development and has endangered internal peace and stability. The existence of an indigenous *lingua franca*, Swahili, is also an important cohesive force. It is at least understood, if not generally spoken, throughout the country, and could be proclaimed the official language.

The representatives of external aid organizations have repeatedly pointed to the constructive and realist attitude of the government, and most of the public officials, as an even more valuable contribution to Tanzania's progress. No demagogic statements have been issued; policies are not being adopted purely on the basis of their appeal to popular prejudice. Corruption has been nearly non-existent. Nyerere did not promise his people a rapid improvement in their lives when the country became independent, but instead called upon them to work that much harder. The official attitude toward European and

Asian minorities, who previously dominated the modern sector of the economy, and whose skills and resources are still difficult to replace, has been far more tolerant than in neighboring countries. Tanzania has adopted a pragmatic approach to foreign aid and private investment. Aid has been accepted from both the East and the West with the provision that it comes without strings attached and does not conflict with the general policies of the country. The scope of private investment has been gradually reduced, but nationalization of existing investments did not create a major problem because compensation was granted to the investors.

The First Five-Year Plan for 1964 to 1969 had fixed on an average rate of growth of Gross Domestic Product of 6.7 per cent as its main objective. The money economy would grow at a rate of 8.5 per cent while the subsistence economy, which still accounts for more than half of the agricultural output, would naturally have to progress more slowly. With an estimated increase in population per year of 2.1 per cent, the per capita income would rise at the rapid rate of 4.6 per cent.

The major emphasis of the Plan was placed on expanding agricultural production. As the Arusha Declaration pointed out also, this was essential to ensure a large enough domestic food supply, and above all to generate more export proceeds. The Plan outlined a program of developing co-operatives and extending services and local initiative within the framework of community development. In addition, there was a project to organize several pilot village settlements. Most of the funds allocated to agriculture under the Plan, which represent 14 per cent of all investments, would be devoted to them.

Investment in industry would require only 24 per cent of the total and would be used primarily in the private sector to establish or expand import-replacing consumer goods industries. Both private trade and co-operatives would participate in the effort to improve distribution. Substantial investments were made in economic and social infrastructure: transport, health, and education in particular.

Because of the low per capita income in Tanzania and the small ratio of domestic savings—which did increase, however, under the Plan from 7 to 12 per cent of the G.D.P.—it was absolutely essential to bring in a large amount of external resources to finance all these projects. Domestic resources could cover only 46 per cent of the overall investment planned. This was already an improvement over the 40 per cent of the early 1960's. But more than half of the sum total still had to come from outside sources, through loans and private investments, and about 10 per cent through grants. The Plan here seemed to disregard Nyerere's caution about the hazards of foreign capital.

The targets of the First Five-Year Plan unfortunately were not reached. Gross Domestic Product at constant prices did grow on an average of 4.4 per cent a year. But the 2.7 per cent rate of increase for population was higher than had been anticipated, and per capita income rose only by 1.7 per cent.

The catastrophic fall in the world price of sisal, Tanzania's main export product, was largely responsible for the failure of per capita income to fulfill the Plan's expectations. From 1963 to 1968 the value of the sisal crop dropped from 442 to 155 million shillings—that is, by 65 per cent—while in actual volume it only went down from 214,000 to 194,000 tons, less than 10 per cent. This loss of revenue could not be fully compensated for by an increase in cotton and coffee, the other major crops. The overall production of cash crops, therefore, declined from 1,038 to 974 million shillings.

Another serious failure was the experiment of transforming agriculture along socialist lines with village settlement schemes. New villages were created to permit the mechanized cultivation of land, and in many cases their fields had to be irrigated or drained. The venture turned out to be completely out of line with Tanzania's needs and possibilities. It was a wasteful use of such scarce resources as capital and skilled personnel, and had to be discontinued in 1966, in spite of the high hopes which this experiment had raised. The less ambitious and dramatic assistance given to farmers in providing them with technical advice and marketing services proved far more effective.

The Five-Year Plan called for far more external aid than was in fact received. Foreign aid financed 35 per cent of government development expenditure, instead of the 78 per cent that the Tanzanians had counted on. Therefore, investments that were actually made under the Plan represented only 86.2 per cent of the original amount planned. If one takes into account the rise in prices, one sees that the discrepancy was even greater. The accuracy of Nyerere's warning about the role of foreign aid in a developing country seems in hindsight all the more impressive. The reasons for the reduction in external aid were political, a consequence of Nyerere's deliberate decision to prefer the right to assert the independence of Tanzania's policies over any foreign aid that he might receive. His attitude provoked the United Kingdom and West Germany, two of the largest donor countries, to suspend their aid. (Later this proved to have been only a temporary interruption.) Tanzania broke diplomatic relations with Great Britain in protest against the latter's policy toward Rhodesia. She established relations with East Germany although she was quite aware of the fact that this might well preclude any further aid from the Bonn government.

Employment, too, did not progress according to the Plan. In estate agriculture, especially in sisal, it dropped by one third. In spite of the expansion of non-agricultural employment, there was no overall increase in employment. This left the new members who were added on every year to the labor force without hope of finding a job. In part the considerable upgrading of the wage scale, and the legal minimum wage rate, was a definite factor in cutting down employment in the sisal plantations at a time when prices were falling.

But there were some significant achievements during the First Five-Year Plan. Manufacturing grew at the rapid rate of 11 per cent a year. The production of textiles quadrupled. The supply of cotton goods expanded to the point where it could nearly satisfy local demand. A start was made in oil refining and in the production of cement.

The Second Five-Year Plan, which covers the period from 1969 to 1974, has taken all these results into account. Far more emphasis, for instance, is placed on domestic resources, which are supposed to cover 60 per cent of total investment expenditure. There is a target of 6.5 per cent for the average growth in GDP. On the more realistic assumption that population will continue to grow at an annual rate of 2.7 per cent, per capita income should increase yearly by 3.8 per cent, again a more reasonable figure.

Rural development and agriculture are given first priority in the Second Five-Year Plan. Ninety per cent of the country's population still lives on farms, and agriculture in 1968 accounted for 50 per cent of the G.D.P. The creation of new *ujamaa* villages will be stressed, but once again only through persuasion, never by force. Government assistance and guidance can be made more effectively within the framework of the *ujamaas*, and it is easier to accustom the villagers there to the notion of "self-help" which can then become a major tool of development. Whatever improvement shall be made in agricultural methods and equipment will be kept in line with the resources and skills accessible to most farmers. Thus, for instance, it makes more sense to switch from the hoe to the animal-drawn plough than to tractors, which are out of reach for the majority of farmers.

The Plan outlines a program to improve conditions in the rural areas and to make the standard of living there more on a par with that of the urban population. A sense of fair play alone would have called for such a move, but it was also necessary in order to combat the lure of the cities. Here again the Plan turns to the *ujamaas* because it is much easier to improve the quality of education, health, welfare, and public utilities for farmers there than for those who live dispersed in a multitude of small hamlets.

A reform of education, and of primary education in particular, is being introduced gradually in Tanzania to integrate schools into the work and life of the community. Each primary school will be associated with a farm where the pupils will work, since most of them will eventually become farmers. The danger that the young will desert the farms seems easier to overcome if they can acquire knowledge about their future work and become proud of their profession.

New laws were passed in 1967 to bridge the gap in income between the urban and rural areas, and to put an end to the inflationary rise in wages. In accordance with this legislation, increases in wages should not exceed increases in productivity. In any event the annual increment cannot go higher than 5 per cent.

After the Arusha Declaration in 1967, the government acquired control of a number of factories previously owned on the whole by foreign interests, and a basic change took place in industry. (The government at the same time also nationalized the big sisal plantations and operates them now as state farms.) The government-owned National Development Corporation (NDC) is now at the center of industrial development. It controls the operation of fully or partly government-owned enterprises. In accordance with the Arusha Declaration, the industries which are not slated for public ownership are open to private investors and guarantees will be given to them. The government has invited foreign interests to establish enterprises on their own or in association with the NDC. The second alternative has been more attractive for foreign capital since it promises greater security.

Industrial investment under the Second Five-Year Plan will concentrate primarily on industries which can replace imported consumer goods, and on plants processing raw materials, such as large-scale sisal pulp and paper plant. Integration within the East African Economic Community, which includes Kenya and Uganda, has offered broader opportunities, but there are also some special problems which must be resolved. This association should have facilitated industrialization by creating a large domestic market which would justify the establishment of huge plants benefiting from economies of scale. Tanzania, however, is far less industrialized than Kenya and feels therefore that she will not profit as much from the East African Economic Community. To compensate for this, she is levying taxes on some of the industrial imports from Kenya.

In the field of transportation the prime aim of projects started under the Second Five-Year Plan is to establish a convenient link between Tanzania and Zambia. This would permit Dar es Salaam to become the outlet for Zambia's exports, for its copper in particular.

The desire to attract this lucrative transit trade is secondary here to the political motive. Imperative in the thinking of a passionate African like Nyerere is the necessity to break Zambia's dependence on the railroad of "white supremacist Rhodesia" and on the harbors of Portuguese Mozambique. Up to now these have been Zambia's only export routes. Tanzania therefore applied to the World Bank for assistance in the construction of a Tanzania–Zambia railroad. But the Bank's preliminary feasibility study found that traffic projections would not justify the heavy costs of a railroad, and they recommended instead the construction of a highway as a more economical alternative. This road is in the process of being built with outside financing from the United States.

Public opinion in Africa, however, felt very strongly that the only real substitute for the Rhodesia–Mozambique railway would have been this Tanzania–Zambia railroad. The World Bank's rejection was deeply resented in Tanzania, and it is not surprising, therefore, that Communist China's offer to build the railroad, and to provide financing, equipment, even manpower, was accepted with gratitude. Now both the railroad and the highway are being built at the same time.

Only fragmentary data were available on the results of the Second Five-Year Plan when this book went to press. In its first year we do know that per capita income went up more or less according to schedule. Exact figures in any event, however, would not be sufficient to determine the future success of Tanzania's experiment in introducing through gradual and peaceful means a socialist system that is largely rural. Far more telling, in this case, is the degree to which the peasant masses and the ruling élite, the President's own TANU party, have actively espoused and committed themselves to the ideals and ideas of Nyerere.

Nyerere's policy demands strict adherence to high moral standards, especially from the country's leadership. It offers them few material rewards. On the President's own initiative in 1966 his salary was reduced by 20 per cent, and those of his ministers and high government officials by 10 to 15 per cent. Reports suggest that these sacrifices were made willingly, sometimes even with pride. But actually there is no evidence to indicate the extent to which they were voluntary.

Tanzania's economic progress since independence has been steady, but relatively slow. The per capita income, which was estimated at $98 in 1970,[14] is one of the lowest in Africa. Obviously, with a capitalist system of development the prospects of rapid advancement would have

14. *United States AID Economic Data Book, 1971.*

been much greater for the most dynamic sectors of the population—the efficient cash crop producers, the managers, and the professionals.

At the same time, Nyerere's moderate attitude in racial matters, in his dealings with the West, in his relations with domestic and foreign capitalism, with the latter in particular, is known to irritate many younger leaders of TANU.[15] They are impatient with his gradualism and are calling for more drastic and violent methods. The appeal of Marxism, of Communist China especially, is growing stronger. They feel that China's system of equalitarian rural socialism would be far more effective in Tanzania and would yield swifter results than Nyerere's own approach. The support that China has given in the construction of the Tanzania–Zambia railroad—a symbol of African resistance to the vestiges of Western colonialism—when the project was turned down by the World Bank, is naturally reinforcing the bond of friendship with China. China's example is having a greater impact on Tanzanian thought today.

But the decisive influence is probably still Nyerere's own personality. He enjoys universal respect and admiration, even from those who do not approve of his policies. Reports also indicate in particular that his rural policy of gradual reform is easier to comprehend and accept for the peasant masses than either Marxist socialism or capitalist individualism would have been. If this is in fact the case, then Nyerere's base of domestic support is secure. This should allow sufficient time for his experiment to achieve its results. We have one important caveat, however. This optimistic prognosis does not take into account possible developments in the international field. An attitude on the part of the West which would be offensive to African nationalism might very well force Tanzania and her leader to adopt more extreme policies.

Latin America

CUBA: CASTRO'S COMMUNISM, SEMI-FAILURE, OR SEMI-SUCCESS?

In the period which preceded Castro's revolution, Cuba's economy maintained a close symbiotic relationship with the United States. One could almost say that Cuba was a *de facto* American colony, with most of the negative aspects of a colony and few of the advantages. Thus in contrast to Puerto Rico, it did not enjoy the right of free emigration to the United States, which would have absorbed its excess popula-

15. Henry Bienen, *Tanzania: Party Transformation and Economic Development*, Princeton University Press, Princeton, 1970, pp. 252–253.

tion and relieved the pressure of unemployment. Neither did Cuba have free excess to United States' markets, with the exception of a fixed quota for sugar. Thus there was no possibility of attracting United States capital and of taking advantage of low labor costs to develop an export industry. Yet American industrial products benefited from preferential tariffs which precluded competition from other industrial countries and effectively blocked the establishment of any domestic import replacement industry which could have competed with the big United States corporations.

The dominating factor in the economy was the sugar industry, which had been developed largely since Cuba's independence from Spain in 1898 with American capital for export to United States markets. At its peak it contributed 30 per cent of the gross national product, and accounted for about 80 per cent of total exports.[16] American corporations owned most of the large sugar plantations, covering an area of 3 million acres, as well as 63 of the largest sugar refineries.[17] During the depression of the 1930's, when world prices of sugar fell catastrophically, American sugar interests in Cuba negotiated the free admission of a sugar quota on the American market which would represent 28 per cent of all sugar consumption in the United States. Cuban producers were thus guaranteed the sale of an important part of the crop—usually half or more—at United States domestic prices, which were considerably higher and more stable than world prices. The importance of this quota, which the United States taxpayer might have considered as a subsidy to American-owned sugar companies, can be seen if one examines the quota for 1958, the last year before Castro. It stood then at 2.9 million tons, and with the average difference of 3 cents a pound between world and United States prices, brought the sugar companies roughly $150 million extra. This corresponded to above 20 per cent of the value of total Cuban exports, which had reached $733.5 million in 1958.[18] Although highly profitable, the concentration on sugar was not an unmixed blessing for Cuba. The sugar industry was very labor-intensive during the harvest season, but provided only seasonal employment; large numbers of landless laborers remained idle for the rest of the year in the absence of alternative employment opportunities.

16. Celso Furtado, "Economic Aspects of the Cuban Revolution," in *Economic Development of Latin America*, Cambridge University Press, Cambridge, 1970, p. 215.

17. K. S. Karol, *Guerillas in Power?* Hill & Wang, New York, 1970.

18. *Yearbook of International Trade Statistics, 1968*, United Nations, New York, 1970, p. 211.

American interests were also heavily involved in cattle raising, the second largest agricultural activity.

Industry in Cuba concentrated on producing consumer goods for the domestic market. Most of the factories were owned by subsidiaries of big American corporations and were designed for the final processing of intermediary products imported from the United States. They operated on a high level of efficiency and technical sophistication, with capital-intensive production methods similar to those used in the United States. There were few independent enterprises. Most of the small or medium-scale concerns provided services or supplied the capitalist foreign-owned enterprises.

In the 1950's the tourist industry attracted increasing numbers of Americans. While it poured valuable foreign exchange into the economy, tourism had a deplorable impact on the social and moral climate of the island. With the establishment of casinos, Havana became the favorite playground of American professional gamblers, an open city where organized crime and vice could flourish undisturbed. The contrast between the impudent luxury of the tourist hotels and the wretched misery of suburban slums was particularly flagrant and insulting. It nurtured the seeds of a violent rebellion.

The ruling class in Cuba consisted of plantation owners and the wealthy urban bourgeoisie who were closely linked to business interests in the United States. The governments which they controlled encouraged foreign investments and were thus supported by the United States. This was the case even of Batista's unusually corrupt dictatorship, which maintained close contact with the gambling circles. Only the professional class, which was also the most highly educated and had retained the ideals of democracy and national independence, expressed any real opposition to government policies. Industrial workers were relatively few in number and they were strongly unionized. Their wages were rather high because of the great productivity of the industrial sector, in contrast to the low pay of urban workers in the overcrowded and inefficient service sector. The poorest section of the population lived in the rural areas. There some peasants managed to survive on the yield of tobacco and various food crops, but most of the rural inhabitants were seasonal sugar workers.

The close ties between the United States and the Cuban economy awoke in most of the urban population a yearning for the materialistic values of the consumer society. The middle class in particular tried to imitate American habits of consumption. In 1959 there were some 300,000 automobiles and 500,000 TV sets in Cuba which, in comparison to the population, represented one of the highest ratios in all of Latin

America. True the per capita income of $400 was equally unusual for a developing country. The level of education and literacy was also high. In 1950 there was only 22 per cent adult illiteracy in Cuba, in comparison with 51 per cent in Brazil, and 43 per cent in Mexico. Argentina's 14 per cent was the lowest in Latin America.

The revolution in Cuba started with Fidel Castro, an upper-class professional, and a tiny group of his followers in a rural mountain area. Although they opposed a dictatorship which had forcibly ousted a legal democratic government and was universally hated, they found little active support in the cities. The official communist party, heavily represented in unions which negotiated wage agreements with the government, was adamantly opposed and called them irresponsible adventurers. But the courage of the Castro group gradually won respect, admiration, finally widespread support. Deserted by his supporters, Batista had to flee to the United States where he found refuge.

The Castro movement had no comprehensive or clear-cut platform. It included both socialist revolutionaries and liberal democrats who shared the common goal of overthrowing Batista. The official plan was to restore the democratic constitution which had been adopted in 1940 and then annulled by Batista. This included land reform and some other moderate social measures. With national and social liberation as its objectives, and supported in this by the great majority of the population, this program would obviously have reduced the influence of American and foreign capital on the Cuban economy. Initially, however, there was apparently no intention to affect a total break in relations with the United States. The new Cuban regime gave no indication of refusing mutually acceptable solutions of the conflicts which of necessity arose between the opposing interests of both parties. But the American business interests in Cuba were not inclined to negotiate in a spirit of conciliation or compromise, and in their intransigent attitude they enjoyed the full support of the United States government. When the large sugar estates were nationalized under the general program of land reform, the American sugar companies rejected the indemnity that had been offered to them: bonds with 20 years maturity at 4 per cent interest. Instead they demanded immediate payment of full compensation. Since Cuba was manifestly unable to comply with such a demand, its only purpose could have been to provoke retaliatory action on the part of the United States government, leading hopefully to Castro's overthrow.

The first of such American reprisals was to trim the Cuban sugar quota from 2.9 to 1.9 million tons. In adopting this policy of economic pressure—if blackmail is too strong an expression—American business-men, and the government in Washington which backed them, made a mistake which had far-reaching consequences. They totally misjudged Castro's temperament, his passionate will to assert Cuba's national dignity and independence. They discounted too quickly his ability to obtain the support of the great majority of his people in his decisions, regardless of any cost they might entail. It seems very clear to us that this confrontation which was initiated by American corporations pushed Castro more quickly into a far more rigid course of action against all capitalists, and especially American interests, than he intended at first.

From reprisal to counter-reprisal the escalation of the Cuban–American confrontation proceeded inexorably. The cut in the sugar quota precipitated the spread of nationalization, which was extended to all industry and large-scale trading enterprises. In order to compensate for the loss of the United States sugar market, when the quota was completely abolished soon afterward, and the ensuing loss of dollar receipts, Cuba had to look for other outlets and sources of imports, countries where purchases could be made without spending convertible currency. The Soviet Union naturally offered their co-operation and the Cuban–American struggle thus became an important part of the world-wide East–West conflict. The final breakdown of relations occurred when, on the one hand, all American investments, totaling about $1 billion, were nationalized without indemnity, and on the other, the United States discontinued all exports of oil and other essential goods to Cuba. American technicians were recalled, as well as the managerial teams who were operating Cuba's industries and public utilities. The economic blockade was explained to the American public by the necessity to forestall any Soviet penetration in their own backyard—a danger which in part United States policy had itself created—and to restore democracy on the island. The latter seems to us a somewhat less than convincing argument.

The conflict with the United States created considerable economic and political difficulties for Castro, even within his own government. A substantial number among his followers were opposed to total socialization. This sentiment was shared by most of the members of the middle class, which had initially welcomed the revolution but who were closely tied to and dependent on American business. Many of them left after failing to prevent socialization, and their departure stripped Cuba of her small nucleus of competent economic leadership. It also pushed the political pendulum even further to the left.

The Cuban revolution had no prepared blueprint for the reorganization of the economy. More than any other contemporary revolution it was the brainchild of a single individual. Fidel Castro was not the head of an organized party with carefully defined political and economic doctrines, but the charismatic leader of a loosely structured movement. Far from dogmatic Marxist, Castro was rather a populist type of socialist, moved by an aversion to materialistic capitalist society and by the ideal of social justice and equality. The course which Cuba has followed since the revolution has varied greatly, reflecting both the subsequent events and a tendency to spontaneous improvisation, which is characteristic of the movement and its leaders.

The first move of the revolutionary government was to redistribute income in order to increase the purchasing power of the masses. As Celso Furtado points out quite correctly, this was quite different from the usual practice of socialist economies.[19] In the USSR, for instance, the emphasis was on maximum accumulation of capital by the government to increase public investment, at the cost of limiting or even reducing private consumption. The Cuban land reform nationalized the large estates in order to transform them into co-operatives or state farms and allowed some 100,000 tenant farmers and sharecroppers to own the land which they were cultivating. As a result, the government gained direct control of 11.4 million hectares of arable land, and 7.2 million hectares were held by small farmers. The purchasing power of these farmers obviously was increased with the abolition of rents. Urban rents at the same time were reduced by 30 to 50 per cent, and the wages of industrial and agricultural workers raised. Government expenditure for social services, which would benefit primarily the poor, was also increased. With such measures, about 15 per cent of the national income was transferred between 1959 and 1961 from property owners to workers.

The domestic impact of this redistribution of income at first was quite salutory. The growing consumer demand stimulated food production by the small farmers. The output of industrial consumer goods also increased as long as supplies of intermediate goods lasted. Since in the past a good part of the income from property had been sent abroad, these measures also had an immediate positive effect on the balance of payments.

But the country was bound to run into serious trouble, primarily because of the total break in relations with the United States. As we mentioned earlier, alternative export markets had to be found, as well as new sources of supply for capital goods and intermediate products for industry. American and Cuban managers and technicians

19. Furtado, *op. cit.*, p. 240.

of the nationalized industrial plants, who had left for the United States, had to be replaced at once.

Cuba's first development plan was prepared with the aid of experts from socialist countries of Eastern Europe. Its main objective was to achieve economic independence by de-emphasizing the country's previous exclusive reliance on sugar as the sole export crop and by diversifying agriculture and industry. Cuba expected the socialist countries to replace the United States in supplying them with equipment as well as technical personnel. Unfortunately, the results of this policy were quite disappointing. New crops were introduced without sufficient study or adequate preparation. The results did not compensate for the reduction in sugar production and exports. In industry the situation was even worse. Cuban factories were designed to function with the help of American machinery, and were run according to efficient American methods of production for consumer goods. Socialist countries, with a somewhat backward consumer goods industry, proved unable to supply the equipment or the technicians which the Cubans required. In the absence of spare parts, and unable to procure the intermediate materials which they were supposed to process, many industrial plants had to shut down. In addition, harbor installations suddenly needed considerable investments in order to handle the large ships which trade with Eastern Europe would require. With the drop in exports food imports had to be reduced. All this created a shortage in most consumer goods and left farmers without great incentives to deliver foodstuffs to the cities. Food rationing had to be strictly enforced. The nationalization in 1963 of all retail trade and handicrafts, along with the complete collectivization of agriculture which occurred somewhat later, even further dislocated the system of distribution and aggravated the shortages of foodstuffs and consumer goods.

The campaign to diversify the economy was abandoned in 1963 and 1964. With the approval of the Soviet Union, Cuba decided once again to focus on sugar, the one export item which it could produce cheaper than the rest of the world. The socialist countries agreed to import most of the annual harvest at prices well above the world level. This subsidy served somewhat the same purpose as the aid which Cuba had previously obtained from the United States through the import quota system, and was also more or less the equivalent in dollar value. For the years 1965 to 1968 it averaged out to about $200 million.[20] The high cost of domestic beet sugar in the USSR made the purchase of cane sugar from Cuba quite economical, even at a subsi-

20. *The External Financing of Economic Development,* United Nations, New York, 1970, p. 51.

dized price. By 1970 Cuba planned to expand its sugar production to 10 million tons, an increase of 40 per cent over the previous record crop of 1952. Of this total, 5 million tons would go to the USSR and 2 million tons to the other socialist countries. The 2.5 million that would be left over after domestic consumption would remain available to obtain convertible currencies on the world market and to pay for imports of industrial products from Western Europe which the socialist countries could not supply.

Furtado, who is quite sympathetic to the Cuban revolution, points out that the decision to concentrate on sugar, and the choice of an extremely ambitious production target, were not prompted so much by hard economic thinking as by Castro's impetuous temperament. Nothing seems to fascinate him more than meeting challenges head on and mobilizing all possible energies and resources. The target of 10 million tons of sugar would demand costly additional investment to expand existing capacity. Huge numbers of urban workers would be pulled away from their normal productive activities at harvest time. Worse yet, 10 million tons of sugar would be a glut on the world market. Prices would fall, and this would reduce, not increase, the net proceeds of sugar exports.

Still, the gigantic effort was made. Masses of city workers and youths more or less voluntarily enlisted for the arduous task of cane cutting. A propaganda campaign proclaimed that the 10 million record crop would be a historic milestone on the road to socialist development. As we know now, the harvest of 1970 did indeed surpass all records, but fell considerably short of its objective. In 1971, Castro set a goal of 7 million tons, but although this was a more realistic figure, again the harvest did not live up to expectations.

Table XXI
CUBAN SUGAR PRODUCTION
(in million tons)

1952	7.2	1961	6.8	1965	6.1	1969	4.3
1958	5.8	1962	4.8	1966	4.5	1970	8.5
1959	6.0	1963	3.8	1967	6.1	1971	6.5
1960	5.9	1964	4.4	1968	5.1		

It has been twelve years now since Castro's government first took hold of Cuba, but the situation is still too unsettled and full of contradictions to permit a simple assessment of its performance.

An enormous effort was made toward economic development. The ratio of investment is reported to have gone as high as 31 per cent, which is unprecedented for a developing country.[21] It is higher than in other socialist countries and comparable only to the ratio of Japan. This has imposed a heavy burden on the population, and is in large part responsible for the strict rationing and the general shortage of food and consumer goods. Up to now, however, the results have not been commensurate with the energies and resources deployed.

This is visibly the case in agriculture, which has received the most attention since the decision to abandon the policy of diversification. Considerable investments have gone into improving agriculture. The capacity of storage dams has been multiplied by 40, and a great deal of planning has been involved in anti-erosion work and pasture development. Even in industry, investments have been concentrated in goods such as fertilizers, which have a direct impact on farm output. Yet with sugar and cattle as the major exceptions, the value of agricultural production declined from 1962 to 1970 by 23 per cent. This appears to be the result mainly of a centralized and bureaucratic control of production. Political motives, such as reaching a specific target prescribed by Havana in a given time, frequently prevailed over principles of sound management. With little opportunity to display their competence or initiative, farmers have had no incentive to increase their effort. In view of the shortages in consumer goods, more work could not bring them tangible benefits.

This centralized direction, with frequent changes in policy and emphasis, more often than not improvised rather than based on careful study or preparation, has brought about a stagnation in industrial production. It has totally dislocated distribution. Both suffer from absenteeism and reduced productivity.

On the other hand, the productive capacity of the economy has increased substantially because of the massive investments. If and when improved management and increased incentives ever allow a better utilization of the greatly expanded resources, there will surely be a corresponding rise in production.

To arrive at an overall assessment of the Cuban revolution, one must compare its achievement with its goals. In the absence of a definite party doctrine, these objectives are described in the statements of Castro and his lieutenants, especially those of Che Guevara. The first and foremost of these was to assert the country's independence and dignity, to liberate Cuba from the semi-colonial yoke of American capitalism. The final goal was to establish an equalitarian civilization

21. Charles Vanhecke, *Cuba: De L'utopie aux Realites,* Le Monde, Paris, 18 and 20 March 1971.

which rejected the materialistic values of capitalism and replace them with a feeling of solidarity between all members of the new socialist society. Everyone would enjoy an adequate standard of living, and there would be no emphasis on private wealth.

One cannot deny that Castro's most stunning victory is his successful resistance to the United States. He has gained and maintained the independence of his country, withstood economic and political pressure—and in one instance, at least, also military pressure—from the hemisphere's superpower. This contest between the Latin David and the Yankee Goliath is probably still the prime reason for his popularity at home. He has offered great satisfaction to his people by gratifying their pride and self-respect. It is obvious that it has also been the basis of his legendary popularity throughout Latin America, where fear and resentment of the United States are nearly as strong as in Cuba. To some extent this is the case even in the other countries of the Third World.

But what is not so well known is the fact that American influence could only be dislodged at the cost of following the lead, both economically and politically, of the Soviet Union. This dependence implied of necessity a growing alignment with Soviet policy and methods, and led to the erosion of what had been the most attractive aspect of the Cuban revolution: its spontaneous, non-dogmatic character. Initially there had been great leeway, cultural freedom, and creativity, far more than in most socialist countries. Now the recent trial, followed by a "confession" of his political sins by one of Cuba's outstanding poets, confirms the suspicion that Castro has adopted some of the more repugnant of Stalinist practices. This is aggravated by a personality cult which, if at first somewhat justifiable as an expression of hero worship, has grown beyond all bounds of reason.

The goal of establishing an equalitarian, non-materialistic society, such as the one pursued in Mao's China, has proved far more difficult to attain in Cuba. A major triumph has been an improvement in the condition of the most disinherited groups: the landless cane cutters in the rural areas who are only seasonally employed, and the unskilled unemployed in the cities. They have finally been granted equal status and security in employment. Public services in education, health, and welfare were made available to all, and progress in this area must be considered an important step.

But as we said earlier, the de-emphasizing of material incentives for individuals and the rejection of the whole concept of profit-oriented government enterprises, along with Castro's preference for agricultural work—even at the lowest level, such as cane cutting—has discouraged hard work and efficient, cost-conscious management. These factors are mainly responsible for the decline in production, the general and persistent shortages. As we stated before, the majority of Cubans—60 per cent of whom are urban dwellers—were deeply imbued with the values of a consumer society. Even if the population at large did not enjoy it at first hand, the standard of consumption of the middle class was relatively high. After an initial spurt of patriotism, most Cubans, therefore, grew increasingly reluctant to obey Castro's repeated commands and exhortations and to devote all their energies to hard work from which they could reap no effective reward. With a strict system of rationing and price control, the cost of rationed foodstuffs and other necessities absorbed only part of even minimal wages. Yet there was nothing else left to purchase. Thus increased absenteeism, and diminishing productivity of labor, was accompanied by a drop in the actual participation of women in the labor force. There is indeed little justification to supplement a nominal income which cannot be spent. The time is better used in foraging for food in the countryside, or queuing in the endless lines.

In spite of the example which Castro personally has shown, enthusiasm for "voluntary" unremunerated work, such as cane cutting in the rural areas, is decidedly on the wane. The promises made on each of these occasions—for example, during the campaign for the 10 million tons *zafra* in 1970 when the claim was that success would remove all restrictions—have become less and less plausible.

Not surprisingly, therefore, Castro has intimated that he has basically given up all hope of convincing the present generation. He feels that they have been irretrievably poisoned by the lure of capitalism. The government has even authorized the emigration of a relatively important number of people to the United States—1,000 per week. True, this reduces the strength of the groups who are most at loggerheads with the government.[22] Attention is now focused on the new generation, and enormous efforts are made to ensure that with proper education there will emerge the truly socialist being who is free of egoistic individualism. To rally the youth to the cause of equalitarianism, a number of special schools have been established in rural areas, where the importance and dignity of farm work is stressed.

It is too early to tell what the fruits of all this will be. Eventually the extraordinary blend of improvisation on the decision-making level, and bureaucratic centralization in the actual implementation, which has been characteristic of the Cuban revolution so far, will probably

22. In September of 1971, the Cuban government withdrew its consent to this exodus.

disappear. The country will move forward along the same lines as the other socialist countries. Using as a base the considerable productive investments which have already been made, such a development might even be quite rapid. Cuba thereby will be relinquishing, however, the primary objective of her revolution, which initially aroused so much hope and sympathy for her throughout the Third World—to create out of a semi-developed capitalist economy an equalitarian socialist society which would be less dogmatic and more humanistic than the Soviet model.

MEXICO: AN EXAMPLE OF SUCCESSFUL DEVELOPMENT THROUGH
PRIVATE ENTERPRISE IN A MODERNIZED SOCIETY

Mexico alone in Latin America is able to show rapid and continuous economic growth over several decades. The average rate of growth of gross domestic product in real terms; that is, at constant prices, amounted to 6.3 per cent per year from 1950 to 1960, rose to 6.7 per cent during 1960 to 1967, and reached 7.4 per cent for 1969 and 1970. In spite of the very large increase in population, the real per capita income expanded at an annual rate of 3.0 per cent in the 1950's and 3.1 per cent during the 1960's.[23]

During the same period Mexico enjoyed a political stability which is quite unique in Latin America. It cannot be coincidence that Mexico is also the only country on the continent to have experienced a real revolution which swept away the traditional oligarchia of large estate (hacienda) owners. This class, as we said earlier, still yields considerable political and economic power in most other countries of Latin America.

Before the revolution, under the long dictatorship of Porfirio Díaz from 1876 to 1911, Mexico experienced significant economic growth. Railroad lines were extended to unify and expand the domestic market. Metal mining was developed with financing from foreign, largely American, capital. In agriculture nearly all the land was owned by a tiny minority of hacienda owners. One per cent of the population controlled 97 per cent of all arable land.[24] The government abetted this excessive concentration of land by relieving Indian communities of communal lands they had tilled since time immemorial and transforming them into plantations for modern cash crops.

23. *United Nations Statistical Yearbook, 1969,* United Nations, New York, 1970, table 180.
24. Celso Furtado, *Economic Development of Latin America,* Cambridge University Press, Cambridge, 1970, p. 218.

Rogen Hansen has emphasized in his book *The Politics of Mexican Development*, the dual origin of the Mexican revolution.[25] On the one hand, it represented a revolt by the Indian peasantry who were desperately fighting to retain or to recover their ancestral lands. On the other hand, it was fueled by the active discontent of largely middle-class mestizos who felt robbed of any possibility to advance economically or politically in a society where the élite alone had a say in the government.

The revolution completely destroyed the power of this ruling class. It is more doubtful whether it had the same success in establishing a society which reflected the lofty ideals embodied in the constitution of 1917. The most liberal of its kind at the time, the constitution was conceived essentially to protect the rights of the underprivileged workers and peasants, and to ensure in particular land reform, collective bargaining, and social security.

Today, more than 50 years after the start of the revolution, official statements and publications pay constant lip service to its ideals. One is reminded of this even in the names of streets in Mexico City, where one of the main shopping areas is called *Insurgentes*. The name of the ruling party, *Partido Revolucionario Institucional* (PRI), offers a perfect illustration of the political temper in Mexico today. The revolution has been institutionalized. The PRI has been in power for over 30 years and its hold on the people appears as strong as ever. Hansen attributes its success to an ability to integrate all the major sectors of the electorate: the peasants and the urban workers, as well as the industrial and agricultural élite who are the new ruling class.

The development policy which Mexico has followed for the last 30 years has granted peasants and urban workers only the minimum satisfaction of their demands to keep their allegiance and their confidence in the survival of the revolutionary ideals. With this minor reservation, it is designed solely to favor the new ruling class.

One must not confuse Mexico, however, with Latin American countries dominated by the traditional oligarchia. In the latter the oligarchy is interested mainly in preserving its privileges, is less concerned with development; it even suspects sometimes that economic development will undermine its position. The new ruling class in Mexico, first of all, is much larger. It includes the rapidly growing middle class and encompasses now about 30 per cent of the population. The essential difference, however, is that its profits are mainly entrepreneurial. It pockets most of the proceeds of economic growth

25. Johns Hopkins Press, Baltimore, 1971.

and increased productivity, leaving only crumbs to the lower classes. Thus it is vitally interested in rapid economic development, and consequently economic development has been the major objective of government policy. Pursued with great determination and skill, this policy has attained a considerable degree of success.

The dual obligation of meeting the basic demands of the masses while reserving most of the benefits to the upper classes has been particularly obvious in the government's agricultural policy. Under the land reform which was part of the 1917 constitution, the land expropriated from the haciendas was to be incorporated in peasant village communities, the *ejidos*. The members of the *ejidos* could usually cultivate their small family plots independently, but could neither sell nor even rent them out. Thus there would be stability and equality within the peasantry.

On the whole, this land reform did indeed bring a certain social equilibrium and peace in rural Mexico, although it was carried out very slowly. The transformation of land tenure started only in the 1930's on a large scale and is not yet complete. It has been marred by many inequities. Still, 52.7 million hectares, or about 27 per cent of the total area of Mexico and 47 per cent of all cultivated land, by 1964 had been handed over to 2,385,000 farmers, who represented with their families about half of the total peasant population. Hansen points out quite correctly that the peasants who have received land, no matter how little, are usually pacified. The *ejidos* have also managed to retain most of their surplus population. Although they are underemployed, even unemployed for part of the year, they prefer to remain on the land in order not to lose their rights. The rapid growth of population in the whole country has also extended to the rural areas, but land for redistribution is still available. The hope of receiving land is a powerful tranquilizer.

The *ejidos* have been somewhat less successful in improving the standards of the rural population. In large measure this is due to overcrowding on small plots, usually of 4 to 6 hectares, in the central part of Mexico, where most of the *ejidos* founded on former estates are located. This has not deterred the *ejidos* from raising their productivity and their total output, although the government gives them relatively little support in technical guidance and credit facilities. Still, the rate of growth has been slower in the *ejidos* than in the private agricultural sector. Thus between 1940 and 1960, the total crop output increased in value by 123 per cent in the *ejidos* and by 222 per cent on private farms, usually of 5 hectares or more.[26] In the 1960's, newly developed

26. Hansen, *op. cit.*, p. 62.

irrigated land was reserved for the creation of new *ejidos*, and more rapid progress was made in that sector.[27]

But during the early years in particular, private farms were largely responsible for the tremendous breakthrough in agricultural production. The government deliberately encouraged this by developing new land in the northern and northwestern regions. This was to compensate for the temporary dislocation of traditional agriculture because of the land reform in Central Mexico. A massive program of public investment financed irrigation and the construction of rural roads, and from 1930 to 1963 represented on an average nearly one third of all government investments. Estates of up to 100 hectares of irrigated land were exempted from expropriation, and these exemptions were even more liberal when certain crops were involved. One hundred fifty hectares might be allowed for cotton, which was considered particularly important to the economy, and 300 hectares even for bananas, coffee, or sugar.

With modern methods of production and easy access to public and private credit, medium and large-scale commercial farms flourished. Making extensive use of mechanized equipment, fertilizers, and selected seeds, they expanded rapidly and became the most dynamic sector in agriculture. The value of their total output in 1960 amounted to 7.4 billion pesos, in comparison with 5.8 billion for the *ejidos*, and they figured even more prominently in the production of the major export crops.

From 1935 to 1967 the average annual overall rate of growth for agricultural production was 4.4 per cent. This included privately owned farms of less than 5 hectares, which lagged far behind the larger ones. It is an exceptional record among developing countries that are also engaged in simultaneously promoting rapid industrial development. Hansen points out that it may be the basis of Mexico's "miracle." The development of agriculture has made Mexico largely self-sufficient in food, and in spite of a rapid increase in population, food consumption has gone up in volume and in quality. Agricultural exports, which have been increasing at an annual rate of 6.2 per cent since 1940, provided most of the foreign exchange to pay for the imports of industrial equipment. The greater purchasing power of the rural population has created a growing domestic market for the developing Mexican industry.

The government policy for agriculture is a typical example of the general approach in Mexico to development. The pattern was to create profitable opportunities for private enterprise by facilitating

27. Furtado, *op. cit.*, p. 220.

and encouraging its activity. This was done through legislative measures and public investment in productive infrastructure. The decision on direct government participation in any area has been entirely pragmatic. Efficiency rather than ideology was the determining factor, and policies, therefore, were extremely flexible. The government stepped in with public financing of private enterprise when necessary, participated in joint public–private companies, or developed projects on its own as the situation required it.

Public corporations were set up not only to run transport, utilities, and oil wells, but also to launch those essential industries which private enterprise could not and/or was not willing to undertake on its own. Public investment was designed to "break bottle-necks," to overcome shortages in key sectors which stood in the way of economic development. Thus the emphasis switched from agriculture (irrigation and road building) to basic industries, including steel and oil, electric power, and transport.

The rate of public investment has been high and has gone up steadily from 4.4 per cent of the G.D.P. from 1940 to 1946, to 6.2 per cent for 1960 to 1967. About three quarters of these investments from 1939 to 1959 came out of the public sector—that is, out of the government budget and the profits of public enterprises. The rest was divided fairly evenly between domestic and foreign loans. Deficit spending and ensuing inflation were prominent in the early days, but since 1954 there has been a monetary stability which is quite uncommon in Latin America.

One should note that Mexico's large public investment programs were essentially financed out of the national budget in spite of the fact that during most of this period the ratio of government revenue to the G.D.P. was quite low, never more than 10 per cent. Taxes went up on both corporate and personal income at the end of the 1960's, but until then more than half of all revenues came from regressive indirect taxes, the bulk of which was paid by low-income groups. Yet from 1940 to 1963, only 16 per cent on the average of the budget was allotted to social programs benefiting the poorer classes. Expenditures for economic development accounted for 45 per cent. Thus one can say that for most of the period the national budget took charge of redistributing wealth from the poor to the rich, since only the latter truly profited from economic development.

The private sector felt the impetus of public investments and other government measures and responded very favorably. The rate of private investments rose from 4.2 per cent between 1940 and 1946, to 14.5 per cent from 1963 to 1967. At first, private investment represented less than half of the capital available, but subsequently it was responsible for 70 per cent of the total. Overall, the ratio of investment to G.D.P. rose from 8.6 per cent from 1940 to 1946, to 20.7 per cent from 1963 to 1967, a ratio rarely reached in developing countries which do not impose mandatory restrictions on consumption.

Government policies to encourage private investment in industry offered substantial tax concessions. Exemptions were granted for a period of 5 to 10 years to new enterprises which the government considered important to industrial development. Rebates were made on import duties for raw materials and equipment. Investment subsidies were given in some cases and credit was supplied at low rates. In addition, tariff protection was substantially increased to guarantee a profitable domestic market for new industries or for those which were expanding their capacity. Later, in the 1950's, import licensing was introduced as another protective device. At first it applied mainly to luxury items, in order to discourage their import and save foreign exchange for the purchase of more essential products. Gradually, however, licensing was extended to cover approximately 80 per cent of all Mexican imports, and in particular all industrial products which could be produced domestically. All these measures represent a quasi guarantee of high profits to a reasonably competent entrepreneur, and they are powerful incentives to private investment in industrial development.

Institutions such as the *Nacional Financiera* have also encouraged private investment and private savings. Their contribution has been invaluable in mobilizing the mass of small savings which previously were hoarded, and in directing them to productive investments. The monies initially were put in government securities. Gradually they were also invested in bonds, and in shares of stock of utilities and industrial concerns set up by the *Financiera* independently or in cooperation with private domestic or foreign interests.

Naturally, therefore, industrial production has developed very rapidly in Mexico. This has been true both in the expansion of output by industries already established and in the proliferation of products. Manufacturing has grown at an annual rate of 8.1 per cent from 1940 to 1950, 7.3 per cent from 1950 to 1960, and 8.2 per cent from 1960 to 1968. From 1963 to 1969 the index of manufacturing output rose by 75 per cent.[28] Manufacturing also now plays a more important role in the economy. It provided 12.7 per cent of total employment in 1940, and 20.1 per cent in 1964, and produced 17.8 per cent in the G.D.P. in 1940, 26.5 per cent in 1967.

28. *Monthly Statistical Bulletin*, United Nations, New York, July 1971.

The most rapid growth has occurred in heavy industry—iron and steel and chemicals—rather than in basic consumer goods such as textiles. There is an increasing variety of durable consumer and capital goods, automobiles, and even color television sets.

Industry in Mexico has reached the point where it can meet more of the rapidly increasing local demand. The scope of the Mexican market is becoming large enough to enable producers of many manufactured items to compete on the world market and to export their goods in increasing quantities, although the total volume for the time being is still small. Local producers obviously have a natural advantage in processed foodstuffs such as canned fruit and sugar. But in addition, other manufactured products made up more than 18 per cent of the value of all exports in 1968, in comparison to only 3 per cent in 1940.[29]

As we said earlier, it is important to note that domestic resources have provided nearly all the necessary funds for Mexico's economic development in the last three decades. But policies on foreign investments have been very lenient and pragmatically conceived. Foreign capital before the revolution had dominated the mining sector, at the time the most productive and dynamic in the economy. Although the 1917 constitution stipulated that ownership of subsoil resources be vested in the nation, existing concessions nonetheless were all confirmed. But no serious conflict arose until the depression of the 1930's. Then an American oil company and a British concern, which together were responsible for nearly all of the country's oil production, refused to abide by a ruling of the Mexican Supreme Court in a wage dispute. Thus they openly violated the laws of their host country and flouted both the government and public opinion. Nationalization of these companies became inevitable. Naturally this expropriation in 1938 spoiled the mood for foreign investments in Mexico, although in view of the depression everywhere in the world at that point the times in any event were not very auspicious for investments. The companies attempted unsuccessfully to prevent the sale of Mexican oil abroad and eventually accepted compensation from the Mexican government. After some initial difficulties the National Mexican Oil Company (PEMEX) acquired enough technical skill and equipment to make a fairly reasonable go of their operations. It concentrated on supplying the domestic market at the lowest possible price. Already by 1938 about half of the country's total oil output was reserved for domestic consumption, and the cheap cost of fuel to industry was certainly an

29. Calculated from data contained in *Yearbook of International Trade Statistics, 1968*, United Nations, New York, 1970.

important factor in its development. Seen in retrospect, the nationalization of the oil industry seems to have been a tonic for the Mexican economy as a whole.

The climate for foreign investments improved after World War II and the flow of capital resumed. Most of it came from the United States, lured by Mexico's rapid economic development and by her political and social stability. The monetary stability which has lasted since 1954 and the absence of restrictions on the transfer of profits or capital abroad have encouraged foreign investors. Mexico's favorable financial position has made it possible for her to raise funds in foreign capital markets with better terms than those granted to other countries in the Third World and Latin America in particular.

Most of the new direct investments have gone into manufacturing, which is moving ahead at a noticeably rapid pace, and where additional profits are to be found in the government's various tax and tariff incentive programs. Thus, while less than one third of American private investments in 1950 was in manufacturing, by 1967 it had gone up to two thirds. In absolute figures United States investments in industry rose from $133 to $890 million. But in spite of this tremendous increase, American capital does not dominate the Mexican economy or even the manufacturing industry, as it does in several other countries of Latin America where it has aroused hostility to "Yankee neo-colonialism." Hansen estimates that American-controlled enterprises account for only one sixth of all Mexican manufacturing output. They are of relatively minor importance, therefore, in comparison to domestically controlled enterprises.

The economic development of Mexico has been an outstanding success, probably the most impressive since World War II of any developing country within a system of private enterprise. Today, after three decades of continuous, rapid, even accelerating growth, Mexico is practically at the level of a developed country, although the per capita income is still low ($511 in 1968) and the distribution of wealth very uneven.

As we have already indicated, the single most important factor in this success was the removal of the former ruling oligarchia with its concern to preserve the status quo, and its replacement by a dynamic class of modern entrepreneurs. Mexican development can be viewed as a twentieth-century version of the economic progress made during the nineteenth century in Western Europe and the United States. In both instances development was directed by entrepreneurs for their own benefit primarily, with little thought given to improving the material well-being of the peasants and workers in the lower classes.

Government policies have influenced much more actively Mexico's development than they have in the similar phase in the West. The government itself created favorable conditions for the expansion of industrial and agricultural production by setting up a material infrastructure of power, transport, fuel, and irrigation, and an institutional framework with credit, tariff protection, and tax privileges. Here again one must note the government's all important role in maintaining political and social stability. It took skillful manipulation on the part of successive presidents to convince peasants and workers that the government had remained faithful to the ideals of the revolution, that it was striving toward the establishment of a welfare state for the benefit of the underprivileged. They succeeded in creating the illusion, although the substance of government policies definitely favored the privileged classes. Only the *ejido* land reform and a few legislative measures to protect the rights of industrial workers in fact benefited the urban and rural masses.

A survey of the Mexican National Bank reveals that inequality in the distribution of personal income grew worse from 1950 to 1963. During this period the personal income of the poorest half of Mexico's families declined from 19.1 to 15.5 per cent in relation to overall personal income, which had risen considerably. With a substantial increase in population, it seems likely—although no accurate data are available—that the real income of the bottom 20 per cent did not go up, and may in fact have even dropped.

In addition, social services for the poor are less developed in Mexico than in most other countries of Latin America. As late as 1967 only 6.1 per cent of the Mexican population as a whole and 18.9 per cent of the labor force was covered by social security. The extremely high rate of population growth has obstructed all attempts to broaden the scope of social services and to improve the standard of living of the masses. With a rate of growth at a record level of 3.6 per cent per year from 1963 to 1968, Mexico's population explosion has also been a major obstacle to economic development. As is the case in other countries with the same population problem, it has increased demand for food, consumer goods, and social services, and thus reduced the savings available for productive investment. Up to now no major effort has been made to introduce family planning.[30] It is one of the few obvious gaps in a development policy which in nearly all other aspects has been well thought out and executed.

30. A change in government demographic policy seems to have occurred in Spring 1972, when a major campaign in favor of family planning has been launched. (*The New York Times,* June 22, 1972.)

The prospects for further rapid economic development in Mexico depend to a great extent on the country's social stability. Will the government be allowed to follow the same general course of action as before? Will it go on limiting the fruits of development to the upper and middle classes? Will it be able to satisfy the demands of the masses with relatively minor and marginal concessions, such as an increase in social services (education, health, and social security), in minimum wages, and in the distribution of land to the *ejidos*?

Pressure is building up for improvements of far greater import. It can only become more insistent as the formerly passive attitude of peasants is radicalized with the spread of literacy (illiteracy has declined in the 1960's from 33 to 22 per cent) and with snowballing unemployment in the urban and suburban areas.

Still, three decades of rapid growth have given a certain resilience and momentum to the Mexican economy. It can now afford to be more generous to the poor without sacrificing future growth. The same was possible, and did in fact happen, in Western Europe and in the United States in the early part of this century. One can see a first sign of this change in policy in the very substantial increase which the government introduced in minimum wages for both urban and rural workers in 1970. It corresponded roughly to 15, 16 per cent, whereas in previous years it had not exceeded 7 per cent. The changes in the tax system, to reduce the impact of regressive indirect taxation and to redistribute wealth to the poor rather than the rich, and the accelerated allocation of irrigated land to the *ejidos*, are other indications of this same trend.

On the whole we feel that an optimistic view of Mexico's future is justified by the pragmatic approach of her government and her ruling class. Both have demonstrated over several decades an extraordinary ability to face facts and adapt policies in accordance with changing times and situations.

Asia

CHINA: THE ESTABLISHMENT OF EQUALITARIAN COMMUNISM

When the communist regime took over mainland China in 1949, the country was the typical example of an underdeveloped economy, although considerable progress had been made in the coastal regions and particularly in Manchuria. About 80 per cent of the population still derived their livelihood from agriculture, with an extremely low productivity. The cultivation of an hectare of arable land necessitated 244 man hours as compared with 30 in the USSR and only 7 in the

United States.[31] The distribution of land was extremely unequal: 10 per cent of the farming households, including both landlords and rich peasants, owned 53 per cent of all farm lands, while the poor peasants who comprised 68 per cent of the rural population held only 22 per cent. More than half of the total number of farmers—54 per cent in 1937—were part-tenants or tenants.

Because of the shortage of arable land, high and steadily increasing rents were exacted. The crushing burden of rents and land taxes made it impossible for farmers to invest in land improvement, and the insecurity of tenure further removed any incentive to do so. Landlords, 27 per cent of whom were absentee owners, had little reason to improve their land since the rate of return on their investment in land was already highly profitable and mounting. Yet with these drawbacks, and in spite of the diminutive size of most farms and the lack of modern tools or fertilizers, the extraordinary industriousness of the Chinese farmers enabled them to obtain the best possible yields under the existing system of land tenure and available technology. The yield for major crops per acre was substantially higher than in India, with more or less similar conditions of farming.

But the great majority of Chinese peasants still lived in extreme poverty. They faced the sure threat of starvation when catastrophe hit, whether it were a natural one, such as a drought or a flood, or man-made, such as the civil war which devastated China throughout all of 1937 to 1949.

Most of China's industrial production consisted of traditional handicrafts. In the rural areas this provided part-time occupation to the peasants during slack periods on the farms. Urban handicrafts created masterpieces of exquisite traditional craftsmanship, but had a very low level of productivity in turning out items of average quality. In 1933, 72 per cent of all manufactured goods were handicrafts.

Foreign capital and foreign enterprises had created modern industries in the regions and cities dominated by foreigners: in the treaty ports of Shanghai and Tientsin, where foreign concessions enjoyed extraterritorial status, and in Manchuria. Manchuria in particular had been chosen by the Japanese as the heavy industry center of their empire after they occupied it in 1931. They developed there an important iron and steel industry.

Foreign trade also evolved out of the initiative of foreign powers, starting with the Opium War of 1840 when Great Britain forced China to open its ports to traders. China exported mainly primary products;

31. Nai-Ruenn Chen and Walter Galenson, *The Chinese Economy under Communism*, Aldine, Chicago, 1969, p. 5.

the traditional ones of silk and tea were gradually replaced by others such as soya beans. Imports consisted mainly of industrial consumer products with capital goods slowly growing in importance. China's foreign trade remained relatively small during that period as most of her G.N.P. was generated in her subsistence economy. Still she found herself in the same state of economic dependence on the developed market economies—her main outlets and sources of supply—as the other developing countries.

Even more relevant to our discussion were the political implications in China's relationship with the developed countries. With one of the most ancient and highly developed civilizations, China for thousands of years had viewed herself as the center of the universe. Her nationals referred to her as the Empire of the Middle. Yet for more than a century she had been subject to deep humiliations. She had been forced to open up her ports to foreign commerce, to grant extraterritorial concessions which violated her sovereignty, to accept unequal treaties. Her right to control her own finances had been abrogated. She was forced to mortgage part of the proceeds from her taxes as security for foreign creditors. Her numerous defeats lost her territory; finally she was confronted with the sight of foreigners on her own soil flaunting their power and wealth before helpless and wretched Chinese and discriminating against them in their own country. The bitterness accumulated through many decades of such flagrant inequality is at the root of the intense pride and aloofness which Communist China demonstrates to all foreigners, not only to those from capitalist countries.

After the unification of China under the Kuomintang government in 1925, China's international status was somewhat improved. She regained control of her fiscal administration, for instance. But other more grating restrictions were not lifted. In particular, one notes that foreign concessions maintained their position in the major coastal cities.

One can understand that with such a background one of the first objectives of the Maoist regime was to restore China to the position of a major world power, equal if not superior to any other. The yearning to build up the nation's self respect after a century of painful humiliation was as strong as the usual patriotic drive for national strength.

The Chinese communists started off with several advantages which the Russian Bolsheviks did not possess in 1917. They could profit from the experience of Soviet Russia and avoid some of her mistakes and pitfalls, while following the same general pattern and adapting it to the conditions of their own country. One must remember, too, that they had the benefit of their own experiment on a relatively small scale in Yenan, where they had ruled since 1934 and which served as a pilot project, especially in the field of agriculture.

Because of the essential difference between the Russian and the Chinese communist revolutions, the latter is much closer to the events that take place in nearly all the countries of the Third World. For the most part the October Revolution in Russia was made by and for the urban industrial proletariat, and was headed by a group of urban intellectuals. It was imposed on the peasantry, who remained for some considerable time indifferent, even hostile on occasion. In China, on the contrary, where the urban proletariat represented only a minute part of the population, the communist revolution grew essentially out of a peasant movement. Some of its principal leaders, including Mao himself, were of peasant extraction, with rural inclinations and rather suspicious of city sophistication. Its peasant origins strongly affected agricultural policies in particular and the general orientation of the revolution.

China followed at first the Soviet example in placing the main emphasis in her investments on the development of heavy industry. But from the start she was conscious of an urgent need to increase agricultural production, food especially. She also realized quickly the advantages of using the immense manpower resources of her rural population for development.

Land reform was very rapidly effected in agriculture. The estates of the landlords and all the land of rich farmers, over and above what they could cultivate without hired help, were expropriated and parceled out among the tenants, the landless laborers, and the poor farmers. About 46 million hectares were distributed out of a total of 97.9 million hectares under cultivation in 1949. In spite of the difficulties which arose because of insufficient credit and the absence of marketing facilities, which the landlords and merchants had provided previously, although at an exorbitant price, agricultural production increased considerably. According to the official index it rose by 48.5 per cent from 1949 to 1952. It is true that this growth in output is due probably not only to the fact that former tenants who now owned land for the first time had new incentives, but also to the end of the civil war. With the advent of peace, public works, in particular irrigation installations, could be restored and cultivated areas expanded by 10 per cent.

The second phase of land reform in socialist countries usually consists in regrouping small holdings of individual peasants into large-scale co-operatives or collective farms. In China this occurred in several stages. It started off with mutual aid teams whose members worked together but retained ownership of both their land and the tools of production. Such teams had existed in the past in certain regions of China and had been tried out by the communists in Yenan. Agricultural producers' co-operatives were set up next. In the lower grade of semi-socialist co-operatives, tools and land were both pooled and the proceeds were distributed in part to repay each member for his contribution in capital (land, livestock, tools) and the remainder according to the labor performed. In the more socialist co-operatives, all of the income was distributed as remuneration for labor. It is difficult to ascertain to what extent participation in these co-operatives was voluntary and based on the mutual benefit of the members, as official statements would indicate. The improved efficiency which was achieved through the specialization of labor and the preferential treatment in securing government credit, seeds, or fertilizers must have been important incentives. At any rate, China did not experience a period of forced collectivization with measures of mass repression, such as the crisis which devastated Soviet agriculture during the early 1930's and resulted in a catastrophic decline of production.

The process of integrating the rural population into co-operatives started in 1950, when 10.7 per cent of peasant households belonged to mutual aid teams. By 1956 it was practically completed, and 96.3 per cent had become members of producers' co-operatives. Out of those, 87.8 per cent belonged to higher types of co-operatives, also called collectives.[32] At a later stage the collectives, which had initially been founded largely on the basis of former villages, were integrated into larger communes. For the purpose of organizing production, however, the collectives were subdivided into production brigades and production teams. In China as in the Soviet Union, there were also state farms where labor was remunerated by fixed wages. These were usually established in new settlements, which were founded in regions inhabited by non-Chinese ethnic minorities. A vestige of private individual ownership was also preserved. Each farmer could own a small plot adjoining his house where he usually grew vegetables and raised poultry and small livestock, primarily for home consumption.

Agriculture was certainly not neglected in the early stage of the Chinese revolution. But in accordance with Mao's pronouncement in 1955, the emphasis in this area was placed on effecting institutional changes. Agriculture's share of capital investment during that period

32. Audrey Donnithorne, *China's Economic System*, Praeger, New York, 1967, p. 39.

was quite small. During the First Five-Year Plan, 1952 to 1957, the overall ratio of investment to gross national product was about 20 to 25 per cent, roughly equal to that reached in the Soviet Union, but actually one which implied a much greater sacrifice in consumption because of the lower level of income in China. Industry accounted for 47.9 per cent of total investments, a ratio in this case even higher than in the USSR, where it was only 40.9 per cent during their first plan. Only 14.9 per cent of total investments were allocated to agriculture, compared with 19.2 per cent in the USSR. Eighty-five per cent of total industrial investment went to heavy industries.

The concentration of effort in industry, which this very high rate of investment reflects, resulted in an extremely rapid rate of growth for industrial production. While estimates vary according to sources, the consensus seems to be that total industrial output about doubled during the period from 1952 to 1957. Absolute figures for the increase of output of a number of key products during that period are shown in the following table. As one might expect, the manufacture of intermediate products and capital goods grew much faster than that of industrial consumer goods, especially mass consumption items such as cotton textiles.

Table XXII
INDUSTRIAL PRODUCTION
HEAVY INDUSTRY AND MACHINERY

	1952	1957	Increase in Per Cent
Pig iron (thousand tons)	1,900	5,936	212
Steel	1,348	5,350	297
Electric power (million kwh)	7,260	19,340	166
Coal (million tons)	66.5	130	96
Crude oil (thousand tons)	436	1,458	234
Metal cutting machines (units)	13,734	28,000	104
Cement (thousand tons)	2,860	6,860	140
Sulfuric acid (thousand tons)	190	632	233
Chemical fertilizer	181	631	249
LIGHT INDUSTRY			
Rubber footwear (thousand pairs)	61,690	128,850	109
Cotton yarn (thousand bales)	3,618	4,650	29
Cotton cloth (million meters)	3,829	5,050	31
Cigarettes (thousand crates)	2,650	4,456	68
Edible vegetable oil (thousand tons)	983	1,100	12
Matches (thousand cases)	9,110	10,250	13

Source: Chen and Galenson, *op. cit.*, table 111-4, pp. 62 and 63.

The enormous expansion in the output of heavy industry in particular could not have been achieved without considerable assistance from the Soviet Union. This included massive supplies of equipment and complete plant installations. About half of the total industrial investment mentioned in the First Five-Year Plan was given to projects supported by the Soviet Union. Thus the three major iron and steel plants were equipped with Soviet machinery, as well as the first Chinese automobile factory, an oil refinery, two major hydroelectric plants, and 19 thermal plants. Moreover, the USSR provided considerable technical assistance. About 11,000 Soviet experts worked in China during the 1950's and 28,000 Chinese technicians and specialized workers were trained in the Soviet Union. While Soviet economic aid enabled China to accelerate its economic development during the 1950's, it was granted only on a credit basis. Chinese goods, mainly primary products, paid for these credits during the next decade, and in the absence of new Soviet credits this represented a heavy drain on the Chinese balance of payments.

In industry, just as in agriculture, the transformation of ownership and organizational structure was achieved in China in a much more gradual and flexible way than in the Soviet Union. The sweeping nationalization of all private enterprise by the October Revolution aroused the bitter opposition not only of the owners but also of the managerial and technical personnel who were unwilling to knuckle under to manual workers. When this class had largely disappeared after the end of the civil war, by dying off or emigrating, Soviet industry was faced with a critical shortage of key personnel which was particularly serious during the crucial period of industrialization. Only after a new generation of Soviet-trained technicians and managers had emerged and was able to take over was the balance at all redressed. China, on the contrary, succeeded to a great extent in holding on to the technical and managerial skills of her private industrialists, skills which were far scarcer there in 1949 than in Russia in 1917.

At the time of the communist takeover a substantial part of China's modern industry, which accounted for a third of the country's output, was already under government ownership. Most of it represented confiscated enemy assets, primarily Japanese-owned plants in Manchuria. Most of the non-Japanese, foreign-owned enterprises had been destroyed or damaged during the war and were of relatively little importance. These were gradually taken over by the state, with the last British-owned woolen mill still in existence as late as 1959. At first most of the privately run factories were not affected. During the early period, from 1949 to 1953, they even grew in number, and were able to expand their production considerably because of the country's economic revival after the end of the civil war. Gradually, however, the government exerted pressure to transform private firms into joint state/private enterprises. The former owners were kept on as managers and received a dividend on their capital. At a later stage this dividend, which could vary according to the rate of profits, was replaced by a fixed interest rate, usually of 5 per cent. The transformation of private enterprises was virtually completed by the end of 1956. Interest payments to about 250,000 former owners were made at least up to the start of the Cultural Revolution. Thus these enterprises remained under the direction of experienced managers who were under the same obligation to follow strictly government instructions and to carry out their part of the production plan as state officials. Most likely the sum total of the interest payments granted to them was far smaller than the losses which would otherwise have been incurred had these managers been prematurely replaced. All the newly established enterprises, of course, operated under full government ownership.

The First Five-Year Plan was unquestionably successful, and strikingly so in the most important area of industrial development. But it appears not to have given full satisfaction to the communist leaders and in particular to Mao himself. Industrialization by developing heavy industries, which used capital-intensive techniques, had not provided much additional employment. From 1952 to 1957 total employment in the modern sector rose only from 30.2 to 31 million. This scarcely made a dent in the problem of finding employment for a rapidly growing labor force. It was estimated that during the Second Five-Year Plan 15.3 million additional jobs would have to be created, just to cover the already unemployed and the anticipated increases in the labor force. Furthermore, this did not even take into consideration the mass under-employment of labor on the farms. The Soviet model from the point of view of employment had not proved satisfactory. Greater emphasis on labor-intensive activities would be more suited to the needs of China and could take advantage of the opportunities which her vast manpower resources offered. The notion of adopting an original Chinese format of socialist development also flattered their national pride. In addition, there was growing concern on Mao's part about the "revisionist" trend of Soviet policy, especially after the anti-Stalin speech which Khrushchev gave at the 20th Congress of the Soviet Communist Party. The communist ideal of equality seemed to be slanted in favor of a new privileged class of party bureaucrats and technocratic managers. If China were to go on following the Soviet example, a revisionist trend might emerge there also, and this danger had to be avoided at all costs.

The Great Leap Forward, which was initiated in 1958, was based on the conviction, reinforced by the success of the First Five-Year Plan, that it would be possible through the mass mobilization of the rural population to accelerate both economic development and the socialist transformation of society. The emphasis on industrial development was preserved and even strengthened. The plan was to maintain a 25 per cent annual rate of growth in industrial output. But this accelerated expansion would be first seen in the construction of plants and dams, in digging irrigation canals, and in other public works. For such projects a great number of laborers with shovels could replace bulldozers and other costly mechanized equipment. In industry the same approach would be followed with the construction in rural areas of a multitude of small plants using simple and inexpensive equipment and significantly more labor than modern larger-scale factories. Industrial management at the same time was decentralized in order to allow more scope for local initiative in setting up and operating the new small-scale industries.

The organizational framework for mobilizing the rural masses was found in the people's communes, which were a consolidation of agricultural producers' co-operatives. The replacement of some 740,000 co-operatives by 26,000 communes had been accomplished very rapidly in the fall of 1958. The official explanation for this extraordinary speed was the spontaneous enthusiasm of the rank and file, but meticulous organization and preparation is probably closer to the truth.[33] The communes represented a far higher degree of collectivization than the previous agricultural co-operatives. They took over the administrative functions of local government and were responsible not only for agriculture but also for industry, trade, banking, education, and cultural activities within their territory. Their most important task was to promote the establishment of new industries, to employ local manpower, and, when available, local resources and raw materials. The plan was to make the communes self-sufficient as far as possible for most consumer goods and even basic capital goods. Thus factories were created to produce building materials (bricks and cement), textiles, and shoes, as well as agricultural tools, fertilizer, and even iron and steel, the so-called backyard iron furnaces. Public works, including

33. K.S. Karol, *China, the Other Communism*, Hill & Wang, New York, 1967, p. 155.

irrigation and flood control, were undertaken on an expanded scale, and agricultural work was intensified with such methods as deep ploughing in order to increase productivity. The communes decided on the allocation of the manpower for all these activities.

The progress which was made toward socialization in the communes was reflected in the method of remuneration. The last vestiges of the former co-operative sharing of proceeds disappeared and agricultural as well as industrial workers were paid fixed wages. Private plots were abolished and communal mess halls were established to serve meals to the workers in order to permit women to assume their full role in the labor force. Babies and small children were taken care of in communal nurseries. The essentially political character of the Great Leap Forward can be seen in the arguments used by the enormous propaganda campaign which was conducted to arouse the enthusiasm of the people. It was represented as a giant step forward to the advent of communism. The communal dining halls and even more the free distribution of rice in a few communes were depicted as the start of the ideal communist system of giving "to each one according to his needs." Thus, in a few years China would have advanced further on the road to communism than the USSR in over 40 years. Moreover, this would be achieved by the people themselves, whose creative power could not be too much praised, and not by experts, and, what was worse, foreign experts. For the first time the advice of specialists would be replaced by the wisdom of the people.

The drive for the Great Leap Forward started with what seems indeed to have been genuine interest on the part of the masses, fanned into enthusiastic approval by an intensive and all pervading propaganda campaign. The first reports pronounced it a great success. New factories were built and put into operation by the hundreds and public works proliferated. Production statistics for those years—and none have been published in China since—seemed to justify this optimism. The official index of industrial production rose from 196 in 1957 (1952 = 100) to 272 in 1958 and 371 in 1959, an increase of nearly 40 per cent for each of these years. It was soon discovered, however, that the expansion was more apparent than real. Much of the output of the new factories was of such poor quality that it proved unusable. This was especially true of the pig iron produced in the backyard furnaces. Some of the public works which were started without sufficient study and preparation did more harm than good. Thus in several regions large reservoirs and the irrigation canals that were dug lowered the level of ground water and reduced soil fertility. Not all of the new methods proved useful; deep ploughing in certain areas contributed to soil erosion.

In many communes enthusiasm for industrial development was so great that most of the available labor force was assigned to it. Thus in 1958 there was a shortage of labor for harvesting the crops in several provinces, and the yields were affected. Special bulletins had to be sent out to prevent the repetition of these drastic miscalculations. The proliferation of projects, which all were started at the same time, resulted in the haphazard allocation and inefficient use of human and material resources. Enthusiasm alone without organization and professional skills proved inadequate to the gigantic task of expanding the economy and changing the society over to a socialist pattern. The elimination of all material incentives, by introducing fixed wages for farm work and confiscating all private plots, may also have weakened the impact of the mass propaganda on the farmers. Without the hope of reaping profit for themselves or their families, they may have been discouraged from intensifying their efforts. Frequent cases of absenteeism were reported in many communes.

The failure of crops three years in succession, from 1959 to 1961, aggravated the already disastrous consequences of these policy errors. The output of agricultural raw materials, such as cotton and sugar cane, which were required for industrial processing, was seriously reduced. In spite of all this, however, the generalized famine which would have been unavoidable in the past under similar misfortunes did not occur.

A period of retrenchment then occurred. Industrial production drastically declined, in part because of the shortage of raw materials, but primarily because of the dismantling of all new plants which had been unable to attain minimum standards of efficiency in quality and cost of manufacture. Priority was given in investment to agriculture and to industries with direct impact on agricultural production: fertilizer and farm machinery. There was a change in policy for the communes. Private plots were returned to the peasants and fixed wages were abandoned in favor of remunerating farm work according to individual performance. The practice of collective mess halls and free distribution of rice was also dropped. Agricultural production was further spurred by the establishment of a great number of state-owned agricultural machinery stations. These had at their disposal most of the limited supply of tractors and farm machinery and could lease them out to communes for a minimal fee. The role of the communes in production was thereby reduced. At present they still appear to administer the few industrial activities which have not been discontinued, but their primary functions are mainly administrative, social, and cultural. They serve also as the main channels of communication between the government and the people at large.

Since the failure of the Great Leap Forward, no official economic statistics have been published in China. But one can be fairly certain that industrial and agricultural production did recover after the low mark reached in 1960/61, and expanded considerably further until the Cultural Revolution which started in 1966/67. This progress can be seen in the increasing availability of industrial consumer goods for domestic markets and for exports, and in the fact that rationing has been removed from most foodstuffs.

These happy results were the consequence of more rational policies. Thus in agriculture the emphasis was no longer on ambitious new constructions but on improving and repairing existing facilities, on putting them to better use. A systematic effort was made to ensure that irrigated lands became fully drought resistant, and that the maximum possible of cultivated land produce high and stable yields. New seeds, different from the miracle varieties of wheat and rice developed in Mexico and in the Philippines, but with similar high yields, were developed in China. The consumption of fertilizer increased from 2.3 million tons in 1961 to 9.5 million in 1967. In the same period domestic production rose from 1.4 to 6.0 million tons, and imports from 0.9 to 3.5 million tons. Tractors and farm machinery began to be manufactured locally, and by the mid-1960's practically all farm machinery was of Chinese design and construction.

This progress is particularly impressive in view of the fact that not only had Soviet aid completely stopped, but that even past credits owed to the USSR had all been reimbursed. Moreover, China had already started her own foreign aid program, and was expanding it. The crisis which had followed the Great Leap Forward had not noticeably slowed it down. From 1953 to 1965, according to unofficial estimates, the Chinese committed a total of $2,038 million (out of which about 60 per cent went to communist countries) to foreign aid.[34] Soviet credits to China for a period roughly two years longer, 1950 to 1964, came to only a slightly higher total of $2,294 million, and from this amount one must subtract $2,244 million which were reimbursed. Chinese terms for foreign aid are far more generous than those of the other socialist countries; most of it is in the form of grants or interest-free loans.

The creation and rapid expansion of a nuclear and thermonuclear

34. Chenn and Galenson, *op. cit.*, pp. 210 and 213.

force is a particularly impressive demonstration of China's technological, economic, and consequently military advances. Unquestionably
the USSR gave her a helping hand at first in that direction. Too,
China benefited from a concentration of all available human and material resources, which is possible only under a system of total government control. Still her achievement is extraordinary, coming as it did
faster than in any of the other nuclear powers, including the Soviet
Union, and overcoming the handicap of a far less developed economy.

There is no question, then, that China's economy thrived under
communist rule, and that she made faster progress in development
than most other countries in the Third World. But this was not sufficient for Chairman Mao Tse-tung, the leader and prophet of the
Chinese revolution. Mao felt that the main objective still had not been
reached—the goal which obviously Mao considered even more important than an economic development that could be measured purely
in a greater availability of material goods. This goal was the establishment of a fully equalitarian society which would have totally rooted
out all élitist domination or egoistic craving for private advancement,
and would have done away with the difference in status between
classes of farmers, urban workers, and intellectuals. With the exception
of the Great Leap Forward, development was still directed by a
highly competent and skillfull group of managers and communist
party officials. The practice of material incentives had been encouraged rather than abolished. In imitation of the reforms introduced
in Eastern European socialist countries, there had even been an
attempt to emphasize the profitability of enterprises. To Maoist communists this smacked not only of Soviet revisionism, but of outright
retrogression to capitalism.

The "Great Cultural Revolution" came of Mao's deep fear that
China would soon follow the example of the Soviet Union. There he
felt that the revolutionary fervor had subsided after the generation of
the original founders, and had been replaced by apathy; the government had been taken over by a self-serving bureaucracy. To avert this
danger Mao took the deliberate risk of jeopardizing not only future
progress, but also the normal operation of the economy, by dislocating
the government and destroying his own brain child, the communist
party apparatus. In the middle of 1966 he unleashed the "Red Guards,"
masses of young people who were fanatical believers of the truth as
set down in the "little red book," and pitted them against the leadership of all existing institutions, were they party, government, education, agriculture, or industry. With or without justification they
attacked violently all higher officials, accused them of violating Mao's

precepts, and threw them out, replacing them with their own followers. Their assault inevitably met with strong resistance. Serious
clashes, bordering on civil war in several regions, resulted. The country was partly at least in a continued state of chaos, with transportation frequently disrupted and production disorganized and neglected.
The struggle for control went all the way up to the highest level of
the party and government leadership. Mao's main opponent was Liu
Shao-chi, whom Mao himself had placed at the head of government
when he resigned from the post of Chairman of the Republic in 1959.
Liu Shao-chi had presided over the recovery of the economy and the
development achieved since the end of the Great Leap Forward, and
at one point it seemed doubtful that Mao would ultimately prevail.
As we know now, Mao finally did emerge the victor, in great part because of the support of the army, whose chief up to very recently was
the most powerful man in China after Mao. The army gradually took
over control of all major aspects of government and the economy; the
Red Guards were returned to their schools or given productive work
to do in agriculture and industry. The former leaders were sent out
as ordinary laborers to be re-educated through manual labor.

It is difficult to know exactly what happened during the Cultural
Revolution, which lasted approximately from 1966 to 1969. The generally secretive posture of the Chinese communists was particularly
pronounced during that period, and the country was for all practical
purposes sealed off from foreigners. Students who were abroad on
official scholarships had to return home for indoctrination in the spirit
of the revolution. Chinese diplomats were recalled from their posts for
the same purpose.

Gradually China's isolation was relaxed, to the point where the
government, in full control obviously and feeling quite secure in its
power, not only permitted but invited inspection by foreigners in the
spring of 1971. Those who had known pre-revolutionary China found
an entirely different country. All visible indications of the appalling
misery of the majority of the population—the malnutrition, sickness,
ignorance, and filth—had gone, together with the insolent luxury of
the "happy few." Instead there was a drab uniformity in food, clothing, and to some extent already in housing in the rapidly growing
major cities. Although it is barely adequate according to the most
modest of standards, and inferior to what even the underprivileged
enjoy in the affluent countries, still for the Chinese masses this represents an enormous improvement over their previous state of abject
poverty and total insecurity. Such conditions continue in most underdeveloped countries.

The economy seems again to be operating normally, without trace of the turbulence which had marred the period of the Cultural revolution. The masses of Chinese workers and peasants are applying their traditional industriousness, although it has been reported that two hours of their working day are devoted to the study of the precepts of Mao, and not to productive work. The recent successes of China with atomic weapons and rocketry suggest that there was no interruption in their technological progress, or that it was resumed after the Cultural Revolution.[35]

Several sources have also confirmed the fact that most of the former managers and leading specialists in such various fields as industry, administration, and education, who were relieved of their positions during the Cultural Revolution and sent out to the communes for re-education, have now returned. The administration at present is under the control of the "Revolutionary Committees" which have assumed tight political control and imposed ideological discipline and work patterns in keeping with the Maoist philosophy.[36]. They are usually headed by a triumvirate consisting of representatives from management, the army, and workers or peasants. Former managers no longer give orders, only advise. Although their advice is usually taken, the basic principle of equality for all categories of workers, regardless of their particular work or level of responsibility, is thus maintained, along with competent management. The same reasoning dispatches urban workers, particularly those involved with non-manual tasks, to spend a certain amount of time each year on the farms. This stretch of farm work obviously does not produce a significant increase in agricultural output, but it emphasizes the importance of agricultural labor.

Another reform was recently introduced in education, which may have far reaching consequences, and which seems also to stress the importance of equality within Chinese society. In addition to part-time work on farms or industries during their high school careers, something which has also existed in other socialist countries, graduates of secondary schools are now obliged to work for three years in communes or factories before they are entitled to continue their studies. At that point candidates for higher education will be selected not only on the basis of their academic performance—the number of posts

35. For the first time since 1959 some figures have been published on China's economic growth in 1971. The value of industrial and agricultural output increased by about 10 per cent compared to 1970, and steel production reached 21 million tons, 18 per cent above the 1970 figure and about four times the 1957 level (*The New York Times*, 2 January 1972).

36. *The New York Times*, 2 June 1971.

which will need to be filled in each field is also a consideration—but at least as much on their political attitude. The duration of this higher education has been substantially reduced and study is intermingled with productive work. The aim is to prevent students from acquiring an élitist mentality, divorcing themselves from the mass of ordinary workers.

A very high rate of investment, estimated at around 25 per cent of gross product, has expanded production and permitted an increase in individual, and especially in collective, consumption. The complete control over production and consumption by the government enabled it to devise ways to find these investment funds which would not disturb most Chinese. The main sources of revenue were government enterprises and the turnover tax; neither affected much the average worker. There was no income tax. At first investment followed the Soviet theory of giving the first priority to heavy, capital-intensive industry. But at a later stage the allocation of investments took more into consideration the natural resources of the country. Greater emphasis was put on labor-intensive projects in order to make use of the country's prime wealth, her large and hard-working labor force. In China today research concentrates on the problem of adapting labor-intensive methods to areas of production which in other countries would require more sophisticated capital-intensive methods.

In the absence of official statistics and in light of the general veil of secrecy in which the country has shrouded itself, it is rather difficult to evaluate in quantitative terms the development achieved by Communist China since 1949. One can judge more easily whether or not the main goals of the revolution, economic development, a respected international position, and the establishment of an equalitarian communist society, have been attained. Then it seems quite clear that some very positive results have been achieved.

The ability of the communists to gain the active, frequently the enthusiastic, support of their people, and thus to mobilize fully their energies, has been a very important factor in their success. To us who are citizens of countries with a strong democratic tradition, who take for granted the right to freedom of thought or speech, the Chinese practice of massive indoctrination and brain-washing, their personality cult which has surpassed anything in Stalin's Soviet Union or Hitler's Germany, seems repugnant. But one must remember here the abject poverty and the flagrant inequality, in a climate of demoralizing corruption in pre-revolutionary China, which made the oppression of the masses even more unbearable. Maoist communism offered the hope of improving their material condition and justified this improvement with an inspiring ideal of human equality and solidarity. How can one be surprised by the fact that it was embraced by the masses as a "quasi-religion," with a fanaticism such as the Muslims displayed at the beginning of Islam?[37] We must admit that on the whole the trust of faithful Maoists has been well rewarded.

Although the Maoist revolution has not been free of violence— and respect for human life is not one of its more outstanding features —what bloodshed or killing of class enemies has existed has been on a much smaller scale than in the Soviet revolution. However distasteful the brain-washing that is practiced in Communist China may be, it seems less reprehensible than mass extermination.

There is obviously no freedom of any kind in China. But freedom has never been part of the communist ideal, as historically it has not been an element of any religion in its first stage, when it still claims to have the monopoly on truth and the road to salvation. Mao's government has created in China the most equalitarian society existing anywhere in the world. To ensure its survival the government has abolished material incentives and burned out any egoistic craving for individual advancement. In addition to a standard of individual consumption which is much higher than what they had in the past, the masses benefit from highly developed collective services, such as health and old age protection. Their educational system is more practical and better adjusted to the present requirements and opportunities than those of most developing countries.

Thus China has succeeded in scarcely twenty years in overcoming the drawbacks of economic underdevelopment to become one of the world's superpowers. Only time will tell whether her apparent success in creating a fully equalitarian society will be durable. Will it survive the end of the present austerity, will it still prevail in the greater abundance of the future? China offers an example which quite a number of developing countries would like to imitate. But only in a few are there the resources, as well as the mentality, which are prerequisites for the success of such an endeavor.

IRAN: AN EXPERIMENT IN ECONOMIC AND
SOCIAL REVOLUTION FROM ABOVE

Iran has had a glorious past. In 1971, the Shah celebrated the 2500th anniversary of the founding of Persepolis, the ancient capital of an empire which extended at one point from the Indus to the Nile. But in more recent times conditions in Iran have reflected little of

37. Paul Alpert, *Demain la Démocratie*, Editions de la Flèche, Paris, 1939, Chapitre VI.

her former splendor. Ravaged by numerous conquerors, she was not able to keep up with the course of history and slipped backward. Iran in the early part of this century was a stagnant weak country, unable either to adapt Western civilization or to withstand Western pressures. She had maintained her nominal independence only because of her geographic position as a buffer state between the possessions of Russia and Britain, which competed for control over Asia during most of the nineteenth century. In 1907, however, Russia and the United Kingdom reached an agreement and divided Iran, then called Persia, into two spheres of influence. The North would be dominated by Russia and the South by the British, while the middle, with the capital city of Teheran, would remain neutral territory.

The only large modern enterprise in Iran was located in the South, and was therefore British-owned. It was the Anglo–Persian Oil Company, founded in 1909 on the basis of a concession which had already been granted in 1901 for 60 years to an English engineer for prospecting and extracting oil. The government of Iran was to receive only a very moderate royalty of 16 per cent of the company's profits. During World War I, when the British navy switched from coal to fuel oil, the British government acquired a majority interest in the company. As we mentioned earlier, a secret clause in the company's agreement with the British government stipulated that the British navy could purchase oil at a much lower rate than the current market price.

The terms of this concession were bitterly resented by Iranians, who considered it a scandalous exploitation of their natural resources by foreign capital. The growing discontent in the country finally forced the Iranian Parliament in 1932 to declare the concession invalid and to terminate it. Considerable pressure was immediately exerted by the British government, including appeals to the World Court of Justice, and even the League of Nations. Iran's precarious financial situation at the time left her no alternative but to agree the following year to a compromise. The government ratified the concession and extended it for another 32 years, up to 1993. In return, payments were increased. In addition to a minimum tax of £225,000 to £300,000, Iran would receive 4 shillings on each ton of oil sold, and 20 per cent of net profits after the payment of a guaranteed minimum dividend. The company also agreed to train and to employ Iranian personnel.

During World War II, and especially after the occupation of Indonesia by the Japanese, Iran became the main source of oil for the Allied forces in the Eastern Mediterranean and in Southeast Asia.

The strategic importance of her railroad, which transported nearly all military supplies to the Soviet Union, led to the "protective" occupation of Iran by British and Soviet troops. The latter remained in the northern part of the country until 1946, and were only withdrawn after a complaint was lodged by Iran at the United Nations and strongly supported by the American and British governments.

By then the country was nearly ruined; its system of transportation was completely worn out from excessive use and lack of maintenance. The abject poverty of the overwhelming majority of the population was in sharp contrast to the growing prosperity of the foreign oil company and aroused public indignation. The man on the street in Iran found it impossible to accept that, as shown in the table below, the United Kingdom and not his own country should be the one to profit the most from the extraordinary advances in oil extraction.

Table XXIII

	Iran's Receipts from the AIOC (taxes and dividends)	*Taxes Paid by AIOC to the* UK Government
	(in million pounds sterling)	
1948	9	28
1949	13.5	23
1950	16	50.5

Source: Official Record, United Nations Security Council, 563rd Meeting, Vol. 15 (1951), quoted in Bahman Nirumand, "Iran: the New Imperialism in Action," Monthly Review Press, New York and London, 1969, p. 45.

Iran was paid in all less than 10 per cent of the company's profits. The company had organized and was running their concessions as if for all practical purpose they were a foreign enclave outside the sovereignty of Iran. This was especially true of Abadan, where they had constructed the largest refinery in the world at the time, and where the oil export harbor was located. Senior posts were all still manned by British citizens in spite of the 1933 agreement. Most of the facilities and the luxuries of Abadan were reserved for the use of the company's senior staff and thus denied to the Iranians.

By 1950 the Nationalist Front, headed by Dr. Mohammed Mossadegh, was gaining strength rapidly throughout the country. They demanded the complete revocation of the 1933 concession, claiming that it was illegal because it had been obtained by force. The possibility of agreeing on improved terms had no place in their thinking.

Their campaign against the AIOC was based on political rather than economic motives and had as its objective their country's liberation from colonialist exploitation and domination by foreign capital. This was to be achieved irrespective of the economic cost to Iran. The program of the National Front also included land reform and other proposals which were equally objectionable to the ruling class of feudal landowners.

In order to avoid nationalization, the Anglo–Iranian Oil Company agreed to revise the terms of its concession and to increase up to 50 per cent the government's share in its profits. The revised agreement was duly signed by the government in power but rejected by the Parliament. After new elections and protracted controversy, the Iranian Parliament passed a law nationalizing the oil industry, and in April, 1951 Mossadegh became Prime Minister. All the properties of the AIOC were transferred to a newly created National Iranian Oil Company, with 25 per cent of the profits to go to the former owners as compensation.

The AIOC and the United Kingdom refused to recognize the legality of this move, one which Iran felt it was her right as a sovereign state to make and one which belonged in the category of domestic legislation. The British presented their claim at the International Court of Justice at The Hague and raised the problem again in the Security Council. But discussions at the United Nations were inconclusive and the Court ruled that the matter was outside its jurisdiction. This was tantamount to a nod of approval on their part. The United States tried to mediate in the dispute, but attempts to negotiate all failed. In retaliation the company recalled their technical and supervisory personnel, with the hope that this would paralyze the operations of the oil fields and refineries. They tried also to prevent all export sales of Iranian oil by appealing to the sympathies of other international oil companies, and on the whole this policy was successful. The production and export of oil declined drastically. The British government co-operated with the company by freezing all Iranian assets and deposits in British banks.

The flow of foreign exchange into the country plummeted to a new low as a result, but the blockade did not seriously disrupt the economy of the country. Only the rich, and they were in a minority, suffered from a lack of imported consumer goods, while the bulk of the population, who eked out a marginal existence, were scarcely affected. In this kind of emergency an underdeveloped country with a subsistence economy is far more resilient than a developed country which depends heavily on its international trade. The successful resistance of Mossadegh to the pressure of a great colonialist power and a foreign capitalist enterprise helped him maintain, and even increase at first, his popularity.

But in the course of imposing his domestic policy, Mossadegh tried to restrict the prerogatives of the Shah and aroused his enmity. The struggle for power between the ultranationalist Prime Minister, who was accused of accepting support from the communists, and the monarch ended in August of 1953 by a military coup said to have been engineered and financed by the CIA.[38] This was never confirmed, but once the Shah resumed power in September of 1953 Iran received an emergency aid grant of $45 million from the United States. Her financial resources were completely exhausted, and during the fiscal year of 1954 American aid to Iran totaled $127.4 million.

A new oil agreement was approved in 1954 by the Iranian Parliament. While it upheld the principle of national sovereignty over natural resources, this agreement in substance was on a par with the last proposals of the AIOC before nationalization. The oil fields and all the installations in Iran would be owned by the National Iranian Oil Company (NIOC). But the actual operations would be run by an international consortium of the former AIOC and the other foreign companies which had joined in the earlier boycott of Iranian oil. American oil companies managed to control 40 per cent of the consortium. Iran would receive the proceeds of a 50 per cent income tax on the profits of the consortium. Oil for domestic consumption would be supplied at cost to the NIOC, which had a monopoly over sales within Iran.

Since 1954 the payments of the consortium to Iran have increased considerably, in line with the generally more favorable terms exacted now by all the oil-producing countries. In all, payments have gone up to $900 million per year. In addition, the NIOC has negotiated even more lucrative oil and gas agreements in areas where the consortium does not operate. Under the terms of these new agreements Iran will receive 75 per cent, and in one case even 90 per cent, of all profits.

As late as the 1950's, however, the oil sector with its capital-intensive, modern technology was still largely a foreign enclave. Other than the foreign exchange which it provided, it had little impact on the rest of the economy. Agriculture supported 80 per cent of the population, and had an extremely low rate of productivity because of primitive farming methods and an entrenched system of land tenure. A tiny class of feudal absentee landlords owned most of the land, which was then worked by sharecroppers without security of tenure.

38. *The New York Times Magazine*, 21 May, 1961.

They comprised 90 per cent of the rural population and received on the avereage only 30 per cent of the harvest. Modern industry was scarcely developed, other than the traditional handicraft of rug manufacturing. There were a few factories, mainly government-owned, which produced cement and basic consumer goods such as sugar and cotton textiles.

At the end of World War II attempts were made to plan and co-ordinate economic development and industrialization. They led to the creation of a body called the Plan Organization, which was put in charge of planning *per se* and also of operating the major development projects. This Organization had a major role in Iran's economic development after the middle of the 1950's, when oil revenues, which were supposed to be reserved for development expenditures, were increasing rapidly. One can imagine the difficulties that planners encountered in a country where economic considerations are frequently overruled by politics as well as personal intrigues. George Baldwin, one of the foreign experts who had worked in the Plan Organization, describes the situation vividly in his book *Planning and Development in Iran*.[39] Still the body was useful in initiating worthy projects and, just as important, in preventing others which would have been of little value to the economic development of the country. It managed to lay down some guidelines, which have been respected, on the general allocation of resources in the various sectors of the economy.

The major turning point in Iran's development was the Shah's comprehensive program of economic and social reform in 1960. He proclaimed it the "White Revolution" and received the immediate approval of the people in a nation-wide referendum.

The rationale for this revolution from above is not hard to find. The Shah only had to look around him to realize that a drastic transformation of the country's economic and social structure was desperately needed. The parasitic landlord class stood in the way of any progress and their power had to be broken. The peasant masses had to be liberated from oppression and exploitation. The country's youth was becoming increasingly restive and rebellious and lacked direction. The people were clamoring for their rights, for an improved standard of living, for national strength. Iran had to be industrialized, modernized, given a new orientation.

Reforms would have to come quickly. The country would other-

39. George R. Baldwin, *Planning and Development in Iran*, The Johns Hopkins Press, Baltimore, 1967, pp. 195–207.

wise see the full flowering of the revolutionary explosion that nearly occurred during the Mossadegh crisis. The example of neighboring Iraq, where the royal family was exterminated in 1959, left no doubt that in such a revolution the Shah would be likely to lose his life as well as his throne.

The most important step in the Shah's White Revolution was land reform. At the time only 15 per cent of all arable land was owned by the peasants. Tenant sharecroppers farmed the remaining 85 per cent; 15 per cent was owned by religious institutions; 5 per cent by the government, and the crown, and 65 per cent by the large landowners. The harvest traditionally was divided into five equal shares to cover the cost of land, water, power (usually draught animals), seed, and labor. Since the sharecroppers in many cases could only contribute their labor, the landlord supplied the rest and took in four fifths of the harvest. In other instances the tenants were charged more than one fifth of the harvest for water, and saw their own meager share reduced even further.[40] In the absence of written contracts, sharecroppers were entirely at the mercy of landowners who could dismiss their tenants or move them around at will. In view of the fact that most of the peasants were continuously indebted to their landowners for advances before the harvest, paid usually in kind, one can readily picture the slavery in which they existed. The average annual income of some 3 million farmer families in about 50,000 villages was between $133 and $200.[41]

The Shah made his first move to redistribute the land in 1950 when he organized a system whereby the tenants of crown lands could buy their farms on credit. A special bank gathered in the payments and lent out the proceeds to farmers to finance the new equipment and the drilling of wells. When the program ended in 1958 over 200,000 hectares had been redistributed to 25,000 farmers.[42] A somewhat similar sale of government land was started in 1958 and about 100,000 families benefited from this distribution.

In 1960 a proposal to extend land reform to private estates was submitted to Parliament. But the power of the landowners was such that they prevailed to insert loopholes which would have permitted them by various subterfuges to retain all their land. The Shah therefore dismissed Parliament and introduced in January of 1961 a sweeping land bill which allowed only one village per owner. Some 200

40. Norman Jacobs, *The Sociology of Development: Iran As an Asian Case Study,* Praeger, New York, 1966, p. 135.

41. M.R. Pahlavi, *The White Revolution in Iran,* Teheran, 1967, p. 34.

42. *Op. cit.,* p. 33

landowners in Iran had estates which consisted of more than 200 villages. Together that tiny group owned nearly half the villages in the whole country. Landowners would now be granted compensation, based usually on the value indicated by their previous land taxes. In most cases these taxes had been grossly underestimated, so that the landowners suffered a considerable loss in relation to the market value of their properties. The compensation would be paid in ten annual installments while the peasants had 15 years to reimburse the state. At a later date the land reform was enlarged in scope to cover the estates of religious institutions and to abolish the traditional system of share-cropping. Dealings between proprietors of farms exempted from re-distribution and peasants would be based on contracts stipulating rents paid in cash. The government sold shares to the public in state-owned enterprises in order to obtain funds for the land reform.

There also had to be some arrangement to provide the seeds, fertilizer, equipment, and credit, but at a lower cost and on better terms, than previously had been supplied to the peasants by the land-lords. A network of multipurpose rural co-operatives was created, headed by a central organization under the Ministry of Agriculture. This group will instruct the co-operatives and assist them in carrying out their functions until local leadership can take over.

The land reform law included provisions to prevent excessive subdivision of new farms among various heirs, leaving them with uneconomical miniholdings. Moreover, the government suggested to the peasants that they consolidate several family farms into larger farm units, which could more easily take advantage of modern meth-ods and mechanized equipment.

All water resources were to be nationalized; it would be govern-ment policy to ensure adequate water supplies at minimum cost to all legitimate agricultural and industrial users.

Supplementing the land reform was the nationalization of all forest and pasture land. Thus they would be protected from abuse by private interests. The Shah felt this point to be sufficiently important to be covered by the White Revolution.

There has been a lot of controversy about the meaning of the White Revolution and the impact it has had on the economy and society in Iran. The land reform of course has attracted the most attention. Official statements maintain that the principal objectives have been reached, in spite of a resistance which bordered on revolt in some cases. The White Revolution has liberated the peasants from oppression and launched them on the road to improved productivity and a higher standard of living. Over 2½ million farmers have benefited from the land reform; 7,600 rural co-operatives have been established with a membership of 1½ million. Opponents of the Shah assert that on the contrary the whole program is a sham, undertaken to improve international and domestic public relations. They claim that there has been only a partial distribution of rather infertile land on the whole, which has not made much difference in the lives of the few peasants involved, and that most of the co-operatives exist on paper only.[43] Baldwin has a more balanced view of the situation and finds no reason to discredit the Shah's original intention to carry out a sweeping program of reform. There were perfectly valid motives of self-interest and self-preservation. But judging from the record of other similar attempts in Iran, Baldwin doubts "whether land reform is likely to achieve its aims without fundamental changes in the political system."[44]

It is difficult to ascertain the truth from these conflicting statements. But one should note that unlike most other countries Iran did not experience a temporary decline, or even a stagnation, in agriculture during the period of transition to a new system of land tenure. The index of agricultural production rose by nearly 50 per cent from 1960 to 1970, and the per capita rate of agricultural output by 11 per cent. Wheat and sugar, the two most important agricultural products, went from 2,613,000 tons to 3,800,000, and from 113,000 to 553,000 respectively. It seems difficult to believe that the peasants would not have derived any benefits from the expansion in farm production.

One of the most impressive, and potentially far reaching, acts of the White Revolution was to enroll university and high school graduates in programs which replaced military service with work in rural areas to improve living conditions. The first and biggest of these projects was the creation of the Literacy Corps. After completing a four months' training course, its members are sent into the villages to teach in elementary schools and conduct adult education courses. The Literacy Corps seems to have been instrumental in accelerating the progress of literacy, which up to now has been very slow in the rural areas. The cost of this program is about one third of what it normally is for education, and the peasants, moreover, usually agree to build the necessary school buildings at their own expense.

In 1964 the Health Corps was created to provide medical services in rural areas which lacked proper health facilities. Physicians move around in mobile units and are assisted by university and high school graduates. That same year the government also set up the Reconstruction and Development Corps to assist peasants in modernizing their

43. Nirumand, *op. cit.*, pp. 127–133.
44. Baldwin, *op. cit.*, p. 98.

methods of production and in deriving maximum benefits from the land reform.

All these schemes for the most part enlist only youths from the privileged classes, whose parents alone could afford to provide their offspring with higher, even secondary education. It is not clear how much of an impact they have had on development. But as important as any contribution to economic progress that these schemes might make is the fact that they allow these youths the opportunity to become aware of the appalling conditions in which the masses of their countrymen still live. Hopefully they arouse in them the feeling of national solidarity and the desire to participate actively in the arduous but challenging task of improving these conditions. It is too early to tell, however, to what extent the youth have responded.

The Shah's outline for the White Revolution contained also some general principles for industrial development. Industries which involved natural resources such as mining and the production of electric power, railroads, airlines, telecommunications, and other public utilities were proclaimed of national importance and to be operated therefore by national corporations. The manufacture of basic industrial materials—iron and steel, for example—also fell into that group.

But private enterprise and private initiative would be encouraged. The government intended specifically to promote private investment in industry when it sold shares in state-owned factories in order to finance the land reform. Foreign investment should also be made welcome, particularly if there could be an association between foreign enterprise and domestic private or public concerns.

Specific emphasis was placed as well on drawing labor closer to industry, and on labor's participation in profits. A special law stipulates that industrial companies are to conclude agreements with their workers granting them bonuses based on increased productivity or a share in profits. Unless such an agreement is made, the enterprise has to set aside up to 20 per cent of its profits for the workers. The actual rate would be fixed in each case by the Ministry of Labor. The Shah has himself admitted that previous laws have not been very effective in protecting the rights of workers because of lack of enforcement, and this new bill may suffer the same fate.

Iran's policy of economic development and industrialization. is quite pragmatic, and has attracted private foreign capital. The most important foreign investment set up three large petrochemical plants in association with the National Petrochemical Company. The Soviet Union has co-operated in the construction of a steel plant with an initial capacity of 600,000 tons, and a machine tool factory. Both will be financed by exports of natural gas to the USSR.

Domestic private investment has been instrumental largely in expanding and diversifying consumer goods industries. Industrial output has increased rapidly, and the index of industrial production went from 100 in 1963 to 233 in 1969.[45] Industry, including oil, in 1967/68 represented up to 34 per cent of the Gross Domestic Product, while agriculture yielded only 23 per cent. From 1960 to 1968 the growth rate for manufacturing output came to 12.5 per cent and for agriculture 3.2 per cent. The rate of growth for the overall G.D.P. at constant prices has been extremely high for a developing country, and has, moreover, been growing steadily, from 5.6 per cent between 1953 and 1960 to 7.6 per cent from 1960 to 1967. The growth of per capita G.D.P. has also accelerated from 2.4 per cent to 4.7 per cent. The per capita income has gone from $143 in 1958 to $252 in 1968.

Iran has undoubtedly enjoyed a very rapid rate of economic growth since the end of the oil crisis in 1953, and in particular since the reforms of the White Revolution. The question remains, however, if Iran's present policies alone will be successful in bringing about economic development and in establishing a modern industrial economy and society.

Iran's natural wealth, her oil and natural gas resources and her fertile land, are obviously in her favor. In addition, she does not have the pressure of an excess population draining her resources. But of greater importance is the role that the various social classes will play in the future. Up to now economic development has almost exclusively benefited the privileged groups, those who are related to, or favored by, the Shah. Only limited substantive improvements have been made in the life of the rural and urban masses, although these to be sure have been dressed up in solemn pronouncements.

Will the peasants be satisfied with these relatively minor changes, and with the additional benefits that will come if the government has the wisdom and the strength to continue its program of land reform? Will the progress of industrialization provide sufficient additional employment to absorb most of the unemployed already concentrated in cities, who represent at least 5 per cent of the labor force, and part of the under-employed supported by the rural subsistence economy? Will the prospect of rapid economic development and the opportunities it will offer the professional class pacify the rebellious mood of so many Iranian students at present? One must ask further if the Shah's various mobilization schemes for rural development will

45. *Monthly Bulletin of Statistics,* July 1971, United Nations, New York, p. 26.

provide a creative outlet for the students' national and social ideals? Will the Shah himself pursue the White Revolution and transform its slogans into realities, saving thus his country and himself from a more violent, a more destructive upheaval? Only time has the answers.

SOUTH KOREA: THE DEVELOPMENT OF AN EXPORT ECONOMY THROUGH FOREIGN AID

In comparison to most other developing countries, South Korea today seems to have wrought an economic miracle. The country is a showcase for development in an economy of private enterprise, achieved under the most difficult of circumstances. One must remember that South Korea started with an economy which was dislocated by the partition along the 38th parallel, and then completely devastated by the war from 1950 to 1953. But in less than 20 years it has managed to reach an extremely high rate of economic growth, based mainly on the exports produced by newly created industries. An exceptionally large foreign aid program has been responsible on the whole for financing this extraordinary expansion. But growing reserves of domestic savings are reducing the country's dependence on external resources.

When Korea recovered her independence from the Japanese after World War II, she was left with an economy that was well advanced in comparison with most other developing countries. Japan had established there a reasonably modern and efficient infrastructure of transport and power.[46] But naturally, in their role as colonial masters, the Japanese had largely developed those sectors which could best serve their needs and in particular supply Japan with rice and raw materials. They had such tight control over the modern sector that when they left in 1945 there were no trained Koreans to take over their responsibilities.

An additional source of difficulty was the partition of the country, which became definite in 1948. Most of Korea's agricultural land and the major part of the consumer goods industry were in the South, while the North had more of the mineral and power resources as well as the heavy industries. South Korea therefore was faced with a shortage of fuel and power, and lacked the essential fertilizers which previously had been supplied by the North.

The Korean War broke out before these problems could be resolved and wrought complete havoc with the economy. Over 90

46. W.D. Reeve, *The Republic of Korea: A Political and Economic Study*, Oxford University Press, New York, 1963, pp. 102–103.

per cent of the country was invaded and devastated. In Seoul alone 80 per cent of all industry, public utilities, and transport had been reduced to rubble, as well as over half of all private dwellings. About 7 million persons were made homeless.

In the first years after the end of the war, and up to 1961, the United States largely financed South Korea's substantial economic recovery and gave on the average $270 million a year from 1953 to 1960. This represented more than 10 per cent of the country's total G.N.P., and about $13 to $14 per capita.[47] But South Korea's political instability impeded progress. The authoritarian and corrupt rule of its first President, Syngman Rhee, lasted up to 1960, followed by a short-lived interlude of democratic government, which was overthrown by a military coup in 1961. The emphasis placed on strengthening her military defenses rather than on economic growth was also not conducive to real economic development. Relatively little improvement was made in the extremely low standard of living of the population, which remained practically at the same level as under the Japanese domination. The per capita income increased by 18 per cent from 1953 to 1960 but was still below $100. Unemployment in both the urban and rural areas was very high and on the rise. The state of the country's balance of payments posed an immediate and dangerous threat to any future prosperity. In 1960, $32.8 millions' worth of exports amounted only to slightly more than 10 per cent of imports, which totaled $305.4 million. The deficit had to be made up by foreign donations of $275.7 million.[48]

Economic development did not in fact really begin in South Korea until the First Five-Year Plan for 1962 to 1966. The Plan outlined an economic system of "guided capitalism" which on the whole has remained in effect to this day and has been supported by government policies. The government guides and participates in the development of key industries and other major projects. As private initiative and resources are drawn into the development effort, direct government participation is then supposed to decline.

The targets of the Plan were very ambitious. The government aimed at a growth rate of 7.1 per cent for the G.N.P., of 15 per cent for secondary industries (manufacturing, construction, and mining), and of 4 per cent for primary industries (agriculture and fishing). The number of unemployed workers, which came to 2.7 million and represented over 25 per cent of the labor force, was to drop to 1.8 million, or 15 per cent. There would be a rapid increase in exports

47. Reeve, *op. cit.*, p. 126.
48. Reeve, *op. cit.*, p. 141.

and invisible receipts which would include, of course, the rising expenditures of United States military forces in South Korea. At the same time imports would grow at a much slower rate and reduce the deficit in the balance of payments. The necessary financial resources to carry out the plan would come largely from external sources: 42 per cent from United States net aid and other donations, and 16 per cent from foreign loans. Only 42 per cent would be derived from domestic savings. The rate of investment in relation to G.N.P. would go from 13.4 per cent in 1960 to 22.7 per cent in 1966.

In agriculture the Plan's main objective was to make the country self-sufficient in food and to eliminate the food imports which in 1960 had represented about 16 per cent of all imports. South Korea as a predominantly agricultural region had enjoyed substantial food surpluses before the war. The United States occupation authorities initiated a land reform which was carried out at the end of World War II. According to the new law, all land owned by the Japanese or belonging to big estates was distributed to some 1.5 million landless peasants. There were measures to increase agricultural production, including price incentives. Prices paid to farmers had previously been too low because of the large-scale import of American surplus food which the United States sent out as aid. They were now stabilized at a satisfactory level. Considerable effort would be put into reclaiming land and extending irrigation. Here community development and agricultural co-operatives would be part of the Plan to expand land under cultivation and to improve farming methods with double cropping and crop diversification.

In industry the objective was approximately to double the existing productive capacity. This would be achieved by doubling the extraction of coal, by nearly trebling the capacity of electric power already installed, and by increasing the production of steel, fertilizer, and cement. Motor vehicles and machinery would also be manufactured, and a start would be made in oil refining. Thus the major emphasis was on generating basic intermediate products and capital goods. Investments in the production of consumer goods would concentrate on textile manufacturing, South Korea's most important industry, which depended for the moment entirely on imported cotton. But several synthetic and chemical fiber plants would be built to supply domestic raw materials.

The National Construction Service Program was set up to provide productive jobs to a great number of the unemployed. They would work in labor-intensive public works projects, to develop in particular underground water resources, multipurpose river basins, and to build dams, dykes, roads, and bridges.

On the whole, satisfactory progress was made in development during the First Five-Year-Plan. The average rate of growth between 1962 and 1965 for G.N.P. and for mining and manufacturing, especially, went beyond the Plan, with 8.3 per cent and 15.3 per cent, respectively. Coal production more than doubled from 1960 to 1966, going from 5.2 million tons to 11.6 million, and electric power nearly trebled at 4.911 million kwh from an original 1,750 million. Shortages in fuel and power, which had impeded progress in industrial production when traditional sources of supply in the North were cut off, thus disappeared. Moreover, the creation of a new large oil refinery offered an additional and increasingly important domestic source of power, as well as a basis for a new petrochemical industry.

Agricultural production, unfortunately, did not reflect the same advances. With the growing demand for food because of an expanding population and an improved standard of living, South Korea did not progress very far on the road to self-sufficiency in food.

Exports, on the other hand, increased spectacularly, by 662 per cent from $32.4 million in 1960 to $250 million in 1966. By 1966 there had been a considerable change in the composition of exports, with manufactured products gaining in importance and representing now 61 per cent of the total, in comparison to 18 per cent in 1962. In contrast to exports, imports grew only by 134 per cent from 1960 to 1966. Still, their increase in absolute figures was substantially more significant, from $305.4 to $716 million. In 1966 exports covered 35 per cent of the value of imports, in contrast to 11 per cent in 1960, but the deficit in the balance of visible trade nevertheless increased from $272.6 to $466 million. American aid was declining gradually, and had dropped to $106 million in 1966. The remaining deficit was made up largely in $114 million paid by the United States to support their forces in South Korea, and in rapidly increasing foreign loans. The government borrowed $38 million, and the private sector an additional $170 million. Direct foreign investment contributed to a minor extent with $13 million.

In carrying out the First Five-Year Plan, the inability of the economy to generate sufficient domestic savings resulted in a relatively disappointingly low rate of investment. The rate of investment on the average was 14.2 per cent of the G.N.P. Only 5.1 per cent of the G.N.P. came from domestic savings. The rest was obtained from foreign sources.

Non-agricultural employment, in industry and services, increased substantially by 25 per cent from 1963 to 1966, and the number of registered unemployed did decline from 715,000 in 1962 to 666,000 in 1966, or 7.1 per cent of the labor force.[49]

The Second Five-Year Plan for 1967 to 1971 studied the successes as well as the drawbacks of the First Plan in order to find a remedy for the basic weaknesses in the South Korean economy. The main goal was to find an alternative to the excessive reliance on external resources for financing most of the country's investments and import requirements.

A considerable effort would therefore be made to raise the rate of domestic savings from 6.1 per cent in 1965 (the base year when the Second Plan was being prepared) to 14.4 per cent in 1971. With a tax reform and an improvement in tax administration in particular, government savings should increase substantially and represent 5.8 per cent of G.N.P. in comparison to the former 0.6 per cent. Private savings would also grow from 5.5 per cent to 8.6 per cent. The Plan indicated that nearly one third of the total increase in the G.N.P. should be saved and that by the end in 1971 domestic savings should finance 72 per cent of all investments. For the duration of the Plan the annual rate of investment would be pegged on the average at 19.1 per cent.

The hope was that new legislation would provide enough incentives to encourage the growth of domestic and especially foreign private investments. These incentives were designed to facilitate in particular the expansion of export and import-replacement industries. Aid would be granted in obtaining capital, along with special depreciation allowances. Imports of equipment and raw materials would be exempted from customs duties. There would be temporary exemptions from income taxation and reduced rates for rail transport and electric power. Under the Foreign Capital Inducement Law of 1967 foreign investors were authorized to transfer their profits and dividends out of the country without any restrictions whatsoever.[50]

The Plan anticipated a 7 per cent average rate of growth of G.N.P. from 1967 to 1971, less than the advance recorded during the First Plan in spite of a higher rate of investment. One must remember, however, that under the earlier program additional output could be obtained simply by the more effective utilization of existing equipment. This was no longer the case. Moreover, heavy investments had to be

49. *Statistical Yearbook, 1969, and Monthly Bulletin of Statistics,* United Nations, New York, 1971.

50. *Area Handbook for the Republic of Korea,* U.S.P.O. Washington, D.C., 1969, pp. 304 and 334.

made in capital-intensive industries, which required a heavy outlay of capital in relation to the expected increase in output. The average rate of growth should be 5 per cent for agriculture and 8.1 per cent in the other sectors of the economy.

In agriculture the Second Five-Year Plan again stressed self-sufficiency in food. There should be a large enough production of food grains in particular to meet all domestic demand by 1971. In industry the total production should double and heavy industry should account for 34 per cent of overall output, up from a previous 28 per cent. The production of iron and steel materials should nearly treble, accompanied by an even more rapid growth of petroleum products, of chemical fertilizers, and of cement. As before, the textile industry, the main source of South Korea's industrial exports, would be allocated the largest portion of investments. Then would come the chemicals, mentals, and machinery and transport equipment industries. Substantial investment would also be made in electric power plants and coal mines. The Plan stipulated that special efforts should be made to promote the expansion and modernization of small and medium industries which utilize some of the intermediate products of the large-scale industries. With labor intensive techniques these can potentially do the most to increase employment. In 1963 they had produced 56.3 per cent of the nation's total industrial output, but were responsible for 62.4 per cent of total industrial employment. Now they were being given the task of reducing the rate of unemployment from 7 per cent of the labor force in 1965 to a maximum of 5 per cent in 1971. The family planning program which was started under the First Plan would be enlarged and revitalized in order to trim the annual increase in population from 2.5 per cent to 2 per cent.

The anticipated tripling of exports from 1965 to 1971, together with a slower rate of increase for imports, should improve the balance of payments. The cash flow from foreign aid would probably be declining, in spite of an additional $30 million which Japan paid annually in reparations. But the government expected to receive more for its services, for the "export of services to Vietnam," a euphemism which designated the sums that the American government paid for the presence of South Korean military forces in Indochina. Most of the deficit on current account, however, would be covered by capital imports and loans as well as direct investments from Japan in particular.[51]

Final figures on the results of the Second Five-Year Plan were

51. Government of the Republic of Korea, *The Second Five-Year Development Plan*, 1967–1971, Seoul, July 1966, p. 65.

not available when this chapter was written. But we were able to glean some general information from the most recent data published and get some idea of South Korea's progress in economic development since 1966.

The general trends which revealed themselves during the First Plan have persisted. Rapid economic growth has continued and has even accelerated, but little progress has been made in achieving economic independence by relying less on external sources of financing for imports and investment. The G.D.P. at constant prices grew by 8 per cent in 1967, 14.4 per cent in 1968, and by 16 per cent in 1969.[52] From 1966 to 1970 industrial production shot up even faster, at a rate of 23.5 per cent a year. The production of electric power more than doubled for the same period, from 3,888 million kwh to 9,192 million kwh; 5,832,000 tons of cement were produced, more than three times the original of 1,884,000. Agricultural production also increased, although it did not progress as fast as industry.

Employment in sectors other than agriculture increased overall by 25 per cent from 1966 to 1969, but in manufacturing specifically by 53 per cent for the same period. The number of unemployed declined form 666,000 to 471,000, or from 7.1 per cent to 4.9 per cent of the labor force. Thus the goal of bringing unemployment down to 5 per cent of the labor force was reached two years before the target date of 1971.

Foreign trade has developed in a spectacular fashion. The value of exports has increased more rapidly than expected, more than tripling between 1965 and 1970, from $250 million to $834 million. But imports have kept up to nearly the same pace, going from $716 to $1,984 million. Exports now do cover 42 per cent of the costs of imports, an increase of 7 per cent, but the deficit in the balance of trade has still risen from $466 to $1,150 million. As the Second Five-Year Plan recommended, foreign loans are making up the difference. In the breakdown of the balance of payments for 1969, which is the most recent available, private loans from abroad amounted to $431 million and another $203 million came from government loans, while direct foreign investments represented only $16 million. Moreover, if one includes the expenditure of American military forces in South Korea, one sees that the government came up with a surplus of $197 million in the balance of services.

As we have just outlined, South Korea's economic policies have been markedly successful. In the last decade the G.D.P. at constant prices has increased at an average rate of 9.2 per cent and per capita

52. *AID Fact Sheet for the Republic of Korea,* Washington, D.C., 1971.

income at 6.4 per cent. In 1970, the average South Korean received $245 a year, up from $130 in 1960. Government policies have created a modern infrastructure of fuel, power, and transport and have established industries producing basic materials, which can be a basis for the further expansion of the economy. All this has been achieved in spite of the heavy defense costs which absorbed over 30 per cent of total budget expenditure.

At this point in our discussion, however, we should take a closer look at certain other factors which may alter the picture somewhat. They may raise some doubts about the future development in South Korea and the stability of the country's social and economic structure.

We indicated earlier that the rapid rate of South Korea's overall economic growth was largely a consequence of the extraordinary expansion of exports. These have grown at an average rate of 31 per cent from 1960 to 1969. The most important of them have been labor-intensive industrial consumer items, in particular textiles and clothing. The United States bought $4 million worth of textiles and clothing in 1965, $99.4 million in 1969, and $131.1 million in 1970. Increasingly, also, exports have included a wide variety of other goods where the price of labor is the main factor in the total cost of production. The impetus for the development of these exports came from importers and frequently even from the manufacturers in the importing countries. Although the United States has figured most prominently in this trade, Japan, too, has recently transferred over to South Korea labor-intensive manufacturing processes in order to secure cheaper imports in place of her domestic output. Inevitably these imports have had to face the strong opposition of industries in the importing countries that were losing more and more of their domestic market to this foreign competition. The workers in these industries protested even more bitterly. As we have already mentioned, the manufacturers, after all, could, and frequently did, make up the loss in profits from domestic production by themselves investing in the foreign industries. This opportunity for a profitable redeployment of their resources was not available to the workers who had lost their jobs. Their position was made even more precarious by the fact that the accelerated expansion of imports from South Korea and other low-wage countries of Asia coincided with a severe business recession in the United States. It is not surprising, therefore, that in order to stem the flow of textiles, which was still the major import and was responsible for the loss of 100,000 jobs in the American textile industry, the United States government, as we have already mentioned, forced South Korea and other Asian exporting countries in October of 1971 to accept a five-year agreement limiting the annual rise in their shipments of non-cotton textiles to 7.5 per cent.[53]

The United States has considered its demand to be relatively moderate. Since the consumption of domestic textiles in the United States is increasing only by 3 per cent, imports will continue to grow in importance, although more slowly than before. But South Korea has had to view this measure as a brake on the further expansion of sales to their most important export market. The United States in 1970 bought about half of South Korea's total exports, and it has now dealt a heavy blow to any prospects of a continued rapid economic growth in South Korea. It is quite probable, furthermore, that similar restrictions will be imposed on other major exports from South Korea. We see here a good illustration of the danger that can threaten a developing country which wants to achieve economic independence and relies too heavily in its development policy on the export of industrial products. In view of the existing economic balance of power, the developing country may become dependent on the main importer of its products if it has no substantial domestic market of its own. This is especially true when foreign sales are not distributed widely, but are concentrated in one or a few major countries. The developing country may find itself in a position that is not significantly different from that of other nations in the Third World that have traditionally been dependent on the major developed countries because of their exports of primary products.

In recent years Japan has considerably increased her trade with South Korea and has been more active in financing investments. She has displaced the United States as the most important source of imports. Substantial private credits and government loans have come from Japan to launch major development projects in South Korea. These include the construction of an integrated iron and steel plant and several metal and machine factories, the purchase of freighters, and the building of a subway in Seoul. Most of these projects are scheduled for the next Five-Year Plan. But by August of 1971, $782 million had already been provided in commercial credits, and $215 million in government loans. These capital imports have made a major contribution to meeting South Korea's deficit on current account. But their repayment may become a source of serious difficulties in the near future because of the predominance of relatively short-term commercial credits.

In assessing the economic development of South Korea, one must

53. The increase in the imports of cotton textiles is restricted by an earlier international agreement.

examine, too, its political aspects, and here again the picture is not uniformly satisfactory. The competitive confrontation with communist North Korea is a basic fact which the South Korean government has constantly to take into consideration in designing its policies. North of the 38th parallel there has also been rapid economic growth. Which development, North or South, has done the most to improve the lives of the people?

There can be no simple answer to this question, in view of the differences in objectives between the communist and the capitalist types of development. South Korea can boast of such visible achievements as an abundance of consumer goods, including the latest appliances. Its capital, Seoul, has been rebuilt as a modern metropolis of glass and steel. Still we note that economic development has benefited primarily the upper classes: the entrepreneurs, the technocrats, and the ruling military bureaucracy. Some of the fruits of development have apparently filtered down to the industrial working class. They have increased considerably in number and their standard of living has improved. It is less clear if the rural population, who represent the largest group in the country, has derived any significant advantage from the expansion of the economy. A land reform was carried out about 20 years ago, but progress in agricultural production has been much slower than in industry.

How do the masses in South Korea view the development achieved in their country? What conclusions do they draw in comparing its merits to those of the drabber, but also more equalitarian, society that exists in the North? The drastic improvement in relations between South and North Korea, which occurred in June 1972, is not likely to reduce the competition between the two regimes. Rather, to the contrary. Indeed, the comparison of results achieved north and south of the 38th Parallel will become much easier. There is no evidence to suggest that the basically military regime of South Korea has succeeded in obtaining or has even attempted to obtain the active support of the people. No effort along the lines of the White Revolution in Iran has been made. Similarly, it seems even less likely that the government has gone very far in arousing any enthusiasm on the part of the youth and its student élite for its philosophy of development. In Iran, at least an attempt has been made in this direction.

The social and political stability of South Korea seems assured for the time being because of the power of its well entrenched military government. In the long run, however, it will need a broader base of popular support. Its future otherwise, and any further development of the economy, seem in doubt.

Chapter 10. *IS THERE A FORMULA FOR DEVELOPMENT POLICIES?*

Is IT POSSIBLE to draw some definite conclusions from the different types of development which we have examined in preceding chapters? In so far as they bear on the prerequisites of development, yes; one would have some precise observations to make. Can one arrive at a single formula for designing the policies of economic development? We think not.

One must remember, first of all, that under the general heading of development one finds a broad spectrum of particular objectives, political and social, as well as economic, which can be more or less emphasized. As we pointed out initially, this variety of goals inevitably requires an equally wide range of policies and methods in order to attain the desired result. There are also considerable differences in the conditions that exist in various developing countries. All kinds of factors are involved here: the level of development, the density of population in relation to the available resources, the country's political structure and cultural traditions, to name only a few. It would be impossible to devise a single policy or method which would take into account such widely divergent conditions.

There is another reason, too, which is even more important and relates particularly to this study. It is a fact, which we hope to have demonstrated in our examples of development, that development can be successfully achieved within the framework of different political and social systems. It can progress under:

—Capitalism, where it relies essentially on the initiative of private entrepreneurs who then reap most of the rewards of such a development.

—Nationalist socialism of the kind that stresses more the nationalist aspects. The policies which can best serve to expand the power of the country and/or its rulers will overrule any concern for the wishes or interests of individuals if these should happen to contradict.

—Revolutionary socialism, bent on the total transformation of society, at its most extreme, of man himself. With the establishment of a totally egalitarian system, the individual is entirely subordinate to the commands of the state—that is, of the ruling party.

In addition to these three clearly defined types there is the whole gamut of intermediary cases which combine some features of one or the other to varying degrees.

Thus one can see that development is feasible under all the major political systems in the world today. This is a confirmation of the pluralistic character of our contemporary world society, in which the inevitable fact of coexistence should logically point to the need for international co-operation and reciprocity.

In spite of the different orientation of various development policies, there are still some basic requirements which must be met— in whatever way seems most suitable—to ensure the success of the development process.

The most important are:

(1) The mobilization of sufficient resources for development. This would include human, material, and land resources. The people must be made to participate in their country's development, either by luring them with incentives, by more or less voluntary persuasion, or by outright coercion. The maximum of savings must be extracted from the economy by restricting consumption. The government can choose to limit the purchasing power by setting high prices and low incomes, or by direct rationing. Additional resources can also be gotten from external resources through private investments, loans, or aid.

(2) The effective utilization of all these resources in productive investments for development. The criteria for these investments would be determined either by the prospects for future profit, or by the directives of a national development plan. The feasibility of an efficient use of resources in many cases entails wide ranging reforms to abolish outdated customs, institutions, or social structures which impede development. Unfair tax laws and systems of land tenure, rigid caste or class barriers that prevent social mobility, religious taboos that forbid the rational use of resources must be removed. But whether they come into being through legislation or through more drastic action, these reforms must reach far enough to carry out their purpose to the end. The middle road which tempts those who shun the use of violent measures has sometimes led to disaster in arresting reforms before they can accomplish their mission. This occurred in India with the government's failure to abolish the customs that prohibited proper livestock breeding. The persistence of this

taboo, along with the even greater disappointment of a land reform that was only partially carried out, have slowed down the progress of farm production and have been a major cause of social and political disturbances.[1]

(3) A reasonable social and political stability to allow the developing country to concentrate all her efforts on economic progress. It requires the active support, or at least the passive acceptance, of government policies by everyone, in any case by those powerful groups whose opposition would be otherwise dangerous. This can be bought with actual improvements in conditions—in living standards or in equality and social justice—or with promises that the policies will indeed produce these changes soon. The people will also be patient when they have an emotional commitment to the socialist and/or nationalist goal of the development policy, or when they have been persuaded or pressured into accepting these goals.

Thus national policies must take into consideration the general requirements of development, the political, social, psychological, as well as economic conditions of their countries, and of course the particular objectives and ideological orientation of their leaders.

In any case, whatever their goals and philosophical bent, developing countries must always face what Goulet has called a cruel choice.[2] There is no easy and painless road to development. It involves always great effort and sacrifice. The intensity and the duration of the hardships that they impose sets the various strategies of development apart from one another. But the essential difference is whether they assign the burden and the fruits of development to a specific income group or whether they divide them up more or less evenly among the population.

1. *The New York Times*, 12 October 1971. A report from South India describes the difficulties encountered in increasing food production. The tenants who have been evicted by their landlords are preventing the cultivation of their former land and political unrest is spreading.

2. Denis Goulet, *The Cruel Choice*, Atheneum, New York, 1971.

Conclusion: *A WORLD STRATEGY FOR ECONOMIC DEVELOPMENT*

Is A WORLD STRATEGY for economic and social development necessary? Implying as it does a close co-operation and co-ordination of efforts from developed and developing, rich and poor, socialist and capitalist countries, is such a strategy feasible?

On the assumption, which seems unassailable, that development is desirable for all of mankind, the answer to the first question must be emphatically yes. Development cannot be achieved on the outside and imported ready-made into the Third World. It can be achieved in isolation, solely through the domestic efforts of developing countries, without external assistance. But such a development would require enormous and protracted sacrifices from their people, which could easily be alleviated and abbreviated by international co-operation.

The answer to the second question is more difficult. It requires one to assess the possibility and the likelihood of international co-operation, which would be based as much on trust, even faith, as on purely rational considerations. On the basis of our lifetime experience in an international organization, we would be inclined on the whole to respond positively, with the proviso that mankind pursues a reasonable course and avoids suicide by nuclear war.

A major argument in favor of such an optimistic view is the fact that the basis for international relations today is an acceptance of coexistence between socialist and capitalist regimes. This will probably remain the case for a long time to come. There is great competition between the two camps; the leading socialist power has emphatically ruled out the notion of coexistence from an ideological standpoint. Still it does mean that in practical terms national policies are no longer ruled by the fervor of anticapitalist or anticommunist crusades.

As soon as one recognizes the fact of coexistence one has to accept the principle of economic co-operation when it is in the national interest. Both sides have taken important steps in this direction. One of them is the increase in East–West trade, the result of a relaxation of export restrictions for strategic reasons, even on the part of the United States, which lags behind Western Europe and Japan, its political allies but industrial competitors. Another instance of such co-operation is the admission of private foreign firms in socialist countries on joint ventures: a United States oil company is engaged in off-shore oil drilling in Romania; Fiat is co-operating with the Soviet Union in setting up a factory for passenger cars, while Renault and some American companies are assisting in the construction of a plant to manufacture trucks.

One cannot ignore the significance of the change in the approach of prominent Soviet economists to economic development.[1] They now admit that in many cases developing countries may have to make use of private capital, if only as a temporary expedient. While they maintain the superiority of the socialist method of development, and in no way deviate from Marxist orthodoxy, their views on practical development policies are not in contradiction with those of most Western economists.

The policies generally followed by the governments of the Soviet Union and the other socialist countries of Eastern Europe are also becoming more realistic in relation to developing countries. They are ruled as much by self-interest as by a desire to grant aid for development. As we have pointed out earlier, for the socialist countries trade and aid become practically synonymous. Their exports consist mainly in capital goods sold on long-term credit at low-interest rates. The repayment of these exports by imports of tropical foodstuffs and beverages (bananas, cocoa, coffee, tea) and primary products such as rubber, none of which they can produce, is definitely in the interest of the socialist countries as well as the developing ones. The former can thus meet the growing demand of their consumers—or in the case of rubber, of their consumer goods industry—without spending their foreign exchange. Repayment by consumer goods manufactured in plants which the socialist countries have equipped is similarly advantageous.

True, such a calculated and practical approach to the relations of socialist countries with the Third World does not always apply. The aid which the USSR and, to a much smaller extent, the other socialist countries grant to Cuba and the UAR is certainly not based on this sort of reasoning, but on political and strategic considerations. But the same attitude explains the defense support aid provided by the United States to the countries of Asia and the Middle East, all signatories of one or another of the mutual defense treaties negotiated by the late John Foster Dulles.

1. S. I. Tulpanov (Professor of Economics at the University of Leningrad), *Otscherki polititscheskoi economiki,* Moscow, 1969.

Mutual self-interest is generally also, and should be always, the basis for the policies of the developed market economies. This common ground should make co-operation between East and West in promoting the development of the Third World seem less unthinkable than it might appear to the general public, still immersed to a large degree in the rhetoric and slogans of the cold war.

The constructive attitude displayed by the socialist countries in the United Nation's discussion of plans for the Second Development Decade of the 1970's offers some justification for optimism. Both at UNCTAD, and especially at the United Nations Committee for Development Planning, in charge of drafting recommendations for an International Development Strategy,[2] the socialist representatives approved even those recommendations which were addressed to their own countries and required specific actions. These recommendations, which will be analyzed below, have been unanimously endorsed by the United Nations General Assembly at its 25th session on October 24, 1970.

It is true that General Assembly resolutions are not binding commitments and express only the intentions of governments. It is also well known that in too many cases, even when they wish to comply with United Nations resolutions, the governments are thwarted by the resistance of their legislative bodies and the lack of support from public opinion. This contradiction between the intentions of governments and the views of legislators is far less likely to occur in socialist countries, however, than in Western-type democracies.

It seems possible, therefore, and even likely, that if both the developing countries—which obviously will have to bear the major responsibility for their development—and the developed market economies agree to carry through the tasks which have been assigned to them, the socialist countries will also fulfill their own obligations.

The International Development Strategy is a comprehensive and integrated program on all fronts, social, cultural, and political, as well as economic. It requires action on the part of developing and developed countries alike, as well as the international agencies of the United Nations family. Dynamic in its outlook, it is not a once-and-for-all fixed program, but one which will be reviewed periodically and amended to suit the times.

The main objectives of the Second Development Decade have

2. The Committee for Development Planning consists of prominent experts in planning from all major countries, capitalist and socialist, developed and developing. The United States expert before his untimely death was Professor Max Millikan of M.I.T. and its first Chairman was the well-known Dutch economist Jan Tinbergen.

been expressed in figures. An average rate of growth of Gross Product of 6 per cent does not seem too ambitious, although it is high if one looks back on the past. Several developing countries have already reached it and even gone beyond it in the preceding decade, when the average rate growth reached 5.6 per cent and thus exceeded its objective of 5 per cent.[3] Under the assumption that family planning policies will grow sufficiently to curb population growth to a maximum of 2.5 per cent per year—a figure which unfortunately seems rather minimal—the annual growth in per capita G.N.P. would be 3.5 per cent. At this rate of growth the per capita G.N.P. would double in 20 years. The chasm between the standard of living of developing countries would thus grow narrower, in relative terms if not in the absolute. To achieve such a rate of growth, agriculture, which will remain for a long time the most important sector of production, must increase its output by 4 per cent, and industry, the most dynamic sector, by 8 per cent. Expanded production should encourage the growth of domestic savings by at least .5 per cent per annum in order to reach a rate of 20 per cent by 1980. Once domestic savings have arrived at this level, developing countries can start reducing their requirements for the inflow of fresh foreign capital. Import requirements to sustain such an expansion of the economy should grow at a rate of nearly 7 per cent, while exports should increase at a slightly higher rate.

Just as important as these targets for increased income, output, and trade are the cultural changes which must take place in the structure of society in developing countries. There must be more equitable distribution of income and wealth. Unemployment is becoming the most alarming problem of the developing countries, and the unemployed, whose numbers are rapidly growing, especially among the young, must be absorbed into the labor force. Efforts must be made to broaden general education and expand specialized training; the latter is absolutely essential to meet the needs of a modernizing economy. In conjunction with this, improvements must be made in health, nutrition, and housing.

The Development Strategy Resolution in the field of trade has

3. The real product grew in the developing countries during the First Development Decade more rapidly than in the developed market economies, where its rate of growth amounted to 4.9 per cent. However, owing to the far greater rate of increase in the population, per capita product grew by only 3 per cent in the developing countries and by 3.8 per cent in the market economies. OECD, *Development Assistance, 1971 Review*, Paris 1971, p. 116.

recommended international action, including commodity agreements, to stabilize the prices of primary products at an equitable level and to remove the obstacles which prevent their import into the developed countries. They suggest further that generalized and non-discriminatory, non-reciprocal preferential treatment be granted to exports of developing countries, particularly to manufactured and semi-manufactured goods. In the same spirit the socialist countries of Eastern Europe would make allowances for more imports from developing countries in their overall economic plan.

In the realm of external aid each developed country would endeavor by 1972 to transfer a minimum of 1 per cent of its G.N.P. in net financial resources, with a major part of these transfers to be in the form of official development assistance, which should reach 0.7 per cent of their G.N.P. by the middle of the decade. Terms of aid should be softened and aid should as far as possible not be tied to purchases in the donor countries. The resources available to multilateral institutions for financial and technical assistance should be increased and developing countries assisted in overcoming their foreign debt crises.

The Development Strategy Resolution also spelled out measures to be taken by the developing countries. Realistic development plans would have to be formulated that would still be ambitious enough to obtain the active support and participation of all segments of the population. The full mobilization of domestic financial resources and their effective use for development should be ensured in particular through appropriate tax reforms. Projects in family planning would have to be launched. A strong emphasis should be placed on expanding employment with policies which will promote both employment and development, using in particular labor-intensive technologies wherever they do not impair efficiency. Progress in agricultural output must be stressed to ensure an adequate food supply, to increase rural employment, and expand export earnings. For this purpose reforms in land tenure should be introduced in order to promote both social justice and farm efficiency. Industrial development must be stimulated in order to expand rapidly the output of manufacturers, to modernize and diversify industry. The emphasis should be placed on those industries which use domestic raw materials, supply goods essential to both agriculture and other productive activities, and turn out export items. The education system must be enlarged with training programs geared to increasing productivity, and the stress put on teacher training and technical and vocational programs. Efforts must be made in the areas of health, housing, and town planning, enlisting the youth and even the children in the development drive. Developing countries must embark on a massive campaign to apply science and technology and to adapt it to their local requirements in order to bridge the technological gap. An important element is the expansion of trade between developing countries, in particular through regional and subregional trade arrangements and integration.

There will be constant scrutiny of the practical results of policies which are part of the overall strategy. On the national level it will be carried out by the governments; on the regional level, by the Regional Economic Commissions of the United Nations; and internationally, by the central United Nations bodies, including the General Assembly. This assessment at two-year intervals will make possible necessary modifications and changes which may become necessary.

The importance of mobilizing public opinion in both developed and developing countries to support the objectives of the Development Decade cannot be overemphasized. This is mainly the responsibility of the national governments. In the developed countries, the public must be made aware of the benfits which will accrue to them through international co-operation for development and of the interdependence of all nations. The governments of the developing countries must seek out the active participation of their population in achieving their development goals.

What are the prospects of reaching the goals set by the International Development Strategy in the 1970's, the Second Development Decade? Will this Resolution of the General Assembly, as so many equally lofty proclamations of previous years, disappoint the hopes it aroused in the nations of the Third World, thus adding to, rather than reducing, international tensions? The Resolution won unanimous approval at the General Assembly. But in the preliminary stages of discussion in the Committee, a number of countries, including some of the most important developed nations, expressed serious reservations. One can only assume, therefore, that these governments will probably not support fully all the provisions of the Resolution.

The most important of these reservations focused on the targets set for financial transfers and official development assistance. As we said earlier, the target of 1 per cent of G.N.P. was rejected by both the United States and the Soviet Union. The United States delegation pleaded the staggering load of domestic needs and external obligations which made it impossible to say when, if at all, this target could be met. They suggested instead greater reliance on private resources, which would not require approval by Congress. The socialist countries argued along political, even propagandist lines. Their position was that this goal was not an expression of human solidarity between nations, but an indemnification for former colonial and economic exploitation. Since the socialist countries had not participated in this exploitation, one could not expect them to share in the compensation. But they also presented a less controversial, more realistic argument. The socialist countries were not supplying private investments or loans on commercial terms; their aid was all in the form of long-term loans at very low rates. They had no responsibility, therefore, in the growing debt of the Third World. There were other quibbles from certain Western countries on the fulfillment date, but not on the target itself.

The developing countries for their part felt that the development strategy did not express adequately their own aspirations. They accepted it, however, as representing an optimum on which under the existing circumstances agreement could be reached.

Far more critical were Peru and Chile, who stated that the development strategy did not emphasize sufficiently the need for commitments. Would the developing countries make the required structural changes—those which they had failed to make in the past—and fully mobilize all their domestic resources for development? Would the developed countries carry over into their national policies the spirit of solidarity which had inspired the General Assembly Resolution? Would the political commitment of the development strategy be fulfilled?

This indeed is the crucial question. In substance, the development strategy, which was evolved by some of the world's leading planning economists, represents a comprehensive set of principles. With some minor contradictions which stem out of a need to reach a compromise acceptable to all major blocs of countries, they appear realistic and could achieve the objectives of the Development Decade, if they are fully implemented.

Important political decisions will have to be made in countries all around the world. The most far reaching of these decisions, as well as the hardest, will take place in the developing countries. With allowances made for varying political structures and conditions, what is involved basically is the determination to mobilize all available human and material resources and to use them in the most effective way possible in the drive to attain the objectives of development.

Will the governments of developing countries have the courage, the wisdom, and also the power which will be necessary to make these decisions, many of which, if not most, may be highly unpopular?

The countries may be forced to break with ancient and cherished traditions, postpone if not put off entirely hopes for rapid improvement. Can they appeal to national or revolutionary ideals, or to self-interest, by promising future rewards, and thus inspire their population, especially the youth, to greater efforts? Will they succeed in overcoming the pressure of rising expectations and by persuasion and/or coercion induce their people to forgo higher consumer standards, at least until an increased output justifies it? Will they be able and willing to stand up to their privileged classes and impose structural changes which would introduce a minimum of social justice in the society?

Such changes should include a fundamental land reform which would be designed to benefit the whole peasantry, including the poorest farm laborers, freeing them from starvation and servitude. This has not happened up to now in India where land reform, according to Gunnar Myrdal, worked mainly in favor of the well-to-do farmers.[4] Agriculture should be restructured to achieve maximum efficiency and to ensure justice and human dignity for the rural population. This can be done in various ways, by introducing individual, co-operative, or collective systems of land tenure.

Tax reform is equally essential to guarantee the full use of domestic capital resources for development and to force the wealthy classes to participate equitably in the national effort. This should also put an end to the demoralizing practice of fiscal desertion through tax evasion and capital flight abroad. Measures such as these which strive to establish greater social justice would also strengthen the government's moral position in asking all its citizens to make sacrifices in other areas as well.

Once domestic resources have been mobilized, the political orientation of the country will determine how they will be allocated. In our discussion of specific developing countries, we showed that development can be achieved gradually and without excessive hardships or sacrifices in a private market economy, where material incentives, the expectation of profits, or high wages decide the allocation of both physical and human resources. The socialist approach, where the emphasis is on the establishment of an egalitarian society rather than a rapid improvement in standards of private consumption, can also succeed. In this case the allocation of resources, including labor, is

4. Gunnar Myrdal, *The Challenge of World Poverty*, Atheneum, New York, 1970.

dictated by the state, and the compliance of the population is assured through persuasion or pressure or a combination of both. Naturally the government must choose the development strategy most in keeping with its objectives and the condition of the country.

Government policies, however, may be misdirected, or they may fail because of the successful opposition of vested interests to reform. In such an event it often happens that these reforms are finally imposed by a government which is more resistant than its predecessor to pressure. The new government is likely to be quite hostile, even ruthless, in its dealings with the opposition. The privileged classes might be well advised to recognize how counterproductive and dangerous their resistance to reforms may be.

There is one temptation which few developing countries so far have been able to resist—namely, to deploy their scarce resources in areas which contribute little to development. Usually this is either to enhance the prestige of the country and/or its leaders, or to serve the interests of powerful domestic lobbies. This waste of resources, either on ostentatious economic projects such as luxury hotels, gigantic stadiums, jet airliners, or on excessive military expenditures, can only retard economic development. If it occurs on too large a scale it can jeopardize the entire program.

There is obviously no guarantee that even only a majority of developing countries will succeed in carrying out the development strategy recommended in the United Nations Resolution. But many of them have made considerable progress in recent years in understanding their economic problems and in taking suitable action. Barring unforeseen events, natural or man-made catastrophes such as floods, followed by a disastrous civil war in East Pakistan, and finally a war with India, one can reasonably expect developing countries to do their share in the International Development Strategy.

The same is true of the socialist countries. As we stated earlier, their specific commitments are relatively simple and limited—to increase their imports of primary products and particularly of manufactured and semi-manufactured goods from developing countries and to accept them in payment for their own exports of capital goods. This is already being done to a great extent and works to their own advantage. There is, therefore, no reason to suppose that the socialist countries will abandon this policy or change their course.

The main problems touch on the role of the developed market economies in the international development strategy, which is far more important because of their traditionally close economic ties with the Third World. Thus in 1968 they had absorbed 74 per cent of its total exports and supplied 80 per cent of its total imports.[5] They provided an even greater share of the flow of external financial resources to developing countries, both through private investment and official assistance. Most developing countries at some point were under the domination, or at least the strong political and economic influence, of the leading market economies. While these former associations have not always inspired further mutual friendship, they have laid the groundwork for a close economic relationship. The cultural ties have facilitated sympathy and understanding on both sides. Finally, the developed market economies have a per capita income far superior not only to that of the Third World but also to the socialist countries, some of whom are still in the process of development. It would seem only natural, therefore, that their participation in the international effort of development should correspond to the magnitude of their resources.

But the present attitude of governments and public opinion—as reflected in the legislative bodies in several of the wealthiest and most powerful market economies—is not reassuring. In theory they recognize that since they are the main trading partners they will benefit in the long run from the economic progress achieved by the Third World. But threatening this positive understanding of their commitments is the active opposition of vested interests who may be hurt, or at least temporarily inconvenienced, by an increase in industrial imports from developing countries. The policies of many developing countries toward foreign private investments have aroused much irritation and even hostility in influential business and financial circles. Finally, there is a growing reluctance in some of these countries, first and foremost the United States, to continue or expand economic aid to development. The fact that the cost of this aid is relatively minor, in comparison to their national income, does not reduce the strength of the opposition. It is not surprising, therefore, that, as we stated earlier, the amount of aid to development has not gone up much since the mid-1960's. One sees, in fact, that it has actually declined in value, if one takes into consideration the rise in world prices and if one sets it aganst the rapidly growing national income of the developed market economies.

Foreign aid to development is thus facing a crisis now. There is a serious danger that the progress of development as a whole may be jeopardized in view of the vital importance of external resources which can be provided only through aid.

5. *United Nations Yearbook of International Trade Statistics*, 1968, United Nations, New York, 1970, table B.

The major issue is not an economic one but one of basic political and moral attitudes. Will developed countries agree to make this relatively minor effort? The answer depends on the importance which governments in the developed countries and public opinion, which view they are supposed to reflect, assign to aid in comparison with other competing public or private claims on their resources. If the emphasis is placed strictly on national self-interest, as has too often been the case with bilateral aid from the major powers, the answer may not be very encouraging. Past experience in this area has been quite disappointing in most cases. On the whole, foreign aid is unsuccessful as a tool of power politics in international relations.

The question should be raised in a much broader perspective. To what kind of world do people in the developed countries aspire, for themselves, and even more for their children? Will an increasingly small, affluent minority of rich countries feel comfortable or even be able to survive surrounded by an overwhelming majority of desperately poor nations? Would not this abysmal difference in standards of living generate the kind of bitter hate and resentment that inevitably leads to conflicts, which would be equivalent to an international war of classes? We freely grant that the rich countries could maintain military superiority by putting together a highly sophisticated and costly war machine. But guerrilla warfare can easily spread from the jungle to the giant urban centers of the developed countries. There it would be far more dangerous and devastating for the extremely fragile fabric of contemporary industrial society.

Technical progress, moreover, is rapidly reducing the cost of even mass destruction weapons such as atomic arms. It is quite possible that soon even poor and relatively small countries will be able to afford them. Obviously this would impose a heavy burden on their population and postpone raising their standards of living. In all likelihood only totalitarian regimes would be able to inflict such hardships on their people, and the temptation for such countries to resort to nuclear blackmail, eventually nuclear war, might be irresistible, even with the risk of losing a substantial portion of their population. Statements of this kind were attributed to the leaders of China when they tested their first atomic weapons. One can only expect countries to pursue rational policies if they have cause to believe that they will reap thereby some reasonable benefit. How can one demand this of nations in so desperate a situation that no reasonable effort can alleviate it? Speaking in the early years of this century about the attitude of the wealthy bourgeoisie toward the proletariat, the French statesman Clemenceau made a remark which seems quite appropriate in this context: "If you wish the workers to become conservative, you must have given them something worth preserving."[6] Following the same train of thought, one can see that the balance of terror between the two nuclear superpowers, the Soviet Union and the United States, is stable for the very reason that neither is any longer a "have not"; both are "have" powers. The Soviet people know that their standard of living, while still mediocre in comparison with that of the United States, is improving and will continue to improve. One can only hope that China's policies are based on these same expectations and understanding.

Even if we were to assume that the security of the rich countries could be preserved because of their sheer military superiority, their position on the globe would be that of an armed camp surrounded by a hostile native population. It would necessitate strict security measures, both on the frontiers and within national boundaries, a position similar to, and in the long run probably worse than, that existing in South Africa today. In such a world the most precious achievements of our civilization, individual freedom and respect for the dignity of man, would be gradually eroded. Their loss would be the price of surviving as the affluent privileged minority of mankind. The cost of survival under such conditions might be the deterioration of the human environment to the point where it would no longer be fit for civilized human beings.

The above are basically political and security reasons for international development aid, but moral arguments should be marshaled as well. Aid should be granted to avert future dangers, yes, but also for the equally important purpose of manifesting the human solidarity between the privileged and the under-privileged. In even the most advanced and wealthiest of nations this notion of solidarity has come into its own only rather recently. As late as the middle of the nineteenth century, the heyday of *laissez-faire*, the workers in Western Europe and the United States were subject to the "iron law of wages," formulated by the German socialist Lassalle, which set an average level of wages equivalent to the subsistence minimum. If the labor force were in excess of demand, the surplus would be eliminated by attrition through starvation. Gradually, because of the advances in democracy, humanitarian ideas, and also greater prosperity, the position of most workers improved. Measures such as minimum wage

6. "Si vous voulez que les ouvriers deviennent des conservateurs, il faut leur donner quelque chose à conserver."

laws, social and unemployment insurance, and in Western Europe national health schemes, have assured them at least a minimum standard of living. These are financed mainly out of the proceeds of progressive income taxes, paid by the high- and middle-income groups. Thus they have established a modicum of solidarity within the national community of the rich countries.

More recently the attention of the public in the rich countries and especially in the United States has been called to the existence of an underprivileged minority which in spite of these social reforms has scarcely benefited from the progress achieved by the rest of the nation. While this problem is most acute in the United States, where it concerns an old established racial minority, it is already noticeable in the United Kingdom and in other countries of Western Europe. There this underproletariat consists mainly of immigrant workers from the poorer countries of Europe and from the Third World. The measures which are gradually being adopted—to a great extent, one must admit, under pressure of erupting violence—to alleviate this situation are extremely costly. They are a serious financial burden, even for a country as wealthy as the United States, and will probably remain so for some time to come. This heavy expenditure and other non-related drains on the national treasury, created either by the Viet Nam War or by a necessity to halt the steady deterioration of the physical environment, reduce the receptivity of American public opinion to international development aid. The old slogan, charity begins at home, is frequently heard.

Yet the problems of the underprivileged minority at home and the underprivileged majority of mankind are quite similar. The danger of racial war in the ghettos of American cities is only a foretaste of a worldwide racial war which could erupt if the Third World were abandoned, and if the rich countries became indifferent to its plight. On the other hand, the contribution to international aid requested of the rich countries is far smaller than what they must spend to help their own poor. They are only invited to share in a joint effort, with the other members of the world community, and the heaviest burden is carried by the developing countries themselves.

Public opinion in developing countries generally considers that the West has at the very least a moral obligation to assist the progress of the Third World, and that their aid is no more than belated compensation for centuries of colonial exploitation. Stated so boldly, this notion of transferring all responsibility for their underdevelopment onto the West is certainly at least exaggerated. It provides sometimes an alibi for the governments of developing countries whose own efforts in development may not have been particularly spectacular.[7] They find this theory most convenient in justifying to their own people their lack of success. Still, the existence of such a guilt cannot be completely denied, either for the past or even in some cases for the present.

In addition, one must recognize that the developed countries have destroyed the traditional framework of the economy and the fabric of society in the Third World which has afforded stability and security if not prosperity. It is immaterial whether this was a deliberate act or the accidental result of the sheer impact of their superior wealth and power. The developed countries should be willing, therefore, to help the developing countries in finding a new equilibrium.

Goulet's statements that "the rich are responsible for abolishing poverty" and that "maintenance of superfluity alongside massive want is dehumanizing both for those who have and for those who have not"[8] seem valid to us both from the ethical and cultural points of view. One is also tempted to paraphrase the sentence of Abraham Lincoln: "This Government cannot endure permanently half slave and half free." A peaceful world cannot exist if one tenth of its population is affluent and the rest destitute.

In spite of the present reluctance of the United States to accept this concept of active solidarity and to grant international development aid, there are certain indications in other developed countries and even in the United States itself which would seem to contradict this pessimistic trend.

Several developed countries, including Canada and the Scandinavian countries, which have no traditional political or economic ties with any developing country, and no special commercial interest in the Third World, have adopted under pressure of public opinion programs expanding official development aid, mainly through grants. They have been motivated specifically by humanitarian considerations, a feeling of solidarity with the poor nations. In Norway, in particular, this public development aid is being financed by a special surtax on the income tax, which went up in 1971 from 0.5 to 1 per cent of taxable income.

In a number of affluent developed countries, especially in the United States, many of the young have expressed their lack of interest,

7. René Dumont, *L'Afrique Noire est mal partie,* Editions du Seuil, Paris, 1966, pp. 66–67.

8. Denis Goulet, *The Cruel Choice,* Atheneum, New York, 1971, pp. 135–136.

if not their aversion, to their parents' drive for increasing constantly the level of private consumption. These young people have shown serious concern for public and humanitarian causes, including aid to poor countries.

A striking example of the interest of youth in making an active contribution was the enthusiastic response to the creation of the Peace Corps on the part of many American university students. In the early days after its establishment by President Kennedy, the number of applicants far exceeded available posts. Later the Peace Corps gradually lost its unique character as an idealistic venture as it became increasingly integrated in the general framework of American international policy. This reduced its prestige and its appeal to the young. Nevertheless, the fact that American youth accepted this challenge so eagerly is still significant and encouraging. A more recent, though more limited, example was the International Walk for Development organized in May of 1971. About 4 million people, mainly young, were involved, and they came from 51 countries, some 2 million from the United States alone. The participants in this walk received a fixed amount per mile walked from individual sponsors, and in the United States the proceeds were split between national anti-poverty projects and the "Freedom from Hunger Campaign," an organization affiliated with the FAO which promotes food production projects in developing countries.

If this new trend toward decreasing the emphasis on private consumption persists, we can hope that greater resources will become available to meet public needs. The protection and regeneration of our physical environment is frequently put forward as the most important of these needs. But just as crucial is an improvement in the human environment, improving the condition of the underprivileged poor within the rich countries and assisting the poor nations in the world as a whole.

For the rich developed nations to contribute their fair share of international development aid would require only an additional $7 billion. This would double the volume of official aid from the OECD member countries. In 1968, the same countries spent $35 billion for liquor and $15 billion for cigarettes.[9] When one compares aid requirements and military expenditures, which for the whole world are of the order of $200 billion, the contrast becomes even more significant. As Mr. McNamara pointed out in his speech on September 21, 1970 to the Board of Governors of the World Bank, the aid target

9. *Partners in Development, Report of the Commission on International Development,* Praeger, New York, 1969, p. 140.

could be met by turning over to development less than 5 per cent of the arms budget. Relying on his experience in the Pentagon, the former U.S. Secretary of Defense stated that these funds could be derived from convertible waste alone.[10] In a similar vein the Nigerian representative at the debate in the United Nations General Assembly expressed the hope that the countries which had been able to invent the technology and supply the immense financial resources needed to put a man on the moon would agree to provide the much smaller sums required to make life on earth less unbearable for the majority of mankind.

This indeed is the basic dilemma of aid to development and of development in general. Will the rich countries recognize their moral obligations to assist the less fortunate people of the poor lands? The answer may very well decide the future not only of the poor nations, but of all mankind.

10. Robert S. McNamara, Address to the Board of Govenors, Copenhagen, 1970, p. 23.

Index

Index

DATE DUE

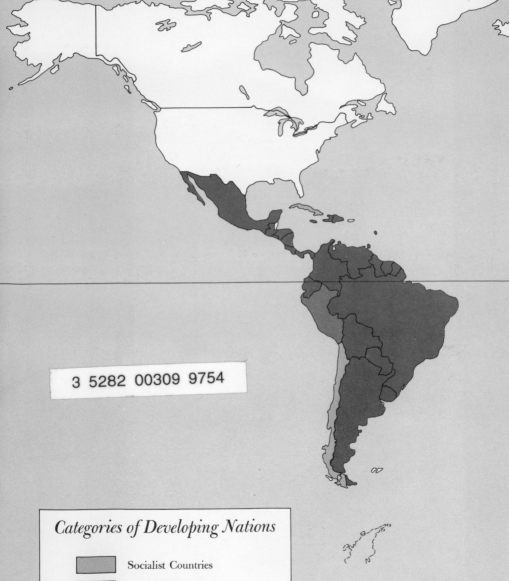

3 5282 00309 9754

Categories of Developing Nations

Socialist Countries

Nationalist Countries

Private Enterprise Countries